How to Be a Power Agent in Real Estate

DARRYL DAVIS

How to Be a Power Agent in Real Estate

McGraw-Hill

New York Chicago San Francisco Lisbon
London Madrid Mexico City Milan New Delhi
San Juan Seoul Singapore Toronto

The McGraw-Hill Companies

Copyright © 2003 by The McGraw-Hill Companies, Inc. All rights reserved. Printed in the United States of America. Except as permitted under the United States Copyright Act of 1976, no part of this publication may be reproduced or distributed in any form or by any means, or stored in a database or retrieval system, without the prior written permission of the publisher.

11 12 13 14 DOC/DOC 0 9 8 7 6 5

ISBN 0-07-138520-7

Library of Congress Cataloging-in-Publication Data applied for.

Editorial and production services provided by CWL Publishing Enterprises, Inc. Madison, Wisconsin, www.cwlpub.com.

This publication is designed to provide accurate and authoritative information in regard to the subject matter covered. It is sold with the understanding that neither the author nor the publisher is engaged in rendering legal, accounting, or other professional service. If legal advice or other expert assistance is required, the services of a competent professional person should be sought.
—*From a Declaration of Principles jointly adopted by a Committee of the American Bar Association and a Committee of Publishers*

McGraw-Hill books are available at special quantity discounts to use as premiums and sales promotions, or for use in corporate training programs. For more information, please write to the Director of Special Sales, McGraw-Hill, 2 Penn Plaza, New York, NY 10128. Or contact your local bookstore.

The terms, "Power Agent," "The POWER Program," and "Next Level" are registered trademarks owned by Darryl Davis Seminars. All rights reserved.

Realtor is a registered trademark owned by the National Association of Realtors.

 This book is printed on recycled, acid-free paper containing a minimum of 50% recycled de-inked fiber.

Contents

Introduction

If you're like me, you probably skim through the introductions of most books, frequently without reading them. Well, I want to strongly encourage you to read this short introduction. Why? Because it establishes the foundation for much of what I present in the following chapters. It'll just take a few minutes …, so let's get started!

This book is designed to help you reach your "Next Level®" in your real estate career. The principles and techniques I reveal throughout these chapters have helped many agents double their income. I know they will work for you as well.

Before I go on, let me give you a brief background on where I came from, because I want you to understand that I wasn't born a top producer. That is, when my parents gave birth to me, they didn't turn to one another and say, "Look, honey, we have a top lister!"

Like most agents, I stumbled into real estate. Before joining the industry, I was a professional actor appearing in movies and commercials. To help support myself while I pursued a theatrical career, I started in real estate part-time at the ripe old age of 19. In my first six months, I was a failure. But I was committed to making it work, so I persevered.

I knew I needed to get better at what I did and I figured, "Why reinvent the wheel?" So, I became a seminar junkie, teaching myself from countless courses, audio tapes, and books. And I became a more effective agent as a result.

Eventually, I left acting and became a real estate agent full time, averaging six transactions a month. I later became a licensed broker and, as a manager, I opened a new office that became the number-one listing and selling office in my market area in just six months.

I soon learned that my true joy in life came from making a difference in the lives of others. I became very good at coaching agents and brokers to achieve their goals, to break through the obstacles that stop them, and to enjoy phenomenally productive and successful careers. Better yet, I found that I truly loved doing this.

In 1993, I created *The Power Program®*, the only training course for agents that meets once a month over the course of a full year. On average, graduating *Power Agents® double their production over their previous year.* Each year, more than 1,000 agents participate in *The Power Program*, delivered across the nation by me and my team of trained *Power Leaders*.

The book that you are holding in your hands is unique in the real estate world precisely because the many tips and techniques I present have been battle-tested and proven by *Power Agents* in markets throughout America.

My goal in writing *How to Be a Power Agent in Real Estate* is to share with you what I know works in the real world and to avoid having you run around chasing some theory about how real estate sales should be. But there's another reason why this book will make a tremendously positive difference in your career, and it goes beyond simple tips and techniques. It has to do with helping to develop your personality and your attitude.

You see, in order to provide their clients and customers with the best possible service, I believe salespeople in our business should master the skills, tools, techniques, and concepts of real estate sales—the technical knowledge that serves as the foundation of the real estate industry. As you know, many excellent courses teach various versions of these building blocks and many of these techniques are described in this book. Yet, after taking courses, reading, books and listening to tapes, why is it that some people go on to be highly successful in real estate sales, while others struggle?

Simply put, there is a wide disparity in production and income between real estate professionals, because the ability to "make it" in real estate sales depends on *personality and attitude* as well as skill and ability. This book is packed with tips and lists and sample dialogues—all wonderfully effective tools—but these items in themselves are meaningless. What is vital is the mental context in which agents perform. Said another way, *your belief structure and personal attitude are the most crucial factors determining whether or not you will succeed.*

This book will give you all the basics of real estate sales, but with a powerful addition. I'll provide you with information that will expand your ability to work effectively with other people, to listen to them, and to help them achieve their goals.

The Three Power Principles of Real Estate

Principle #1: The Coaching Philosophy. If you look around you, you'll find that there are many people who dress differently, drive different cars, like different food than you, etc. The ability to understand what people like and why and to be committed to helping them get what they want is what I call *coaching*. The first *Power Principle*, therefore, is "The Coaching Philosophy."

The old-fashioned approach in real estate was based on *selling*, not coaching. The foundation of this approach was manipulation: you tried to get your clients or customers to do whatever it was that suited your agenda. Your only concern was that they took a particular action (e.g., signing on the dotted line) so that you could get your commission.

In contrast, The Coaching Philosophy asks you to look at what *they're* committed to and give them advice to help them get there. If you truly see yourself as a "real estate coach," you could even go on a listing appointment and, based on what the sellers say, you might determine that it's appropriate that they *don't* list with you. Now, 99.9% of the time, this won't be the case. However, if you are honestly committed to doing what's right for them, you have to allow for this possibility and be more interested in serving the clients' best interests than in serving your own.

When you are coaching others, you have more fun, less stress, and more peace in your career because you are not being combative with your sellers and buyers. You become engaged in what they want and in helping them to achieve it. You learn how to get them excited about buying or selling real estate and to allow them the freedom to make decisions based on what *they* need or want from the purchase or sale of a home. Imagine life as a salesperson without always fighting with people—wouldn't that be great?

One of my own personal goals is to bring *integrity* back into the real estate industry—a concept directly related to The Coaching Philosophy. Listen to this: according to the first *Webster's Collegiate Dictionary*, published in 1898, the definition of "integrity" is "the fair dealings of people in the transfer of property." So, our industry helped create one of the original meanings of "integrity." Yet sadly we no longer associate it with our industry. In my view, part of having integrity is to coach buyers and sellers based on what they're committed to, rather than what's in it for us.

So, how does an agent master the art of coaching others? Most new agents are taught basic information about listing and selling real estate in just a few weeks or even a few days. They are then thrown out into the real world expected to know how to effectively use the information they've just received. Studies show, however, that it takes 21 days to internalize a habit, so how could anyone possibly master all of real estate in only a few weeks?

My solution was to create *The Power Program*, which, as I said above, meets once a month for 12 consecutive months. By focusing on one topic a month for 30 days, agents can really internalize that one area of the real estate, thereby mastering their careers one step at a time. This book can help you do the same thing.

There are 11 skill-building chapters in this book, corresponding to the 12 months of my course. (We spend two full months on "the listing presentation.") Unfortunately, unlike taking *The Power Program*, what you don't get out of reading a book is the actual accountability of implementing these items. So, you'll be left to your own devices to move forward with these concepts. Nevertheless, even if you don't master these items, you can still improve your skill and abilities by 10% in each area. That's substantial and will make a tremendous impact on your success.

Principle #2: The Next Level® Design. *The Power Program* offers radical new approaches to goal setting and personal growth through the *Power Principle* called the "Next Level® Design." Simply stated, the Next Level Design is based on a quote by Oliver Wendell Holmes, Jr.: *"Once the mind of man is stretched, it can never go back to its original form."* In other words, we can measure our lives in levels. When there is a major occurrence in our life, we grow as a person and that growth can never be taken away. For example, when you get married, that is a Next Level; when you have a child, that too is a Next Level. You can't go back to being someone who was never a parent.

When a real estate agent goes from making $50,000 to $75,000 a year, she has to "rise to the occasion" and grow as a person to reach this Next Level. The following year, she may make only $60,000, but she still knows what to do to earn the $75,000. She has the knowledge and experience to get there again.

Now, some Next Levels are reached by happenstance. However, when a person creates his or her Next Level by design, not accident, then the person is truly in control of his or her life. For anyone who wishes to become a top producer in real estate, or any other worthwhile endeavor, it is imperative to learn how to set objectives and achieve them. The Next Level Design encourages you to set long-term goals of a year or more.

But defining your Next Level is only half the battle.

Principle #3: Maintaining Focus. Simply knowing where you want to go won't get you there. The secret is in focusing on attaining this Next Level and in taking action consistent with your commitment.

During *The Power Program* through the years, I often ask my students how many actually make New Year's Resolutions. I've found that typically only 10% follow this custom. The other 90% don't make resolutions because they know they'll break them, so what's the point of making them? You know, in January it sounds like such a good idea, but by March you'll be onto 50 different projects and will have forgotten all about your resolution.

In *The Power Program*, because we meet once a month for 12 consecutive months, we have a built-in solution. Every 30 days while in class, *Power Agents* look at what they did the previous 30 days and set a goal for the next 30 days. Just doing this in and of itself helps them to stay focused. In fact, when graduating *Power Agents* are asked what they think are the main reasons why they double their production after completing *The Power Program*, the number-one response we get is that the monthly meetings help them to stay focused. If you can create a similar support group with other agents and commit to meeting once a month to hold each other accountable for the goals you have set, you will get much more out of this book than if you simply read it by yourself.

You see, real estate is like a marriage. You don't walk down the aisle, say, "I do," close your eyes, and hope it will work out for the next 50 years. Rather, you must wake up each morning and recommit to making your relationship work. That's right: there's actually work to be done.

It's the same thing in our business. You can't just pass your real estate license exam and watch the six-figure income start to roll in. You must constantly recommit to the profession and reinvent yourself along the way, maintaining your focus on reaching your Next Level.

When you systematically look at your goals every 30 days, especially in a group with other agents, you suddenly develop a sense of urgency. You stop putting things off because you know you must be accountable to others in your group who expect to see you move your goals forward and because you are constantly reminded of your commitments.

Let me tell you about Robert Kirby, a *Power Agent* from Virginia Beach, VA. Robert started in *The Power Program* when he had been licensed for only two weeks. In his first year in real estate, he did 97 listings and 34 sales. Even more amazing was the fact that he did this part-time! I'm not kidding—he was driving a truck for Pitney Bowes every day, Monday through Friday, nine to five.

When he graduated, I asked Robert what aspects of *The Power Program* had most helped him with his phenomenal achievement. Here's what he said: "It was the fact that every 30 days, I had to set a goal. It was always, 'What do I need to do in the next month?'"

Now, while this book is not a substitute for the experience of *The Power Program*, it does present the proven concepts from the course and will help you to reach your Next Level. For best results, I recommend you read through the entire book first. Then, go back and review one chapter each month. For the next 30 days after that, maintain focus on that one area of real estate until you master it.

As an independent contractor in our business of real estate, if you can implement the three *Power Principles* we just discussed—to employ *The Coaching Philosophy*, to be *Next Level-driven*, and to *maintain focus* throughout your career—you will soon find yourself walking up to get an award at your company's (or the real estate board's) next banquet.

What This Book Will Provide

Some people can read a book like this and very little of what they read will actually stay with them. Why? Again, it is a matter of *focus*. When you read because you feel *forced* to read, you may glean an idea or two, but for the most part you're just wasting time. I believe that reading is an investment that depends on *you* for its return.

If you approach this book with the attitude that the solutions you want and need are here and all you have to do is discover and understand them, you will find that this book will provide you with tremendous value. Throughout these pages, you'll find the best tools, tips, and techniques, many of them adapted and refined from the original masters of sales literature, like J. Douglas Edwards, Napoleon Hill, Clement Stone, Zig Ziglar, and many others. For over a decade, in my speeches and training seminars, I have been enhancing and customizing these tools to make them appropriate and powerful in today's real estate market. If you read this book with the intention of getting as much out of it as you possibly can and then taking the time to internalize these various skills, you will excel in your real estate career.

Another reason you will benefit from reading this book is that what I've presented here has been proven effective. These aren't my own theories of real estate that I've created in my secret laboratory and have decided to test on you. On the contrary, everything I talk about in this book is proven in the real world environment of buying and selling in various areas across the United States and Canada. When you read about a concept, tool or idea in this book, you'll know that our *Power Agents* have been successfully implementing these same skills, tools and techniques in a variety of marketplaces during various market conditions for nearly a decade.

Who Should Read This Book

Three categories of real estate professionals will derive great benefit from this book: the new agent, the experienced salesperson, and the top producer. Let's take a closer look.

- **New agents** will receive the current, effective, field-proven methods, tools, skills, and techniques they need to accelerate their career. By applying the principles in this book, those new to the profession will be able to succeed in the increasingly competitive world of real estate sales.
- **Experienced salespeople** will use this book to update the skills and techniques they learned long ago and implement new tools and concepts to help them reach their Next Level. By recognizing what has been working for them so far and strengthening the areas where they are lacking, veteran agents will ensure that they can earn a consistent income by selling residential real estate.
- **Top producers** will learn how to break through what is stopping them from reaching their full potential and renew their enthusiasm for this business. By reading this book, they'll rediscover some of the fundamental techniques that helped them to get to where they are now—getting "back to basics"—and become energized to maintain this solid foundation.

In addition to these groups, *managers, brokers, owners, trainers,* and *educators* should really appreciate the value of this book because of the practical, hands-on way it is written and because the information is topical and battle-tested.

Mortgage loan officers will also find this book very valuable because it will give them a comprehensive overview of the real estate sales process and show them how to help real estate agents become more effective. They can also use some of our proven sales techniques in their business to increase their income and boost customer satisfaction.

Here's my final coaching for you before you go on to Chapter 1.

Don't just read this book. Embrace it. Devour it. Internalize it. Become part of the culture in which successful professionals reside. Let the thoughts, words, and concepts become yours to use as you rise to your immediate Next Level and all your future Next Levels. Be committed to giving yourself the foundation to excel; I promise you that all the building blocks are revealed in the pages that follow. Read them with all your might and take the first step to enjoying a more productive career and a powerful life.

Acknowledgments

First and foremost, I thank all of my *Power Agents*. Their commitment to mastering real estate has given me a much better understanding of our business.

To Stu Kamen and Vinnie Romano, for if it wasn't for them this book would never have been written.

To Mac and Pat Levitt, who through their constant coaching have helped me not only be a better salesperson, but a better human being. Thank you for teaching me the concepts of real estate and helping me make a difference in our industry.

To my fellow National Speakers Association members, especially Floyd Wickman, Danielle Kennedy, and Tom Hopkins, for helping me become a much better speaker and trainer.

To my family, especially my son, Michael Raymond DeFina, for putting up with the long hours and being so wonderful in supporting me in my business.

Last, but most certainly not least, to my father Raymond DeFina. I hope he is watching over me and is proud.

CHAPTER 1

Time Management for Real Estate Agents

Power Fact

95% of the problems you and I have in the area of time management are not really about managing time at all. What most of us call time management is really about managing our attitude.

Overview

Chances are good that you've attended a time management seminar before or you've read a book or listened to a tape on the topic. There's also a good chance that after those things you weren't much more empowered or effective with your time than before. That's because, in my opinion, time management is really an attitude issue, not a technique issue. By attitude, I'm talking about being truly focused on and enthusiastic about your goals. You see, when you are really passionate about your goals, your vision, getting to your Next Level, etc., you'll automatically do the most productive things to achieve those goals.

So, as you read the useful information in this chapter, as you learn the powerful techniques and concepts for managing your time, keep in mind that, without the proper attitude, the best techniques in the world won't have much impact.

Let me tell you about the ballerina. When a ballerina is *being* the dance, it's a beautiful sight to behold. When she is simply *doing* the dance, that's when she messes up.

If you want to become effective in your career and you want to really master managing your time, then focus on being real estate and not doing it. When you're doing real estate, that's when it's work; that's when it's all effort. When you're being real estate—when you're being what you say you're committed to—then your actions will just naturally correlate with that commitment.

Fundamental Concepts of Time Management

1. **Think self-management, not time-management.** Time management isn't real. You can't manage a second or a minute. Time just is. But what we can manage is ourselves in that time. We can manage our actions.

2. **Work by objective, not by crisis.** Working by crisis might mean that there is no money in your bank account. Now we've got to go out and list and sell to get some money to get out of the crisis. Working by objective, on the other hand, is having goals, designing who you are, determining your Next Level, and living from that. When you do that, you have less stress. So, the concept is to consciously manage your actions about the goals you are committed to.

   Here's an example. Have you ever cooked for a family event? You have so much to do—you must cook loads of food, clean the house, do the laundry, etc. But when you are in action mode, there are no thoughts, judgments, or opinions getting in the way. You do 10 times more in this short time because you're working with this objective, this goal that you're committed to.

   Take that concept and apply it to your career. When you're committed to something happening in your career and you're crystal clear about it ... when you've got a real desire to reach the Next Level ... your actions will automatically flow. Time goes by quickly and you get the results to show for it. That's when real estate's not hard. That's when it's fun and exciting—a turn-on.

3. **Time management is a system of organized activities.** We have this in certain areas of our personal lives; they're called *routines*. Routines are useful to establish positive behavior patterns that bring about the results we desire. Later in this chapter, I'll give you specific techniques that will help you to build powerful routines.

4. **Time can be invested.** You can invest your time. It's like when you invest $5 and make $10 back. You can invest five minutes of your time and get back great results. For example, when you're in the office, you can return phone calls, clean your desk, or pick up the phone to schedule listing appointments. What would be the best return on your time investment? My point is, start to look at your time as a valuable commodity. Invest it as you would invest in stocks or bonds—as you would invest in anything that would give you a positive return on your investment.

5. **You can't get it all done!** This is a truism. You can't. At the end of the day, you're going to still have things that you didn't get finished, so stop trying to get it all done in 24 hours. It's like a rat on a wheel in a cage. We work longer hours, we come home stressed, we unload it on our spouse, and so on. Understand this concept: you'll get as much done as you get done. Period.

6. **Do *something* as opposed to *nothing*.** This is for the procrastinators. Get busy! If you're sitting in your office and you're procrastinating, or you're taking papers from one side of the desk and moving them to the other side and then back again, you're procrastinating. If you're sitting in the office and it's six o'clock and you're trying to think of what would be the most productive thing to do at this time … you're thinking and thinking and thinking and thinking and you're looking and you're searching…. I'm saying, "Stop all that nonsense and just get busy!"

7. **Live a balanced life.** How many hours are there in a week? 168. We have career, family, personal obligations—which includes sleep. According to Alan Lakein, who wrote *How to Get Control of Your Time and Your Life,* a good workweek consists of two 12-hour days, three nine-hour days, and one four-hour day. That's a total of 55 hours per week. Here's the point of this. If you spend 55 hours in business and let's say you have 73 hours personal (including sleep), that would leave you with 40 hours for family. That would total 168 hours. What most of us in the real estate profession do is we work more than 55 hours and then we take the extra hours from somewhere else, typically our family (see Figure 1-1).

8. **Work a schedule.** In my travels I've met many top-producing salespeople. What makes them top-producing salespeople is that they work a schedule. If something falls outside of their schedule, they do one of two things. Either they'll not do the business or they'll do the business, knowing that they have to make up for it somewhere else. What I would do if I were you

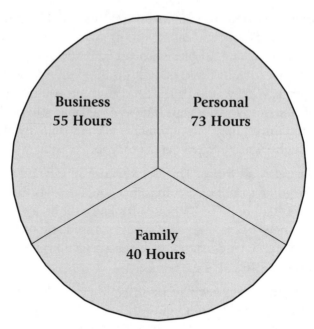

Figure 1-1. A balanced life

(especially if you're having some struggles at home) is to make up a work schedule from Monday through Sunday and give it to your spouse and your manager and tell them that this is what you're committing to.

In one of my training programs, there was an agent in Austin, Texas, who was the top-producing agent in the whole program for a three-month period. What was really interesting is that he was a part-time agent and he listed more houses than any full-time agent in this program. Why do you think that was? Because he managed his time. I asked him how he did it. He said, "When you can only work from six to nine at night, you have to be busy. You can't take the time, when you go into the office, to talk with people. You have to be productive."

If you set a schedule for yourself and you're serious about keeping it, I promise you that you'll be more productive.

20 Powerful Time Management Techniques

1. Set goals constantly. My mother brought me up on goals. She was constantly writing goals and to-do lists—constantly. The thing about goals is that it's OK to change them. You see, it's not just the achievement of a goal but the journey that counts. You've heard that expression before. So, keeping that in mind, what's more important than hitting the goal is your attitude and actions about the goal.

It's really not about the achievement of the goal, but what that goal does for the person. It affects whether you're sitting on the sidelines watching soap operas or out there *being* real estate. You may be thinking that it's important that you reach your goals. No, it's important that you be *committed* to your goals. It's important that your actions correlate to whatever you're committed to. But if you have a goal and it's starting not to turn you on, and your actions show you've lost your commitment to it, it's OK to change it and get committed to something else.

Do you think that when you die it's going to matter how many houses you listed in your life or how much money you saved or earned? What's going to matter is the people you contributed to, the difference you made with your family and community—that's what's important. Goals need to be structured to help us be who we are. So if you've got a goal that's not turning you on and exciting you, change it.

2. **Focus on building your listing inventory.** Although I'll cover this in greater detail in Chapter 2, "The Art of Prospecting," let me share something with you now. If all you did was work buyers, could you make a six-figure income? Yes, but I suggest you would go insane. The best way to increase your production and manage your time is to focus on obtaining listings. You see, if most of your business came from selling houses to buyers, you would have to always be there to work with them. But if you had a lot of listings that should sell in a fair amount of time, you could be on vacation and still be making money. Why? Because other agents are showing your inventory. The more listings in your inventory, the more personal time you can have. Now, if you're spending too much time servicing your listings, it's probably because you're not working that part of the business correctly. We'll address that in Chapter 5, "Servicing Listings to Sell."

3. **Use motivational devices.** I believe that motivational devices clear the cobwebs from your mind and keep you focused on what you're committed to.

   ■ **IMAGE POSTER.** After you design your Next Level and say who you are committed to being for the 12 months, you'll take poster board and cut out pictures and words from magazines that represent that Next Level. For example, if part of your Next Level is to have a Mercedes or a boat, get a picture of that and put it there, maybe with some words to back it up. This will be a continual reminder to focus on your Next Level.

■ **DOT BOARD.** One of the things I have learned from training thousands of agents is that a key factor that holds them back is the stress they impose on themselves. For example, they'll say, "I need more listings" or "I need a sale." As insignificant as the Dot Board technique may sound, it solves this dilemma—and nearly all of my students say this is one of the best things they learned from *The Power Program*®. Here's how it works

Buy a standard piece of poster board and create a chart like the one shown in Figure 1-2.

Month	Listings	Listings Sold	Buyer Sales

Figure 1-2. An example of a Dot Board

Now, whenever you obtain a listing, one of your listings sells, or one of your buyers goes into contract, give yourself a dot in the appropriate column. So the focus is not "I need more listings" or "I need a sale"; instead, it becomes "I need a dot." Once again, as strange as this may be, it puts some fun in your career. What's also great about this is at any time in the year you can look at this board and see how well you're doing in each category. This really works!

You'll get motivated—the peer pressure, the motivation just to get the dot up there is very powerful. I recommend that you put this over your desk or somewhere in the office (e.g., the kitchen) where everyone hangs out and sees it.

4. **Use a daily to-do list with a highlighter.** You should have a planner in which you list the tasks to accomplish. But what do we usually do when we accomplish something? We put a check next to it or we cross it off, right? The problem with this is at the end of the day the focus is more on what you *didn't do* versus what you did. Instead, I suggest that you highlight each item on your list as you accomplish it. This may seem like a little thing, but it makes a huge difference to your attitude.

5. **DWP—Delegate Whenever Possible!** Here's an exercise you may find useful. Make a list of all the low-priority items that you currently do, in business and your personal life, and see how you can delegate these items to others. For example, taking pictures of your new listings, making copies of keys, mailings, filing, housework, gardening, etc. Unless you find a certain amount of solitude in actually performing some of these tasks, I recommend that you outsource them.

6. **Focus on accomplishments.** Let me introduce you to a very effective technique I've used called the "Accomplishment Chart." Have you ever had a time in your career when you were depressed—when it seemed like you were doing a bunch of work, prospecting, showing buyers, etc., but deals were falling through and nothing was going right? Sometimes it just gets so bad, like the more you do the worse things are getting, then all of a sudden you can't see anything possible. You're totally immersed in the box, everything is not working, and it keeps getting worse and worse and worse.

There was a time in my career when I couldn't think how to get out of this whirlwind, except to change my thinking and focus on my accomplishments. So I came up with this Accomplishment Chart. It's a really simple thing and it made a tremendous impact for me.

On this chart are two columns: "Today's Accomplishments" and "Tomorrow's Accomplishments." When I would go home and at night before going to bed, I'd look at this chart and I'd write down all of my accomplishments for that day. During tough times, I'd force myself to find something good. For example, the first day I put on this chart that I had previewed some homes, cleaned up my desk, and made some calls. They weren't earth-shattering accomplishments, but they were accomplishments nevertheless. After I answered the question, "What did I accomplish today?" I'd write on the chart for tomorrow—like a one-day goal—that I'd attend three listing presentations and preview five new houses. The next day I did the same thing, and again and again for three weeks. Before I went to sleep, I kept working this chart. Well, in the third week, I listed three homes and made two sales! Not bad for a week of production. But up until that point, I hadn't done much, because I was so trapped by the negative aspects of the business.

I encourage you to use the Accomplishment Chart whenever you need a boost in your career.

7. **Schedule problem solving.** This is for the top agents. When you get to your Next Level and you've got an inventory of 30, 40, or 50 listings, a seller can't just call and talk to you; otherwise you'd be on the phone most of the time. What a lot of top producers do is schedule problem solving. At the listing appointment they say, "Mr. and Mrs. Seller, if you ever need to speak with me because you have a problem or question, I talk to my clients (for instance) between 5 and 7 p.m. The reason I schedule that time is that the rest of the day I'm out working on getting your house sold. Of course, at any other time you can speak with my assistant, who can usually handle most problems."

8. **Work the *house*, not the *buyer*.** Here's what usually happens. A buyer calls into the office and says, "I want a three-bedroom, two-bath house." What does a typical agent do? She stops everything and tries to find that house for that buyer. Then she takes the buyer out and shows him house after house after house. During that process, if he doesn't buy one of these houses, then the agent makes certain adjustments: "Oh, OK, so you don't like this, I'll make sure I don't show you this, I'll show you another type of house…." This is working the buyer.

Now, sometimes agents ask me, "But Darryl, if I am a buyer's agent, isn't that what I'm supposed to do?" There is no law that says you have to work like crazy showing a bunch of houses. Trust me, this does not work.

Working the house means that, instead of taking one buyer and showing a bunch of houses, you take one house and bring a bunch of buyers through it. Think about it. Which is better, to take one buyer to 10 houses or to take one house and show it 10 times? If you take one house and show it 10 times, your odds soar through the roof. You will sell that house.

I'll prove this to you. When you go to preview houses (a brokers' open house) and your office finds this hot house, the agents run back to the office and get on the phone and call their buyers to come out and see not 10, five, or even two houses. We tell the buyer to come out and see just this *one house*… and what happens? In a very short time, that house sells! In that moment all the agents are working the house, not the buyer.

So make it a system of organized habits and do that all the time. A *Power Agent®* of mine, Angel Schmidt from Long Island, New York, came up with this expression: *"Less stress, income higher, work the house, not the buyer."*

9. **Work the Shiny Penny**™ **list.** You have price ranges. Your buyer wants a house for $200K and you're going to look at houses from $200K to $220K perhaps. For a buyer who wants a house for $220K, you might show houses between $220K and $240K. In other words, you can take buyers and put them into price categories. Let's say in the $200K to $220K category there are 20 houses in your market. Of those 20 houses, aren't there usually three or four best of the best? Forget about style, forget about bedrooms, forget all of that. These are the shiny pennies, the cream of the crop. A serious buyer in that price range will usually buy the best of the best, regardless of the style he told you he wanted, right? That's why at seminars you've been told not to worry if a buyer says she wants this type of house at this price, etc. They don't buy what they call in on. In fact, most of the time they buy a totally different type of house. This is because they buy the best of the best in their price range.

So what I'm suggesting you do is find the shiny pennies in those price ranges and show only those. If they don't buy a shiny penny, chances are they are not ready to buy. Put them in your files and then, the next time another shiny penny comes on the market, call all your buyers in the price range and show just that one house.

What I suggest you do now is go back to your office, make a list of the price ranges in your market, and come up with the shiny pennies. Then make a master list of all those houses: that's the list that you show and you work. If you want to double your sales in the next 12 months, do this and you will!

10. **Preview as little as possible.** New agents need to preview to begin to learn value. But once you understand the value of homes, you shouldn't have to preview. Many agents have made their best sales when they never

saw the house before. There's this thing that happens—not just in the real estate business—called the element of surprise. When you preview the house, you take away that element of surprise.

11. **An idea pad.** This is for those moments when you come up with ideas, like when you're driving in the car. It's not a big item, but it's a useful one. Keep your idea pad with you at all times. Even put it by your bed at night, so when you wake up with a great idea it will be yours forever.

12. **Have an "ad book" that holds your advertising of other homes.** Have a book that has all of your old ads organized by heading or concept or category, e.g., three-bedroom colonial section. That way when you list a house, instead of sitting there trying to think up an ad, just go back to the section that has ads for the same type of house from months ago and use one of those ads.

13. **Improve your technical abilities.** Some agents are really behind the times: you just can't run your business anymore without improving your technical skills. I'm not just talking about computers and the Internet. I bet there are functions with your cell phone or office voice-mail that you're not even aware of. Some of these items can really free up your time when you know how to use them.

14. **Hire an assistant.** When you're ready for this, you'll know. If you want to make more money in less time, pay someone $7 an hour to help you do it. (See Chapter 10, "Working with Assistants," for details.)

15. **Do a listing campaign.** What are the two areas we work in real estate? Listings and sales, buyers and sellers. If you try to do both 100%, what will happen? Nothing—you'll burn out. Here's something I did when I was in sales. You go on a listing campaign. You don't work with buyers. You list, list, list like a mad person for 30 days. You build that inventory. Then you take a break. And when you take a break from listings, where do you work? You play with buyers.

If you keep building your listing inventory, do you have a sense of accomplishment? Absolutely—you're feeling good about yourself. But you need to take a break. You can't keep working listings day and night, night and day, or you'll go insane.

And the reason I call it *playing* with buyers is because you'll find that, once you've built your inventory, you won't care so much if they buy or not. It's more of a game. You show them houses for a few weeks, just the shiny pennies, and you know what will happen? They'll start buying them. Because you're not in the mode of "I *have* to make a sale!" You're showing them only the best. You will close more buyers and you'll have more fun in your career.

Now, after you sell a couple of houses, you write some offers and get them into contract and you've got a few dots on the board, then you're back on the listing campaign. And then you take a break to go play with buyers. Don't try to do both at the same time or you'll go cuckoo. You have to try to pace yourself. Real estate is not a sprint, it's a race; you need to pace yourself.

16. **Move your desk every six months.** I know that some of you can't physically move your desk, but if you can it would be great. You'll get a different view. Or, maybe you can change desks with another agent. Periodically, I just rearrange my whole desk. I'll change my office around whenever I feel that things are getting stale and I need to shake it up. I have agents tell me it's like a shot in the arm or a wake-up call. Plus, you have to clean up your desk to do this. You might be surprised what you'll find.

17. **Have a purpose for each call.** When we get to the section on the telephone and prospecting, we'll be more detailed about this concept. But for now I'm just going to say, *have a purpose for each call.* I think it's really interesting that many of us pick up the phone to make a call without being crystal clear as to our main objective. Before you get on the line, ask yourself, "What's the one thing I want to accomplish from this phone call?" Whether you're talking with some of your existing clients, a buyer, a prospect, or a referral, don't just pick up the phone. Have an intense purpose as to what you want to accomplish and what your objective is. When you do that, you're going to have fewer conversations where five minutes of business gets stretched out with chitchat to 50. That won't happen anymore when you have a clear purpose for each call.

18. **Have a "scrapbook of the future."** One of my students gave me this idea and I think it's the coolest thing. Most of us have a scrapbook of our past (you know, baby pictures, letters we sent when we were at camp—just a bunch of stuff). But you can create a scrapbook of your *future.* Start clipping all the things you want as you design your life, career, etc. Just cut them out and put them in the book. This is really an extension of the image poster we discussed as part of technique #3. But play it out here. Make believe that the scrapbook really shows shots of your life … your future life, that is! I think it's a really neat idea.

19. **Involve your family in your goals.** Put an asterisk next to this one. One of the things I know is challenging in our business is that we tend to work many hours. We spoke about this earlier. We schedule 55 hours this week in real estate and don't manage that effectively, we know we're going to expand out to 65, 75, and so on. When we do that, we're taking those hours from both family and personal life. Family life gets stressful, so I highly recommend that you include your family when setting your monthly goals. Here are two suggestions.

For instance, let's say that I have a wife and two children and I want to get five listings this month. I know I'm going to have to put in extra hours. So I'll go to my family, have a little family meeting, and say, "Here's what I want to do in the next 30 days. I want to get five listings. I'm going to be putting in a few extra hours. Here's my game plan. If we get these five extra listings, honey, you and I are going to go away for the weekend—to that resort you wanted to go to—just you and I with the spa and the whole thing. Kids, I'll buy both of you new 10-speed bikes." Obviously your family may get excited about this. So when you come home at six or seven at night, what do you think your family is going to do? They're going to say, "What the heck are you doing home? Get the heck out of here, knock on some doors, and make some calls. We've only got two listings and we need three more!" Do you follow me? Now, this may put a little pressure on you, but it's the good kind of pressure. I'll call it a "challenge." So have your family be a part of your goals and life will be a lot more fun.

Here's an extra technique my students have told me works really well in helping you to stay close with your family. Typically, whenever we feel guilty because we think we're neglecting our family, we take them out to the movie or to dinner. Instead, make a "Family Fun List." Make a list of all the activities you can do with your family (e.g., picnic, ice skating, horseback riding, theatre, bowling, etc.) and hang it up on the refrigerator. The "game" is you can't do an item twice until you've done everything on the list once. This will force you to do new and creative things with your family. Also, by hanging it up, you'll be more proactive about spending time with them, rather than doing it out of guilt. Oh yeah, make sure you highlight the items as you do them.

20. **Get your file system together.** In technique #13, I briefly advised you to "get technical"—to take full advantage of your computer and your

cell phone and so forth. We have a chapter devoted to technology. Let's talk now, though, about your filing system.

- **BUYERS.** Earlier we spoke about working the shiny penny list—that in each price category of houses there is going to be a handful that are the best of the best, the cream of the crop, the shiny pennies. So with that thought in mind, we want to file our buyers by price range. This way, when you see a shiny penny in a particular price range, you go to your buyer file and call every buyer in that price range to come out and look at that shiny penny. Also within your buyer file should be a folder for what I call "A" buyers. These are people who *have* to buy a house. Most likely they've sold something else, so they've got a bag full of cash and need to place it somewhere. These buyers are the exception to the rule about working the price range. You show them everything and anything, because there's no question about *what* they are going to buy, just *who* they are going to buy it from.

- **SELLERS.** This first (and best) method for filing sellers is by their phone number. Let's say you're working with FSBOs. You take a box that holds index cards and on the tabs you write "0000," "1000," "2000," etc.—with those numbers representing the last four digits of a phone number. So let's say you have two FSBOs (for sale by owner), and the phone numbers are 223-0991 and 526-1234. The first FSBO would go behind the tab that says "0000" and the second FSBO would go behind the tab "1000." Whenever you look at the newspaper and check out all the FSBOs, you cut out each ad and attach it to a separate index card. Then, in the upper left corner of the index card, you put the town that that FSBO is in, if you work more than one town. In the right corner you put the phone number, because that's how we're going to file it. Then you would put some information, like their address and their name. Every time you see that FSBO advertised, you would write the date you saw it advertised. If you note that they lowered their price after a few weeks or months, don't cut out that ad; just use the index card with the original ad and, next to the ad, write their new price. Now, when you call that FSBO, on the back of the index card you can write down your conversation with them.

Here's the real power of this. When an FSBO stops advertising, say, for a month, then you see the new ad with the new price, you can call the owners and say, "Hi, Mr. and Mrs. Seller, this is Darryl from XYZ Realty. I noticed that you started advertising your house again. I remember when you adver-

Front of Card

Escondido	**516 555-1234**

For Sale by owner. 4 bedrooms,
2.5 baths on quiet cul de sac.
Recently remodeled. Great home
for family. Call for appointment.
516 555-1234

Mr. & Mrs. Jack Jennings
2334 Las Viajes Rd.

4/8 ($175,000); 5/7, 5/21, 6/1, (169,000)

Back of Card

4/8 We spoke about ...

Figure 1-3. Keeping track of potential sellers

tised it a month ago for such and such a price." They're going to think you're
Houdini that you remembered this information. So, by using this file system, what will start to happen is that you won't be calling the same FSBOs
over and over without knowing that you've spoken to them before.

When you see any new FSBOs in the newspapers, you cut the ad out and
attach it to an index card. If you already have a card on any FSBOs you see
advertised, you obviously don't need to cut that ad out again. It's a very
effective system for tracking FSBOs. By the way, you obviously need to call
these people and attempt to get a listing appointment!

Of course, you could use a database software program, like Top Producer, to file all this information. As good as I am at technology, I still prefer this file system for FSBOs. The reason is there is something about seeing the "real ad" that gives me a better sense of who these sellers are.

Now that we've got this file system for the prospects—the file box with the index cards—we need another system for our existing clients. Therefore, the second file system for sellers would be individual folders. (I'll give you more on this when we get into the chapter about servicing listings.)

Past Clients

Whether you're computerized or not, I want to say something about past clients. When you're listing and selling real estate on a day-to-day basis, you have a choice to generate business from one of two ways. Either you can go out and generate new business, constantly meeting new buyers and sellers, or you can tap into your existing business—people who know you, people who have done business with you before. Which is better? Obviously, tapping into existing business.

It's amazing to me how many agents live paycheck to paycheck. They get the money and get out of Dodge. They don't stay in touch with those sellers; they don't call them. I know there are a lot of companies out there that offer an automatic follow-up system; that's good, but that shouldn't replace *your* staying in touch with your people. I've met many agents who get 80% of their business from their client base, people they've done business with before. You've got a tremendous amount of listing leads, buyer leads, and referrals from this list, whether you utilize it or not. It's exciting. And I want you, right now, to make a decision and commitment that you need to service and take care of the people who know you and have done business with you before.

I learned this concept from the insurance industry. When an insurance agent sells a policy, he or she gets residuals. Every time the policyholder makes a payment on the premium, the agent gets paid a portion of that. So the more policies the agents sell, the more they keep adding to a steady flow of income that they can count on.

You and I have the same thing available to us. Except in our profession, it's one commission check at a time. But it could be constant. The key here is that you have to stay in touch with your past clients. But you have to put together some kind of system.

And don't do it just once a year. What I've found is that successful agents stay in touch with past clients at least four times a year. They'll send them an anniversary card, a holiday card, and maybe two other mailers, just to say, "How are you doing? Here's my face. Do you need anything? If you know of anybody listing a house, give me a call." Four contacts a year, minimum, and I recommend that one of those contacts definitely be a phone call.

- **FARMING.** You should have a totally separate filing system for your farm. (See Chapter 8, "Farming for Dollars," for more details.)
- **TODAY'S URGENT BUSINESS.** I have a bin for me and for my assistant on my desk. I have a bin for future stuff I have to do and I have a bin for the things I must do today.
- **YOUR TAXES.** I'm not going to go through all the categories, but what I recommend you do is, instead of sitting on your living room floor April 14 making piles, to make the piles as the year progresses by using a manila folder for each expense category.

As I said at the beginning of this chapter, all the best time management techniques in the world are meaningless without the proper attitude. So take a look and see if you're truly committed to achieving your Next Level in real estate. (I already know that you are; that's why you're reading this book!) I don't expect you to implement all of the advice I've just given you. But I do expect you to be willing to do what it takes to move forward in your career. With that in mind, review this chapter once more and select several of the steps to put into action today.

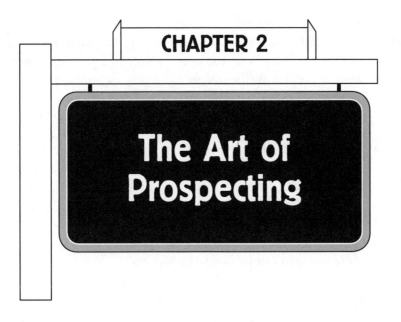

CHAPTER 2

The Art of Prospecting

Power Fact

It doesn't matter whether you're a top producer or a first-month sales-person: when your prospecting efforts dwindle, so does your income.

Overview

No matter how busy you are, you must constantly prospect in order to remain successful in real estate. However, for a lot of agents, picking up that telephone is a very difficult thing to do.

Here's the nasty little secret to prospecting—the toughest point is when you first start. It's no different than when you take on any new activity that requires a change in behavior. Overcoming your old habits requires significant commitment and effort before you can feel comfortable. That's why I want to challenge you. Make the commitment now that for the next 30 days, without fail, you will make *X* number of calls each day or block out *X* number of hours each day to totally devote to prospecting. If you do that on a regular basis for a month, I promise you that picking up that telephone and prospecting won't be such a daunting task. You will overcome something. You'll move beyond this vague fear, or whatever it is that might be holding you back. And, believe me, once you overcome it, then it's easy. It really is a piece of cake.

Now that you've accepted my challenge, let me give you the tools you need to succeed and master the art of prospecting. The material that follows in this chapter is, I truly believe, the best information you will find on how to get through to a seller on the telephone and book that appointment.

Six Key Concepts of Prospecting

Concept #1: Prospecting is the name of the game. We're in a great profession. We do more than just list and sell houses. We make a difference with people by helping them move from point "A" to point "B" in their lives. Now, how we know we're doing a good job of this is by how much money we make. Money is a gauge of how many people we are helping; the more we help people, the more money we make.

Let me share what I call the Links to Success.

- To make more money, we need more closings.
- To have more closings, we need more contracts.
- To have more contracts, we need more listings.
- To have more listings, we need to attend more appointments.
- To attend more appointments, we need to schedule more appointments.
- To schedule more appointments, we need to *prospect*.

So prospecting is the first link to success. If you do more of this, the rest will naturally fall into place. Even if you're *really* bad at it, the more you do it, the more results you will get. Why? Because real estate is a numbers game as shown in Figure 2-1.

Studies show that if you call enough people and just bark into the phone, eventually someone is going to say, "You must be a Realtor®. Come on over!" So you've always got to prospect.

Concept #2: Focus on building inventory. Many of us have listings goals: "This month I am going to get X number of listings." But I want you to start doing what all the top agents do. They don't look so much at how many listings they get in a particular month; they look at how many they have in their inventory.

Before one of my *Power Program* classes, I walked over to my student, Tony Donnino. Tony said that he had gotten three listings and one sale. I said, "Wow. Sounds like you had a good month." And Tony, being a perfectionist, says, "Well, I could have done better." So, since I know Tony loves to set the bar high for himself, I asked him how many listings he had in his

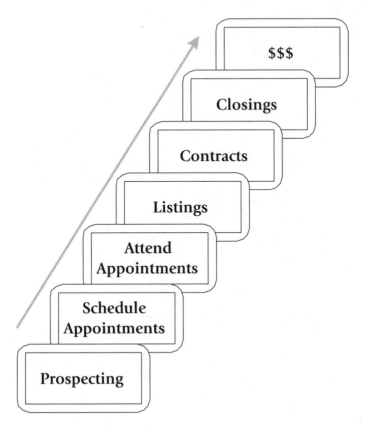

Figure 2-1. It's a numbers game

inventory. He told me he had 26. Again, sounds good, right? But remember, we're talking about Tony here. I said, "Tony, you should focus on building your inventory up to 30 over the next 30 days. Then perhaps next month build it to 35."

What's great about this is that by focusing on *building inventory*, as opposed to just getting listings, you will replenish your listings as they go into contract. So, let's say you have 26 in your inventory and your goal is to get it to 30 in the next month, so you need to obtain four. But, let's say that during the month two of your listings go into contract. How many do you need to get that month? Six, because you're also replenishing the two that went into contract. As a matter of fact, if you just played the game to increase your inventory by only one each month, you would probably be on your way to doubling your income, depending on what type of market it is. You could even create a chart, the Listing Inventory Chart (Figure 2-2).

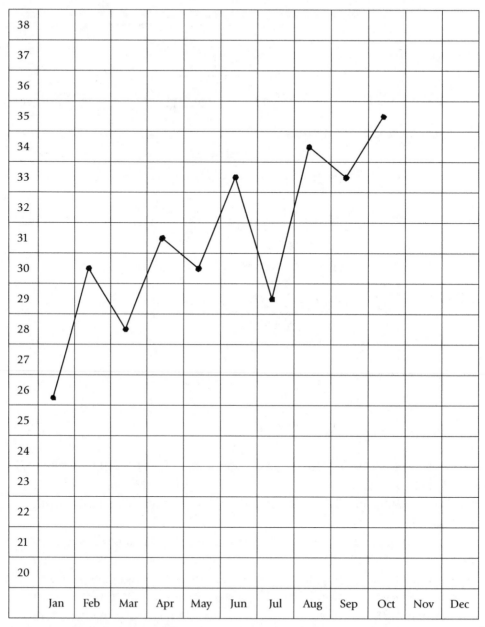

Figure 2-2. Listing inventory chart

Concept #3: If you are in the office, you're not making money. The only way you make money is if you are out of the office seeing people— whether it be buyers or sellers. And if you are in the office, your primary objective should be generating opportunities to go on more listing appointments.

Concept #4: Work a prospecting plan. Here is a very simple—and very effective—plan.

A. Cold-call three hours a week. All the top producers that I know are making six-figure incomes. They are putting $100,000 plus a year into their pocket and they are cold-calling once a week for three hours. Why would that be a good thing to do? I mean, here are people making six-figure incomes; they probably don't need to cold-call, right? Wrong. They do it to keep their skills sharp and stay on top of their game. Not to mention the fact that cold-calling enables them to maintain a high listing inventory in the first place.

B. See two FSBOs a week.

C. See two expireds a week.

Now, just looking at letters A, B, and C, how many listing appointments are you going to attend at a minimum? Four. Do you see that? Two FSBOs, two expireds—four is an absolute minimum. This is what a lot of top producers do. Of course, you might go on more as a result of the cold calls.

Or you can try something that I personally did. We'll call it letter D.

D. Do a listing campaign. I used to go on listing campaigns. For just 30 days, I would list like a madman. I wouldn't work with buyers at all, except for the "A" buyers. I would just list, list, list, list, list. When I got tired of that and I wanted a mental break, I would go play with buyers. Once I got tired of the buyers and I was ready to go back to listing— boom!—I would do a listing campaign once again.

Concept # 5: Refer your B and C buyers out. Here are the definitions of "A," "B," and "C" buyers.

■ An "A" buyer is someone who *has* to buy a home *now*—there are no ifs, ands, or buts about it.

■ A "B" buyer is someone who is *committed* to buying a home, but not in much of a hurry.

■ A "C" buyer is someone who is *not* committed; it's more like "it would be nice" or "it would be a good idea" to buy a home now.

When you're focused on building listing inventory, you should not work with "B" and "C" buyers. "A" buyers are a definite sale, so you keep working them.

Let me illustrate my point this way: Can somebody make $100,000 or more a year in real estate by working with buyers only, not doing any listings at all? Yes, but it would be very tough … and you would definitely be crazy by the time you were through. But if all you did was work *listings* and not work buyers, could you make $100,000 a year? Absolutely.

Now, I am not saying to abandon working with buyers altogether. But you've got to respect what works. And it's not just me saying it. I travel across the country all the time and I'm always talking to real estate people who make six figures. They tell me that 75% of their income comes from listings sold and the other 25% from working with buyers.

So I am telling you to prospect and build your inventory—put most of your efforts into that. And if you are going to work with buyers, make certain that you're just going after the "A" buyers. Why would you work with someone who isn't ready to buy now? We are not chauffeurs; we're real estate salespeople. So if you've got someone who isn't ready to buy now, a "B" or "C" buyer, refer her or him to an agent who hasn't read this book!

Concept #6: Real estate is a pure numbers game. Put an asterisk next to this one. Regardless of how good or bad you are on the telephone, if you just make call after call, eventually you'll get an appointment. Now, I don't know if that helps you or not, but I would think it takes some stress away.

You see, all that we try to do as salespeople, by taking courses, listening to tapes, and going to seminars, is to increase our skill levels so we can then increase our closing ratio. But regardless of your skill level, you should just simply work the numbers.

Just the other day, Sharon, one of my students, came up to me and said, "Darryl, I think I know what you're talking about. I should prospect more. But I'm just not doing it."

"Why?" I asked.

She said, "I just have this fear of calling a complete stranger."

So here is what I told her. I said, "Look, if you don't make the phone calls, are you going to have any listings?"

"Nope."

"Great," I said. "So let's say that you do call and you are really bad and you mess up. Are you going to get any listings?"

"Nope," Sharon smiled. She was starting to catch on.

"So, in other words," I finished, "if you don't call or if you do call and mess up, you are not going to get the listings either way, right? But here's the thing: if you don't even pick up the phone, you're guaranteed not to get the listings."

But if you do call, maybe just maybe you might not mess up. You may even get lucky. Who knows? The right thing could just come out of your mouth and you just might get the appointment and get a listing.

My point is that by picking up the telephone and just making the call, even if you don't get the appointment, you are no worse off than if you didn't make the call at all.

Here's a tip. The key to working the numbers and making calls and prospecting is *don't be so attached to the result*. Let me say that again: don't be so attached to the result.

You know, I believe that the reason you may not pick up the telephone is because you have something riding on what the other person says, meaning, "I've *got* to get this appointment because if I don't, I've failed." Forget all that garbage. This is business. It's not about your worth as a person.

Just pick up the phone and see if you can help these sellers. If they are open to having you help them, well, that's great. If they are not open to it, that's fine too. At least you tried.

Understanding the Mindset of FSBOs and Expireds

To be successful when prospecting, you need to understand the mindset of those you're calling.

FSBOs

First, let's take a look at why a person would be a For-Sale-by-Owner.

- **The person may have had a bad experience dealing with agents.** If this isn't the reason, it's probably that….
- **The person doesn't know any better.** He or she is an FSBO simply because he or she doesn't understand the value that an agent brings to the table. Usually, FSBO are motivated by one or more of three factors:
  - They want to save money. They mistakenly believe that saving on our commission means more money left for them. You and I both know, however, that selling on their own increases the odds that they are going to pocket less in the end. (More about this later.)
  - They think they'll have more flexibility. "I won't be tied to any one broker," they believe. "I will be in more control."

– Their ego gets in the way. "I can do as good a job or better than any realtor," they claim.

Expireds

Expireds are going to be feeling any combination of three things:

- **They are not opposed to working with agents.** They already listed with someone, so we know that at one point they didn't have a problem working with agents. They may still feel that way,
- **They may be upset with agents**—or with the real estate industry as a whole. As in "I was on the fence, then I gave it to this agent. They tied us up for six months and the house still didn't sell. You guys all stink."
- **They feel rejected.** Did you ever call an expired who said, "No, the house didn't sell, and we aren't selling at all right now"? That might be because the expireds are taking it as a personal rejection. They are personally upset. You have to envision the situation here. They are all excited about moving. An agent comes in and says, "No problem, here's what I can do for you." "Oh great," they think. "Our savior." Six months later, 100 buyers through the doors, ads, open houses, exposure, exposure, exposure, and basically what the seller is feeling is that everyone said, "We don't like your house. It stinks."

My question at this point: is the seller in the presence of what he or she is committed to—the reason for starting the whole process—or in the presence of her or his thoughts and feelings—and upset about what happened? Thoughts and feelings, right? What you need to do is bring back to the surface the reason for starting the whole process. (Note: Don't ever address on the telephone what the other agent did or didn't do. You just don't need to get into that.)

What I am telling you to do with expireds is get them out of the box they're trapped in and bring them back to what they committed to by renewing their motivation. I'll tell you how in a minute.

But first, I want to make sure I nail a point down with you. We went through the mindset of FSBOs and expireds. What is the number-one key that you need to focus on in both scenarios? It is to *find out what they are committed to.* To demonstrate this point, I always call FSBOs and expireds during class in *The Power Program* getting them on the phone right in front of the class. And, two out of three times, I get an appointment.

Afterward, agents always come up to me and say, "Darryl, I am amazed at how great you did!" or "I am shocked that you were able to close on that appointment." But the reason I am so successful is because my calls are never intended to manipulate the seller. It is never about me succeeding or even about me getting the appointment. Instead, it is about finding out what these people are committed to and seeing if I can help them. Now, I'm positive that the best way to help these people is for them to meet with me.

Sellers put themselves in a box. FSBOs have convinced themselves that they can save money by selling on their own, that they will have more flexibility, or that they can do a better job than an agent. Expireds are upset with agents or they feel rejected. In either case, we are just dealing with a bunch of opinions and interpretations. These are not facts, not absolute truths. So, when I speak with sellers like these, my only task is to uncover what they are committed to and to help them see this commitment clearly once again.

You see, when you learn what they are committed to and you have a conversation with them about this, you'll find that they really want to give you the appointment—because they want somebody who cares about what they want. The truth is, if you can help them achieve their goals, then, of course, it is in their best interest to speak with you.

Why Sellers Can't Save Money by Selling on Their Own

Think about it. We basically work for free and we are going to take tons of money and promote a home and we don't get paid unless it sells. What a great deal for homeowners! We are going to sell their house for them, which is going to net them the same amount of money as if they went through all that time, expense, and aggravation on their own.

"Darryl, why do you say that?" you ask. Here's why.

1. **FSBO hunters want a bargain.** The only reason why a buyer is going to shop purely FSBO is because she wants—what?—a bargain. She doesn't want to just save the commission; she wants a bargain.

   So, let's take a house that should be listed for $100,000 and we charge X. The FSBO says, "I'll sell it on my own and save X." Now a buyer who calls this FSBO knows the seller is a FSBO trying to save the commission; in other words, this $100,000 asking price has the commission built in. If the buyer doesn't want to pay the commission to the agent, she certainly doesn't want to pay it to the seller, so she takes X commission off the top. But in the buyer's mind, the seller is netting what he would have if he had listed, so she'll usually take another, let's say, 3% off X.

Let's take a FSBO who has been actively selling on her own for a period of time. You can sit at the presentation and say, "Lynn, here is why you are not going to save any money. The buyers you have been having through here, have any made an offer?"

Let's assume she says, "Yes."

"I bet you that they have been offering you about 10% below what you have been asking." Most of the time, the seller will be like, "How did you know?" For some reason buyers read this universal book that tells them, "Pay 10% less than what the seller is asking." Do you get this concept?

This is why a FSBO is not going to save anything. He is going to basically walk away with the same amount of money *or less* than if we sell it for him. And he'll have to do much, much more work just to (hopefully) come out even. This concept may not always hold true, especially in a hot seller's market, but here a few other reasons why a FSBO will not save money.

2. **Third-party negotiating.** With an agent, the buyer and seller don't negotiate directly; we do it for them. The seller wants $100,000 for the house. Odds are she is going to sell for about $90,000 doing it on her own. Because of our negotiating skills, because of everything we have to offer, we are going to be able to net the seller their $90,000 or maybe more. There's an expression you've probably heard: "An attorney who represents himself has a fool for a client." The reason why this is true is because if someone is personally involved, he or she is probably going to make mistakes. Said another way, what we bring to the table for a seller is our objectivity.

We have been trained to negotiate. We do our research and we do this all the time, whereas typical sellers may deal directly with the housing transaction one, two, or possibly three times in their entire life. It's the biggest monetary contract they may ever participate in. Shouldn't they lean on a professional who has negotiated dozens, maybe hundreds of deals? Of course.

Plus, we have a vested interest in getting them more money because we benefit too via our commission. And, once again, if they choose not to work with us, they are going to net no more money or maybe even less for their efforts. Why risk it?

3. **Agents have more available resources.** This is Marketing 101, folks. The seller wants the best possible price. To get the most money, we need to get the most buyers through the door. To get the most buyers through the door, we have to generate the greatest amount of exposure on the home. We get the most exposure on the home through marketing tools. The more marketing tools you have, the more exposure a house gets. The more exposure, the more buyers through the door. The more buyers through the door, the higher the price you will get for the house. The reason why the seller won't save money doing it on his or her own is because sellers don't have nearly as many marketing tools as we have. How many marketing tools does a FSBO have? Two, maybe three. How many do you have? Tons. Here's just one example.

What is the best type of buyer? Relocation. Why? Because they have to buy, they are committed to buy, and they are most likely in a time crunch. Now, let's say a FSBO is selling her house in Boston and there's a potential buyer for her house moving from New York. Guess what? That buyer from New York doesn't get the *Boston Globe,* so he'll never see the FSBO ad. Instead, that buyer has contacted an agent in Boston and she is going to sell him a house that is professionally listed. So, in other words, the FSBO is missing out on the best, cream-of-the-crop buyers. That's just one example of how our marketing tools can get more exposure for a house and therefore a higher price.

So, there you have it: the three basic reasons why the seller is not going to save money doing it on her or his own (see Figure 2-3).

Figure 2-3. Getting the best price possible

Rules of Thumb When Working on the Telephone

Rule #1: Show them that you care. I said this earlier, but I am going to say it again. When you pick up a phone to make your calls, it can't be about you. It can't be about you succeeding or getting a listing or closing. It can't be about any of that. It has to be about the person you're calling and what he or she is committed to!

When I'm in town, I sometimes stop into my students' offices. One time, when I was visiting an office where I had about 20 students, I said that I'd call the first FSBO ad they gave me and schedule an appointment. Somebody gave me an ad. I made this call—my first call—and got an appointment.

The agent went over to the house. She told the homeowner that I was a trainer and the whole story. Then she asked, "Why did you agree to let Darryl in?"

The homeowner said, "Before Darryl called, I must have gotten at least 70 phone calls from real estate agents and he was the only one that I let in." Of course, the agent asked why this was. The woman answered, "I could tell just by talking to him on the phone that he really cared about me and why we were selling."

Everything I am teaching you—the process I am explaining and the script I am going to give you—means nothing if it's about *you* succeeding with it. That's perhaps the toughest thing, because it is part of what motivated you to make the call, right? But you need to learn to shift the motivating force so that it is not about you, but rather about the contribution that you can make to people. Once you do this, you'll be on the right road.

Rule #2: Ask a lot of questions. There are three primary reasons why you probe and ask questions:

1. You want to find out what the person is committed to.
2. It helps display a genuine interest in the person's situation and helps to build rapport.
3. "Whoever asks the last question is in control."

You know that if you call FSBOs and expireds they ask you things like "How much commission do you charge?" Right? And you say whatever you say. Then they ask another question: "Well, how long of a listing do you guys take?" When they ask a question like that, some of us get a little defensive. We start to feel like we are losing control of the conversation.

By the way, don't ever, ever, *ever* handle commission over the phone or talk about multiple listings over the phone or talk about length of listings—anything. Never talk about that because, if you do, then they will decide based on your answers whether or not they are going to let you in the door.

Here is something else, especially with FSBOs and, in a lot of cases, expireds too. If they are selling on their own, do they want to work with an agent, yes or no? No. And if you insinuate on the telephone that the reason why you are calling is to talk to them about hiring you to market their home—said another way, to give you a listing—they won't even let you in the door.

Your approach must be to find out what they are committed to and see if you can help them. Most of the time, helping them means listing the house. Is that always true? No, it is not. But the commitment has to be to help them, whatever that means. And the way to discover how to best help them is to ask questions.

Here are a few questions you might consider asking:

- Where were you going to move when you sold your home?
- Why there?
- Do you have a new house already picked out?
- Have you ever worked with an agent before, either in buying or in selling a house? How was that experience?
- If I had a buyer who would pay you the money you needed to make this move a success, and you wouldn't have to pay a fee out of that money, is that something you would consider?

Rule #3: The purpose of the call is to see if you can help. Am I repeating myself? You bet. When you make this call, there is another human being on the end of the phone who has a book of reasons for selling—some good, some bad. Your job, our job—why we are licensed to do what we do—is to find out what the scenario is and see if we can help that person. If you believe after speaking to him or her that you can help, then your next job is to get in the door. Meaning, don't talk, don't do a listing presentation over the phone. Just get in the door. Got it?

The following section will help you to put the above advice into practice.

The Surefire Process for Scheduling Appointments over the Phone

Even though I've been told by many of my students that this dialogue has gotten them tremendous results, it's important to understand that it's really not the specific dialogue that produces the intended result, but the action of getting on the phone.

I would like you to believe that I am the guru of telephone dialogue, but the truth is that no one really is. What separates the great from the rest is that the great just put in a few extra hours picking up the phone. So, my advice is to use this dialogue as a starting point. Don't worry about memorizing this dialogue or using it as a script. The most important two things to remember are:

1. See if you can help the person based on what he or she is committed to.
2. Assuming you can, get in the door.

Here are some sample dialogues that will help you to succeed.

Step 1: Identify. "Hi. I'm calling in reference to the ad in the paper." You say this first, not "Hi, this is Darryl Davis from Power Realty." If you did that, you would hear "click" … or you may get "Hold on a second. Mom, Dad, a realtor is on the phone for you" followed by "Tell them we're not home!" Instead, just say that you are calling in reference to the ad in the paper. If the person who answers is not the decision maker, she or he will say, "Hold on, let me get my parents."

Then, you ask the second question in the Identify step: "Is the house still for sale?" The reason to ask this question before you identify yourself as an agent is because, if homeowner knows you're an agent before you ask that question, he or she will tell you, "No, the house is already sold." Once again, you say:

"I'm calling about the house for sale"

"Yes."

"Is it still available?"

"Yes."

Now move to the next part, Introduce Yourself.

Step 2: Introduce yourself. "Hi, this is Darryl Davis from Power Realty. How are you?"

Step 3: Clarify. You want to clarify whether the sellers are working with agents or not. "The reason why I'm calling is to see if you folks are open to working with agents in the sale of your property?" The person will answer that question either "yes" or "no."

If the answer is "Yes, we are working with brokers," you have to clarify it. Ask, "Is it currently listed with a broker?" Why would you say that? Because it could be. Sometimes sellers are still advertising on their own, but they just listed with a broker. If they say "no" when you ask if the property is currently listed, great—proceed.

However, if the answer is "No, we are not interested in working with brokers," what do you ask them? "So, you are trying to sell it on your own, huh?" If the person says "yes," you would naturally ask, "Is that because you folks want to save the commission?" She or he will probably say "yes," so now just jump into the next section and ask the following questions.

Step 4: Find out what they are committed to. "Oh, I see. Let me just ask you, where are you folks moving? ... Why there? ... By when do you need to get there?"

How many questions should you ask? Until you have a good sense of what the people are committed to and you think they are ready to let you come over. I've had some conversations go on for over 15 minutes before I got the appointment and some that lasted 60 seconds and then I scheduled the appointment. This is where instinct comes in and you get that only from making a lot of calls.

Step 5: Invite action. (By the way, another way to say "invite action" might be "close." But I like "invite action," because we are going with the consultative approach, not the manipulative way of selling. We train *Power Agents* to tell homeowners that we are inviting them to take action based on what they are committed to and that, if they are committed to selling, they should explore *all* of their options ..., which include meeting us.)

You have a few different ways of doing this.

For instance, you could ask, "Would you be offended if I just stopped by to see your house?" Isn't that a great question? What is the person going to say—"Yes, I would be thoroughly offended!"? I've found that this line works tremendously well with expireds.

What works best with FSBOs is, after you find out what they are committed to, you ask, "If I can help you move to Hunna Hunna and you wouldn't have to pay a brokerage fee out of the monies that you need in order to make this move a success, would that be of interest to you?" This is also great and here's why. This dialogue *sounds* like we are working for free. But if you look at it closely, it says they wouldn't have to pay a fee out of the monies they *need*, not the monies they *want*! What they *want* and what they *need* are two different things. If somebody presses you on the phone with "How can you do that?" your answer should be "There are several ways. For example, are you familiar with how a buyer agency works and that the buyer may elect to pay us? Well, that is just one example of how that could work. But first let me come over, see what you have, and see if I can help you. If I can't, I promise to tell you in the first five minutes that I'm there, so I don't waste your time. Sound fair?"

OK, so that was the telephone process. Now, I want to go through the expired dialogue, cold-call dialogue, and old FSBO dialogue.

Expired Dialogue

With the expired listing, when the sellers put the house on the market, they were excited about their future, about moving and their new home, … or whatever the specifics. Then, after several months of their house being on the market and showing, there are only low offers. Now they feel rejected.

When calling expireds, your focus should be not only to find out what they are committed to, but to help bring them back into the presence of what they are committed to, back into the presence of why they started this whole process in the first place. To refresh your memory, the five steps to the telephone process are identify, introduce, clarify, find out what they are committed to, and invite action.

With this in mind, the expired dialogue would sound like:

(Step 1: Identify) "Hello, may I speak with Mr. Jones, the person who's advertising his house for sale?"

(Step 2: Introduce) "This is Darryl Davis from Power Realty. How are you?"

(Step 3: Clarify) "The reason why I am calling is I noticed your house expired off the Multiple Listing Service and I was wondering if the house is still for sale."

He is going to say one of two things: "yes" or "no."

Now, if he says, "Yes, the house is still for sale," clarify it a step further by asking him if he put it back on Multiple. If he says "no" to this question, we know that he is going For Sale by Owner.

If he says, "No, the house is not for sale," what does that mean? Does it mean that he sold it? Does it mean that he has taken it off the market? Ask him point-blank, "Did you sell it?" If he says "yes," clarify it a step further still. "Is it in contract?" (He may say, "Yes, it did sell" because he has a buyer who is interested but nothing has been signed.) Then you move on ....

(Step 4: Find out what they are committed to) Start off by telling him, "I am looking at a copy of the Multiple and I am a little surprised that it didn't sell. Why do you think that is?"

Let him vent. "Well, it is because the broker or the buyers are stupid."

Then ask several more questions: "Why are you folks moving? Where are you moving? When do you want to get there?" and so on. Find out what they are committed to and bring him back into the presence of why they are selling.

(Step 5: Invite action) Again, you have several different ways to proceed. "Would you be offended if I stopped by to take a look at your house?" or "Let me ask you: if I could help you get to wherever you're going within the time frame you want, with the amount of money that you need, would that be of interest to you?"

Cold-Call Dialogue

This is kind of basic. The thing about cold calls is you are just working the numbers. It does not take a tremendous amount of skill to make cold calls. Let's take a look.

(Step 1: Identify) "Hello, may I speak with Mr. Smith?" Usually, agents will use a Cole's directory (also referred to as a "crisscross" reference) so they have the name of the homeowners right there.

(Step 2: Introduce) "Hi, this is Darryl Davis from Power Realty. How are you?" With a cold call, sometimes it is useful to say, "Are you familiar with our company?" They will say "yes" or "no." Don't do anything with that regardless of what they say.

(Step 3: Clarify) "The reason why I am calling is because [we just listed *or* we just sold *or* we are looking to build our inventory] and I was wondering if you knew anyone who is thinking about selling their home in your neighborhood."

By the way, don't ever, *ever* use "I have some buyers looking in your neighborhood." That is one of the oldest, overused techniques and I hate it. Most sellers out there nowadays are intelligent enough to know that this is just a line that we are using. So, don't use it anymore ... unless it is true. And even then, I would still think twice.

(Step 4: Find out what they are committed to) "How long have you folks lived in the neighborhood?" And so on.

(Step 5: Invite action) Proceed just like we discussed above.

Old FSBO Dialogue

Old FSBOs are people who tried selling their house several months ago and, for whatever reason, didn't sell and stopped advertising. I bet your local library has a copy of all the old newspapers for the past 12 months. Make copies of these ads and call them. For new agents: if the number has been changed, don't call. That means the people sold their house and have moved.

Now the dialogue below is similar to the previous dialogue, but it has a twist.

(Step 1: Identify) "Hello, can I speak to Ms. Johnson?"

(Step 2: Introduce) "This is Darryl Davis from Power Realty. How are you?"

(Step 3: Clarify) "The reason why I am calling is because our records show that you tried selling your home umpteen months ago. Is that correct?" You want to clarify that for them specifically.

To make the transition into finding out what they are committed to, use this sentence: "The reason why I ask about your house is because we listed a lot of homes in your area around that same time and they did sell. Where were you folks planning to move?"

By saying that other sellers hired us to market their homes in your area around the same time and those houses did sell, you are gently zinging the person: "Obviously you folks tried selling. We have clients who were successful. You weren't. Why do you think that was? Maybe it was because you didn't call us to begin with." (But remember to be nice when doing this!)

(Step 4: Find out what they are committed to) Find out what she is committed to, in order to learn if she is still thinking about selling. Bring her back to the presence of why she started the process several months ago and show her that you believe you can help her.

(Step 5: Invite action) Then proceed to invite action and arrange to meet with her.

Before we move on, there is one point that I want to highlight for you. I have given you a lot of dialogue here and spent several minutes going through each category. But you need to know that it is not about the scripts, it is not about the dialogue. I don't want you to take these dialogues and memorize them. I want you to simply be mentally present, find out what people are committed to, and coach them. Know in your bones that it is not about you, it is only about them. You take the concept, you take the process—identify, introduce, clarify, find out what they are committed to, and invite action—and use your own words. This dialogue is just the foundation.

Preparing for the Appointment

There are a few things you need to have in order before you go on your appointment.

1. **Know your market.** Imagine if I did a listing presentation to these people and they talk about this house that sold on Elm Street and this other house on Sycamore. I'd better know what they're talking about, right? The more you know about your market and what houses are selling, the more powerful you will be on the presentation.

2. **Set up your appointments within a time range.** When I say, "I'll see you at 7:30" and I show up at 7:35, I'm already late! To avoid this problem, simply say, "I'll see you between 7:30 and 8:00."

3. **Make sure both parties are home.** This is very important. Like in the insurance business, I call it steering clear of one-legged appointments. Avoid these at all costs. Decisions as important as selling a home always require both husband and wife to be present.

4. **Make sure you have free hours.** Two hours should do it. Instead of telling them this, however, I always asked: "When is dinner? I'll come right after you're done." Or after the kids are in bed. At that time, odds are they are going to be home for the night.

5. **Know how much they want.** Is it important to know how much they want before you go over to their house? Of course. This way you know what you are up against. In the case of FSBOs, you usually know how much they want because they advertise it. When that isn't the case, and when they aren't willing to tell you, you can usually find this out on the telephone by asking a few key questions.

    For example, as you're asking about their house, bedrooms, baths, etc., you can say, "Gee, your house sounds nice. How much are similar homes going for in the market?" If they reply, "Well, my neighbor John sold his house for $200,000 and he didn't even use the heavy-duty nails like we did," then you know that they think their house is worth more than that. Another way to do this is to ask them what their current mortgage is and then, later on in the conversation, ask them how much they need to net in order to make this move work. Then you would add the two numbers and that gives you a ballpark figure of how much they think their house is worth.

6. **Do a preliminary CMA.** There are some agents who believe that, in order to do "the right CMA," they have to first take a look at the house, and then go to the office to pull the comps, and then go back to the homeowner to present this and ask for the listing. That's the "two-stop" approach. I believe this isn't effective, because often the seller won't let you back a second time and, also, because this approach takes longer. I prefer the "one-stop" approach. Here, you get details about the house on the phone (bedrooms, baths, etc.) and then, because you're already familiar with the neighborhood, you run a preliminary CMA. The only difference is that you deliberately leave blank the final price that you would tell the homeowners they should ask for their house when they put it on the market. That part you would put in once you've seen the house. This way, if the house shows really well, you give them the high-end price; if it doesn't, go for the low-end.

7. **Arrive early.** When you're going on a listing appointment, you've got to get the CMA done, make all these calls, file, get the lock box, and, the next thing you know, you're rushing. Oh, and you forgot the yard sign, too. Then, you go over and ring the bell, bringing all this stuff with you to the door.

    Instead, you should get there a few minutes early, park yourself in front of the house, and listen to whatever music gets you psyched before you go in.

17 Powerful Ways to Find Prospects

Some of this may be a bit basic ... and some may seem real daring to a few of you. In any case, here are several highly effective methods for locating prospects in addition to FSBOs and expireds.

1. **Work a high-turnover area.** Work a high-turnover area and find the strengths and weaknesses of your competition. If you're trying to build your inventory, don't go to a neighborhood that has a low turnover. How do you find high-turnover areas? Very simple. Tell MLS to print out everything that sold in the past six months and it will show you. Then,

look and see who the major listing broker is in that neighborhood and do a little research on the strengths and weaknesses of that office. So, when you decide to break into that neighborhood and you are sitting face to face with a seller, chances are you are going to be up against that broker and you will have some ammunition. Be prepared to show the seller that your office has strengths to replace those weaknesses. That is how you blow out the competition.

2. **"Call to action" seminar.** A "call to action" seminar is basically a sellers' seminar or buyers' seminar. Here are some topics you can do for sellers:

- How to advertise a house,
- How to hold an open house,
- How to use today's low interest rates to get your house sold.

There is one drawback to this approach, however: it takes time. But there are some really good benefits.

The major benefits are that it is a way for you to market yourself and your office and, more important, it creates a perception in the market-place that you are an expert in real estate and that you are confident in your abilities because you hold frequent workshops.

If you choose to do this, don't forget the power of synergy. A couple of agents from the same office can combine efforts to do a workshop. Share the money, do promotions, do mailings, and, as a great cold-call technique, call to personally invite sellers to your seminar. (It's an especially effective technique with FSBOs, not to call to look for appointments but rather to invite them to a free educational seminar.) There are so many things you can do with it.

3. **Work orphans.** No, I am not saying that you should cold-call kids without parents! In your office, you've got orphans. Here is a definition of a real estate orphan: "Anyone who has bought or sold property through your office with an agent who is no longer with your office." These are people who bought or sold a house through you two, three, four, five years ago and they are ready to sell now. Here's how a call would sound.

"Mr. and Mrs. Seller? This is Darryl from Power Realty. How are you? The reason why I am calling is I want to apologize. Why? Well, according to our records you sold a house through our office umpteen years ago and the agent you worked with is no longer with our company. The reason I am apologizing is because no one has been taking care of you from our office for quite some time. I just wanted to call and personally introduce myself and let you know that if there is anything you ever need, we are here for you. By the way, do you love the house?"

"It's great."

"Have you done anything to it? Oh, good. By the way, have you folks ever thought of moving?"

If you do what I said and stay in touch with your past clients once a month, you now "adopt" these orphans and they become part of your monthly follow-up of past clients.

4. **Work old FSBOs.** We discussed this one earlier in the chapter. There is so much business out there, it's incredible.

5. **Take the long way home.** This is a little thing, but you will be surprised at what a difference it will make. Try driving to your office on a different route. I know what you do: you go to your office and back home the same way every day. You'll be amazed that, just by taking a different route, you'll see things you never noticed before ... like a few FSBO signs.

6. **Listen to your buyers.** I can't tell you how many listings I got because of this sort of exchange. A buyer told me, "You know we just saw a house that we liked, but it wasn't our style." "Oh," I'd ask, "what did you see? It was off an ad, huh? So it was being sold privately? Tell me, where was it?" If you have a good rapport with your buyer, ask for the address and phone number and they will tell you.

Now you call up the seller. "FSBO, this is Darryl Davis from Power Realty. I heard that you were selling your house. I heard this from one of my buyers. They said I should maybe give you a call. Can I help you?"

7. **Offer an over-the-phone market analysis.** At the time of this writing, a lot of my Power Agents are using this technique with phenomenal results. The concept is this: there are probably homeowners who would like to know how much their house is worth, but they don't want to sit through a long-winded presentation. If you offer a phone market analysis, they get to avoid that.

Here's what happens: they call you, you ask them questions about their house, you tell them you need to do the analysis, and then you call them back. Now, let's say the house is valued around $200,000. You call them back and say, "Based on the comparables, your house is valued somewhere in the $190s to $220s." They will naturally wonder if it is at the high end or low end. What is the only way we can answer that question? We need to actually go see the house. Keep in mind that you have two conversations with them using this method, so hopefully you build some rapport and it will be a lot easier to get in the door.

Here is a sample ad or mailing piece that you can use to promote this approach:

Free Over-the-Phone Market Analysis

If you are thinking of selling or just want to know the value of your property in today's market, just give me a call and answer a few questions—size of the property, how many bedrooms, taxes, Amenities of the house, etc.—all done conveniently over the phone. There's no obligation.
You'll be amazed at how much your house is worth!
Call Power Realty and ask for Hunna Hunna at 631-929-5555.

(By the way, the tag line, "You'll be amazed at how much your house is worth," should be used only in a hot seller's market.) When you use this technique, you'll start getting listings from people who weren't even thinking of selling until you meet them.

8. **The investor ad.** You put an ad in the paper and you have prospects call you. Here's what it would say: "Homeowner/investor looking for three/four bedrooms in …" (whatever market you work). Isn't that great? I mean talk about passive prospecting. Put the ad in and let people call you. Now, somebody who is a FSBO or maybe is just thinking about selling might see your ad and call.

   When people call, tell them that you're ready to buy the right properties at the right price. "How much will you pay?" they might ask. Say, "I can't say until I've seen your house," and make an appointment. After seeing the property, explain that you are an agent … but at this moment you're acting as a buyer. Tell them how much you'd be willing to pay "wholesale." If they don't like the wholesale price, they could list with you and get retail.

9. **Get 15 devoted people.** Devoted people are those folks who like you so much that they'll recommend you first whenever they hear of someone buying or selling. They might be, for example, plumbers, electricians, gardeners, contractors, or divorce attorneys. These are devoted people because they are devoted to you and you have to be devoted to

them. You have to have your own master list of people that you will always recommend, like this plumber or this electrician. You call them and say the following:

"Here's the thing. I am very active in real estate. I want to be able to create a relationship beyond what you and I currently have. What I want to do is, if anyone needs an electrician, I want to refer you ... but here is the fair trade. If you hear of anyone who is thinking about selling, you call me. Now, I plan on doing a big prospecting promotion campaign in the beginning of the year. I will put ads out I will be with my photo, and if you want to share in the promotion, I will give you a little title in the ad."

In a future chapter, I will show you how to put together a PR campaign where you are going to have your name all over the place and you will not have to spend a dime. Begin networking now and get 15 strong, devoted people. You can use them in so many positive ways.

10. **Find "For Rent by Owners" (FRBOs).** This refers to owners of vacation homes or owners renting out their house—investors like that. You want to prospect these types of people because they may own several homes and are collecting rent—an aggravation they might be willing to unload. I have plenty of agents throughout the country who get a good part of their listings by focusing on just FRBOs. Here is a letter you can send them as a follow-up in addition to calling them:

Dear (Potential Customer Name),

I understand that you are an absentee owner of a property in Boyd Acre Subdivision in Clarksville, Tennessee. If that is still so, you may be interested in some things that I want to share with you.

1. I am *the realtor* specializing in your area!
2. Interest rates just *dropped* to 6%!
3. Your subdivision is *hot, hot, hot!*
4. *Now* is a perfect time to *sell!* And I want to sell *your property!*

Since we've never met, and an eyeball-to-eyeball meeting is probably not possible at this time, I have enclosed my personal brochure for you to read. It will clearly show that I am a genuine real estate professional, that I'm serious about my chosen career, and that my track record proves it.

If you are interested in selling, now or in the near future, please contact me by phone at (xxx) xxxxxxx, or by mail, or just drop by if you are in the area.

I look forward to meeting you and working for you.

Sincerely,

Your Name

---

11. **Relo companies.** Here's how this works. Let's say IBM wants to move an employee from here to there. IBM hires a relocation company that manages the move and, if the seller's home does not sell within umpteen days, the relocation company buys the house so the move can happen promptly for IBM. It is then up to the relocation company to sell it; otherwise, it owns a home and loses money. If you build a relationship with a relo company, you can get several listings. How do you find out the closest relocation company? Check your yellow pages. It's also possible that your company/franchise is connected with a relocation company.

12. **Builder accounts.** If you can hook up with a builder, you've got tons of listings. Here are three ways for you to break into a builder.

    ■ If the company builds subdivisions, ask for just a section. For instance, if the builder has 50 houses, ask to try to market in just a section of their lot—say, 10 houses.

    ■ Ask for the builder's old dogs—the houses the company has been trying to sell for a while and just hasn't moved. (Don't call them "old dogs" to the builder!) Say, "Just give me a chance and let me prove myself to you." The builder really has nothing to lose.

    ■ Offer to do an open house. There is no commitment here. Just do an open house. Aside from the opportunity to sell the house, you will also place yourself in front of other interested buyers and sellers.

13. **Do public open houses**. This you already know, but it remains a great way to generate prospects and listings. Here's a unique twist. What you could do to capitalize on this is to hold a "neighborhood open house."

    Here's how that works. Let's say you're going to hold a general open house from noon to 2:00. You would create a special invitation (go to your local printer and use inexpensive wedding invitations) that you would mail to neighbors, inviting them to come by from 11:00 to noon. Now, when these folks come through, you know they are neighbors, so how you speak with them is different than how you would with potential buyers. Your mission here is to see if they would be interested in having you stop by to do a market analysis on their home. This technique works great!

14. **Conduct a farming and self-promotion campaign.** I devote a full chapter to each of these topics later in this book.

15. **Do a low interest rate mailing.** When interest rates are low, there are

always articles about it in the local papers and Realtor Board publications. You can send a copy of an article to neighbors, telling them how the lower rates will generate a lot of buyer activity and that this may be a great time to sell their home and purchase a new home; with these rates, the payments would be less. Now, when you do that, make sure you follow up. Don't just do the mailing and stop there. Mail to 50 people and then, a week later, cold-call those 50 people and ask, "Did you get my mailing?"

16. **Have a spotter for FSBOs.** You tell a bunch of people—kids are great for this one, "If you find a FSBO for me, I will give you $15. Just give me the name and number and I will give you $15." Tell the mail carrier, the garbage collector, the gardener/landscaper, bottled water guy or gal, newspaper carrier. Find the bird dog, the nosey neighbor. These are your spotters. You should do this right away.

17. **Call the immediate area around new listings.** Have you ever noticed that when a new listing comes on the market on a particular block, if another listing is already on that block or near it, the second listing is usually with a different broker than the first? I believe the reason for this is the owners of the second house may think that if they list with the same agency as their neighbor, their neighbor would know all of their personal information. So what one of my top *Power Agents*, Martin Hammer on Long Island, New York, does is each morning he checks all the new listings that aren't his and he calls the neighbors. He lets them know that a house just came up for sale in their area and then tells them he anticipates this house will probably bring a lot of buyers into the neighborhood and he was wondering if they ever thought of selling their house. Martin tells me that this technique is good for an extra 10 listings a year.

Well, I hope you got a tremendous number of ideas on how to be more effective with your prospecting efforts. In closing, I want to ask you a question. Are you serious about your career? Are you really serious about getting better? Are you committed to achieving that next level? Because if you are, you owe it to yourself for these next 30 days to kick some butt. Pick up that phone and make call after call after call. I know that some of you just hate picking up the phone. I know that we love working with buyers. But let me tell you something. I don't care where you are in working with buyers or listings. Whatever the case, for these next 30 days, you should focus on prospecting.

If you make calls and you improve 10%, just 10% in prospecting, you will become a stronger agent and a stronger person and you will feel more in control of your career. So don't wimp out these next 30 days. Pick up the phone, make a bunch of calls, and let it fly!

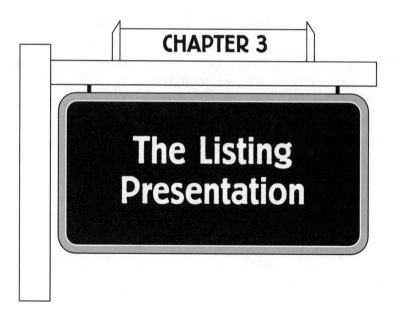

CHAPTER 3

The Listing Presentation

Power Fact

You can be good at many things, but if you can't effectively communicate with the seller, real estate is always going to be frustrating work.

Overview

Shortly before I wrote this chapter, I went into my real estate office and called three FSBOs. I spoke with two of them, scheduled two appointments, and listed both houses. I mention this because I want you to know that I'm not writing about how to do an outdated presentation that I used to do years ago, prior to becoming a national speaker and trainer. In fact, agents who go through my *Power Program* increase their effectiveness to the point where they list two out of three FSBO appointments they go on, based on what I will cover in this chapter.

The approach described here isn't the *only* way to do a listing presentation. I'm sure there are certain techniques that you do really well and I want you to keep doing those things. My objective is not to teach you how to get the listings you've already been getting, but how to get the ones you've been losing. I want you to read this chapter and use what works for you. If there are certain things you do differently, by all means keep them—if they work.

The importance of listing presentations can't be overstated. To succeed, I believe an agent must really master this one area. So I highly encourage you to perfect this presentation in the next 30 days. Read this chapter over and over, practice with your mentors and colleagues, and—most important—get out there and meet face to face with real sellers. Go on as many presentations as you can, if not for the production, at least for the skill level that you're going to achieve at the end of 30 days.

Four Key Reasons Why Listings Are So Important

1. **You'll make more money in less time.** As I mention elsewhere in this book, any speaker will tell you that most top producing agents get 75% of their income from listings sold and 25% from buyers. That's the reason you should spend 75% of your energy building your inventory and 25% of it with buyers.

2. **You'll have less stress and more fun when you focus on building your listing inventory.** It's stressful to take buyers out and show them house after house after house, then hear them turn around in two months and say, "You know what? We changed our minds. We're not going to buy." But when you go on listing appointments, even if you don't get all the listings, you feel a sense of accomplishment because you know you're a step closer to getting one.

3. **With listings, you are in control of your career.** He or she who holds the listings is in control of the marketplace.

4. **If you have listings, you're immune to outside conditions.** You're not a victim of the economy, whether it's a buyer's or seller's market, etc. If you've got a large inventory of listings, you're going to make a sale. Period. Recently, one of my students left a listing presentation and was hit by a truck. He went to the hospital and wound up in a coma. True story. I got the bad news from the manager of that office and, when my student got out of the coma, I called to see how he was doing. When we spoke, I asked him, "How's your listing inventory?" He started to laugh because he knew I was asking because he was laid up in the hospital for a month or two, with no income except for what might be generated from his current listings.

You see, each of us is in business for ourselves and our inventory is crucial to our success ... and to our survival in the business.

Categories of Sellers

There are basically four types of sellers:

1. Sellers who *are more committed to price than to moving.* The problem with these types of sellers is that, if they list with you, the listings become stressful because you wind up being more committed to them selling than they are. You should just move on.

2. Sellers who *are committed to selling but want to do it on their own.* They usually want to do it on their own to save the commission or because they had a bad experience. With this type of seller, what should you focus on? You should focus on having them buy into the value of the real estate industry, meaning that they will sell their house for more money and more quickly by using the services of an agent. Now, if they buy into that and you're the one communicating the message, they will obviously buy into you.

3. Sellers who *are committed to selling* and *interested in hiring an agent.* However, there is nothing special in their minds about you or your company. They're going to hire an agent, but they need to interview a few. What should you focus on in your presentation? Since they've already bought into the need for the industry, you simply have to focus on how your company will serve them better than anyone else.

4. Sellers who *want to hire you and your company only because they've heard of you or your company before or perhaps through a solid referral.* For this type of seller, because they're already sold on you and your company, it's an easy conversation. There's nothing really to sell them on. Just focus on building rapport.

Overview of the Listing Appointment

I can explain either the ABC technique for getting a listing … or the one I teach in *The Power Program.* The ABC version is very simplistic. "A" would be to *ask* for the listing. "B" is when you start to *beg.* "C" is your cue to *cry.* I've met some agents who have been doing the ABC technique for some time now. So I'm going to teach you what we teach our *Power Agents.*

In this method, rather than calling it the "*selling* process," we're going to call it the "*coaching* process." Doesn't that sound better? I want to take the words "selling" and "close" out of our vocabulary because they have a negative connotation. I believe that we *coach* buyers and sellers into making a decision. They ultimately choose, but we coach them to get there.

Step 1: Build Rapport. We've all heard how important it is to build rapport with buyers and sellers. Let me take a deeper cut at this concept with you. We tell *Power Agents* in this step that you want to do a little bit more than just build rapport. You want to connect with the sellers at a deeper level. You do this by "being present."

I believe the reason my closing ratio was four listings out of five presentations wasn't in my dialogue with sellers, my visuals, or any of that other stuff. It was all in this concept of being present. Being present means that you're so tuned into them, so connected, that your focus is more on what they are saying than the next thing you're going to say when they stop talking. When you get this connected with them, you not only *really* hear what they are saying, but you also hear what they are *not* saying.

When you master this skill, the dialogue you use with these sellers will be based on what they need to hear. In other words, instead of "doing a script" (which really works only when they know their "part"), you shape your dialogue based on who they are. When you start to do this, you can "dance" on the listing appointment and create your own objection-handling techniques, and it will feel more like a conversation than a sales pitch.

Step 2: Find Out What They're Committed To. This is the same thing that we mentioned in the prospecting chapter. Other speakers would say, "Find out what their goals are" or "Find a problem and offer them a solution." I prefer my terminology because it's more consultative and more about servicing them. It's a deeper way to connect with them. If they sense that you are really interested in them and care about them, they will choose you over the best salesperson because, quite frankly, they don't want a salesperson—they want someone to take care of them.

When you focus on what they are committed to versus what *you* want (i.e., to get their listing), you can be more creative in helping them.

For example, one of my students in a *Power Program* went on a listing presentation. The sellers wanted to buy a house in the same neighborhood for $275K. Their own house was listed for $169K, which was $10K more than fair market value. So they've got an overpriced listing and the reason they're selling is to buy a house for $275K. Now, based on this scenario, it looked like there was no way they could make all this work. It wasn't going to happen. And that's one way the agent could have listened to them.

But instead, the agent listened to their commitment and focused on what was possible. So he asked the sellers, "If you can buy that house for

$239K or $245K, would you drop your list price $10K to make the move?"

The sellers said, "Yeah, but there's no way that's going to happen."

The *Power Agent* said, "It doesn't hurt to ask." So he called the sellers of the $275K home and made them an offer. They accepted $235K ... down from $275K. His sellers then dropped their price $10K and now they had a line out the door to buy their house. This agent really looked for what was possible, based on the seller's burning commitment to make this move. All that mattered was the commitment. That's what he listened for, that's why he acted, and that's how he achieved success.

Step 3: Coach Them. Based on what they're committed to, what would be the best coaching to give them? 99% of the time it will be to hire a real estate agent. So it's in this step you would actually start sharing with them how you would help them to sell their house and meet their commitment.

Step 4: Invite Action. Here's where we invite them to move forward and hire us to market their home. We do this by putting the house on MLS, doing open houses, advertising, etc.

Now let's break down each step in greater detail and with actual dialogue.

Step 1: Build Rapport

Make sure that you bring the right attitude to the door. Give them a friendly greeting when you arrive and guide them to the kitchen table. Why the kitchen table? Because that's where friends go; it's more comfortable. Here's how I did it.

I would take my briefcase and say, "Let me just go put this down" and I'd walk right into the kitchen. When you walk right in and say those words, I promise you they will follow you.

Preview the House

Before I sat down and opened up my book and did anything, I would preview the house. Here is when you begin to communicate, connect, and coach. I believe that we owe it to them to first preview the home.

My suggestion is to have them take you through the house. You do this to build rapport and show them that you care. This is an opportunity to bond. If you see golf clubs, you can talk about sports. If you see a workbench and you're handy, start a conversation about that. You can spend a half hour previewing the home and there's nothing wrong with that. Why? Because they're not going anywhere tonight. If you need to take two hours with these people, take it. As long as it takes for them to feel comfortable about you and what you're doing. Have a genuine interest in them and their home; don't just zip through.

Another thing here is to acknowledge the pluses and point out some of the flaws. I used to think that if I went through the house and said, "That's a really nice room and it's spacious," they were going to expect me to give them a really high appraisal. But that's not true. When you go through a house and say, "Hey, nice windows," "Cool carpeting," whatever it is, you're acknowledging them personally. After all, a home is a very personal thing, right? Besides, if you don't do this, and if your CMA shows a lower price than what they expected, they won't trust your price because they'll be thinking, "Well, of course Darryl would price it low because he doesn't appreciate the house the way it should be."

Now, you should point out some of the flaws, too, but be subtle about it. I mean if a room smells from the dogs, you can say (sniff, sniff), "Hmmm. So you folks are dog lovers, huh? Yeah, I like a dog or two. Six is my limit." I'm just kidding. The best way to point out flaws is to ask about it and then, whatever they say, jot it down in your notes. For example, if you see a stain on the ceiling, look up at it and ask, "What happened here?" They'll say what they say and you'll make a "hmmm" sound and just make a note of it. This will help with their possible arrogance about how great their house is.

Go back to the kitchen table after you've previewed the home. This is when you sit down.

A Side Note. As you're walking through their house, or just when you sit down to the table, the sellers may throw out a few questions. They might even do this in the middle of your presentation. Here's how to handle what comes up.

Mr. Seller: Now that you've seen my home, what do you think it's worth?

Darryl: Well, Mr. Seller, you know that the price on your home is determined by how much marketing you do. Here, let me show you what I'm talking about. To get the best possible price, we want to get as many buyers to the door to look at the house, wouldn't you agree? It's better to have 100 buyers interested versus just one. How we do that is we give the house as much exposure as possible. That means we expose the house to anybody looking in this price range for this style home. We do that through a number of marketing tools. The more tools you use as a homeowner to market your house, the more exposure, the more potential buyers, and the better your odds of getting the best price. Does that make sense? So I can't tell you the price right now because I'm simply sharing with you the tools that I use to get the best possible price, and you're looking for the highest price, aren't you?

And you pick up where you left off. Don't let them distract you from your presentation. Meaning, if you've got 10 things you want to share— MLS, lock box, etc.—and right around item number three they jump in, don't feel compelled to answer at that time.

(For more about addressing specific questions, see our next chapter, "Objection Handling.")

After we've built rapport, we move forward.

Step 2: Find Out What They're Committed To

We do that by asking questions. When you first sit down with sellers, don't open up your presentation book just yet. Start asking questions about where they're moving, when they need to get there, why they are moving there, etc. You may want to write down their answers, but I don't recommend that. I also don't think your questions should be preprinted. That's too scripted, almost like a survey.

You see, if you're being present, you won't need to write down their answers. Some folks would say that writing it down shows them you're really interested in them. I'd rather show them I'm really interested in them by looking in their eyes, being attentive and empathetic. These questions should flow like a conversation. Ask whatever you need to find out what they're committed to.

I've narrowed it down to a few key questions. (For some of these questions, you'll know the answer beforehand from having spoken to them on the telephone. Nevertheless, it doesn't hurt to recap. Remember, you don't want to take anything for granted.)

- Have you looked at any houses yet?
- When do you need to make this move?
- Have you ever sold a home before? (Why is this question important? They might say to you, "Yeah, we've sold a house before, that's why we think we can do it on our own." If this is the case, ask, "Oh, really, when was that?" "Ten years ago." To this, you can say, "I see. Well, things have changed....")
- Why are you trying to sell it on your own?
- What is the next step in your marketing plan? (They might say, "My what?" You say, "Marketing plan." "We don't have one," they say.

"Well, aren't you lucky that I just happened to bring mine?")
- What is more important to you, price or time? (Watch this. If they say that price is the most important, you follow it up with "So, in other words, if it took you nine months to a year to get the price you want for the house, would that be OK with you?" "No." "Oh, so we're saying time is more important?" See, right there in the beginning, you're putting the entire conversation in its proper context; it's not about price.)
- If I could help you get moved to Florida, would you be interested in me doing that? (That's an important question. After you get clear about what they're committed to, you ask them, "If I can help you do that, would that be of interest to you?" If they say "yes," you're getting permission to give them some coaching, which leads you into sharing about your marketing plan.)
- When you're dealing with an expired, the best question to start off with is "So tell me, what happened?" Let the sellers get off their chest whatever they need to share about their previous experience.

If the sellers say, "The reason why we want to sell on our own is to try to save the fee," should you handle that now? No. When you're getting clear about what they're committed to, some concerns or objections may come up. They're going to say whatever they say. But this is *not* the time to handle any of these things. You just listen and get it. They want to be heard.

Has it ever happened to you that, as you're walking in the door, the sellers say to you, "Listen, I just want to be clear with you, we're not listing our home tonight" … and then two hours later, they've listed with you? My point is that whatever concerns and objections they put out in the first 15 to 20 minutes that you're there will in most cases disappear after you've spent an hour or two with them. If not, you handle it at the end.

Step 3: Coach Them

This is the step when you use your listing presentation book. So, before we go on, I want to review how you put together your book and what the sections are. In *The Power Program*, we teach that there are four sections. However, it doesn't *have* to be four. It could be five or 10. Four is just an easy way for you to understand the flow of the presentation.

The first section should be *validating you*. The reason that you validate yourself first is because sellers have to buy into you—your credentials and power—before they'll buy into anything else. Here is where you talk about your certificates, your license, the code of ethics, the fact that you're a member of NAR, your community involvement, etc.

You may not use all the pages you have. Once you get a sense that they've bought into you and your abilities, even if you have more pages validating yourself, skip them and go to the next section.

Section two is where you sell the "bigness" of *your company*. Here's where you'll probably have a picture of your broker, business cards of the agents in your office, your mission statement (if you have one), your office stats, your market share, etc.

If you belong to a national franchise, your company may have something like a national relocation service, national advertising, or a very recognizable yard sign. Do *not* use those items in section two, selling the "bigness" of your company. The reason I say this is because in section three you will speak about how you market homes. All these above items are part of a marketing effort. Instead, speak about the franchise in terms of how many offices are located throughout the U.S., Canada, and Europe, how long it's been around, etc. Don't get into the specific tools that you use until section three.

Again, once you sense that the sellers have bought into your company and your franchise, move to section three—the *step-by-step process* you go through to sell the home. Here's where you speak about the yard sign, MLS, fact sheets, brokers' open house, opinion sheet, local advertising, public open houses, qualifying buyers, mortgage info, etc. My personal preference is to begin with MLS. I believe that this is the foundation of what we do and it's one of the most powerful tools that we use. Everything else I speak about after MLS ties into it.

Section four is *additional support material*. This is where you may have your CMA, your objection-handling visuals, your net sheet, etc.

How to Present Your Marketing Plan

There are three components to conveying each step in your marketing plan: features, benefit/relate, and acknowledgment.

- **Feature:** This is simply the statement of the item you are presenting. For example, "One of the great tools we use to get your home sold is a brokers' open house."
- **Benefit/Relate:** Here you share how this tool works, why it's so effective, and how it relates to the seller. For example, "Here's how the brokers' open house works. Within the first seven days of the house being on the market, we have one day, for about two hours, where we invite the brokers to come check out the house. My office usually gets about

30 to 40 agents to attend. There are a few benefits of holding a brokers' open house. Instead of 30 to 40 agents coming over 30 to 40 separate times to see your house, we can accomplish the same thing in just two hours, meaning it saves you a lot of time. Second, to help have your house stand out among all the other houses on MLS, this open house acts like a grand opening of a department store."

■ **Acknowledgment:** Here we want to see if they've understood how this tool can help them accomplish their commitment to selling. For example, "Do you see how the brokers' open house could save us a lot of time?" Or, more assumptively, act as if they are going to list by saying, "So, I was thinking Thursday would be the best, just before agents prepare to show houses on the weekend. Would that work for you?" By the way, don't use this after each tool you share; otherwise you'll sound like a used car salesperson.

Let me go through an example of a dialogue on using MLS, which, as I stated earlier, was usually the first tool I discussed:

Darryl: Mr. Seller, another thing we do in putting your house on the market is to put it on the multiple listing service, MLS. Almost every broker belongs to MLS, where we put information about your home, including a photo, into a computer and immediately many agents know your house is for sale. It goes onto a list. *(Feature)* Let me give you an example. This list [show the list] is all the current homes that are for sale on the MLS, meaning these homeowners hired a broker and all the brokers are working together to sell these homes. This is just in our town of [name their town]. Look at this. These are all for sale right here. Can you believe that?

Mr. Seller, right now you're not on the list. Until you're on the list, in my opinion, you're not even on the market. This is your competition. I don't care if it's with me or another broker, but you need to get on this list. Now, once you hire an agent, his or her job is to make sure that once your home is on the list it stands out among all the other homes—like if I took a yellow highlighter to this list right now. This is a powerful tool that we use. And do you know what it costs you? Nothing. You only pay me if I get the job done—that means that I get this sold and you're off to Florida. (Benefit/Relate) You told me you wanted to get to Florida in the next three months. Do you think that MLS could be a great tool to help you do that? *(Acknowledgment)*

Here's one last thought for this section of your listing presentation. As you go through each item (MLS, yard sign, etc.) when you're talking to a

FSBO, focus more on having him or her buy into the real estate industry than into you specifically. FSBOs aren't sold on the industry, which is why they are FSBOs. If they buy into the industry and you're the one communicating the message, they will naturally buy into you.

Step 4: Invite Action

After you've finished explaining how you market homes, move into Step 4, which is to invite the sellers to take action based on their commitment. Once again, the appropriate action, most likely, is that they list with you. In just a few pages to follow, I'll share the dialogue for this step. But first I need to address something important.

Most homeowners make the mistake of hiring an agent based on the *price* the agent tells them. And, unfortunately, some agents tell the homeowner what she or he wants to hear so they can get the listing. The other mistake many homeowners make is they shop for an agent based on the *commission* they charge. I say this is a mistake because, most likely, their home is one of the most valuable assets they own and they look to put someone in charge who will discount his or her fee just to get the listing. My point is this: a homeowner should hire an agent based on her or his skill and ability to get the job done.

That said, the dialogue you can use to lead into talking about price is this:

"Mr. and Mrs. Seller, putting price to the side, based on what you've seen and heard about how I market houses, do you feel it's better that we work together?"

If they don't say "yes," then you need to find out what their concern is and handle their objection. Once they are ready to hire you, then discuss price.

Here is how I believe you should go through price. You have your CMA done prior to the appointment. I'm going to tell you how to present your CMA, because you have to be careful here.

Maybe you present your CMA, the sellers disagree with it, and then you tell them why they're wrong. You may do it nicely, but still, if you disagree with their point of view, they're going to hear it as if you're saying that they're wrong. What you need to do, before even pulling out the CMA, is to sell the concept of the CMA itself. This way, they'll have a different way of relating to the CMA once it's presented.

Let me ask you: which is better, to present your comps and *then* justify them, or to justify your comps *before* you present them? You should justify the comps *before* you show them. Here's how you do it.

Darryl: Mr. Seller, based on what you've seen about how I market homes, my credentials, and my company, are you ready to work with me? I mean with the exception of price. Obviously we have to figure the best price to put the house on the market, but with the exception of that do you feel comfortable working together?

Mr. Seller: Yes.

Darryl: OK, great. Then let's look at how to price your home. Because here's what I did. After I spoke with you on the phone, you sounded serious about selling, so I invested a little time. I did what we call a CMA, which stands for a "comparative market analysis." This is a listing of all the houses that are on the market in this area, what houses sold for, and what listings have expired. What I've done is exactly what a bank appraiser will do. For instance, let's say we put this house on the market and it's on the market for a couple of months. Then, a buyer offers us $500K and we accept. Now they have to get a mortgage from the bank, so the bank sends an appraiser who says our house isn't worth $500K. The appraiser tells this to the bank, the bank calls the buyer, and the buyer comes back and says, "Thank you, but we're not going to buy this house." Sometimes, it can take up to one or two months to find this out. We already had been trying to sell it for two months, so now it's taken us four months of our lives and we have to start the entire process all over again. I'm going to guess that we don't want that to happen. Right?

Mr. Seller: Of course not.

Darryl: So let me show you what I came up with, and I want you to look at it the way a bank appraiser looks at it. In fact, just to add some validity to what I'm saying, here are some letters, Mr. Seller, from bank appraisers, asking me to give them comparables so they can do their own CMA. As you may know, comparables are houses similar to your home in size, features, condition, location, and so forth that have sold recently. Agents and brokers and appraisers use comparables to establish the fair market value of a property. You see, bank appraisers often call us because we're out there with our fingers on the pulse of what's happening. So this information I'm going to share with you is the exact information a bank appraiser is going to look at, and we're getting a jump on it. Isn't that great?

Now you present your CMA.

By the way, the next time the lender's appraiser calls you up and asks, "Can I have some comps for XYZ property?" tell her or him, "That's no problem. As a matter of fact, for that particular piece of property I've got some really good ones for you." (See, you've got to sell them!) And then you say, "But, by the way, there's a new policy in my office. I need you to just fax a handwritten letter on your letterhead saying that you're requesting comparables for XYZ Street and sign it. That's all you need to do and just fax it to me. Can you just do that real quick? Great."

So you do this a few times, and you get two, three, a half a dozen letters to put into your presentation book. Then you use them to validate your CMA by showing the seller, "These are the exact same items bank appraisers are going to look at, and we're going to see them before they do. Isn't that great?!"

If a homeowner disagrees with the comps that you show him, explain to him that it doesn't matter whether we agree with them or not—this is what the bank is going to look at and there's nothing we can do to change that.

Filling out the Listing Agreement

Make sure you agree on price and "assumptively" start filling out the form. Just say, "Let me just get some information."

Get them involved. Remember, to keep the momentum going and to break the silence, just ask them, "What is today's date?" Ask other minor point questions, for example, like "Are you folks leaving the washer and dryer?"

Hand them the pen and direct their signature—e.g., "Press hard, it's cheap carbon" or "This is my good pen, so make sure I get it back."

Ask the significant other a question. This is a simple yet powerful technique. When you hand the pen to one spouse (it doesn't matter which one), he or she usually will look at the other and say something like "Well, honey, what do you think?" This is when you start sweating, because you know an objection is probably coming. To avoid this, ask the other spouse, the one without the pen, a question. Perhaps inquire about their new house. While you're talking with the other person, the spouse with the pen can't talk with that person and so, more times than not, will just start signing.

The Brag Book

The purpose of the brag book is to keep selling you in the event you don't get the listing from the first appointment. You do your presentation, you coach them, and you try to handle their objections and concerns. You try your hardest to get them to list with you and they don't. Now you leave behind your brag book.

Darryl: So, Mr. Seller, you know we've spent a couple of hours together and, based on what you say you're committed to, I really believe that hiring an agent is the best thing for you. And I feel good about our conversation. But something's holding you back. I think that maybe you're not seeing Darryl Davis the human being. I think if you knew me more as a person maybe you'd trust me more. So what I've got is something I call the brag book. It tells you more about myself, my credentials, in a little more detail than we've gone over today. I'll just leave it and be by in a day or two to pick it up. And you know what? Here's another thing. If you interview any other agents, and I recommend you do, make sure you ask to see their brag book.

So, number one, this brag book keeps selling you after you've already left. (You use this only in the event that you don't get the listing the first time you're there.) Now they'll go through it, you'll come back in a couple of days, and they may say, "You know what, Darryl, I think we're ready to put this on MLS." Second, it gives you a reason to go back another time. The third thing it does is it gives you an edge over other agents.

Elements of Your Brag Book
Your brag book should include photos, certificates, awards, letters of recommendation, advertising and open house information, photos and listings of sold homes, community involvement, family, etc. It's similar to section one of your presentation book, but it's more elaborate—with much more detail.

Agent Qualifier
Although I have devoted the next chapter entirely to dealing with sellers' objections, I would like here to share a neat tool that you can use in the event you don't get the listing the first time you meet a seller. It's called the Agent Qualifier. You would use this if the seller plans on interviewing other agents. You give the homeowners this form and tell them that when they interview other agents, it will help them determine who is the most qualified.

What's great about this is it turns the tables on the agents. They'll go on the appointment with their listing agenda and instead spend the whole time being interviewed by the sellers: it's really great!

Here are some of the questions you can use when creating your Agent Qualifier:

1. How long have you been in real estate?
2. Are you full-time?
3. How many houses did you sell last year and how many did you list?
4. How many listings do you currently have?
5. What profession were you in before this one?
6. Do you have a copy of the Realtor Code of Ethics?
7. How much money do you spend each year on education and sales training?
8. Will you stay in communication with me? If so, what system do you use?
9. Will you advertise my home in the paper every weekend?
10. How do you conduct brokers' open houses?
11. Do you use a notebook computer? What are your Web site and e-mail addresses?
12. Do you use the Internet to generate business?
13. If I get an offer and need you to cut your commission, would you?
14. Do you have a list of past clients that I can call?
15. Do you follow up on all showings and give me feedback?
16. Do you send a copy of all the advertising to me?
17. When you make a flier on my home, what do you do with it?
18. How much time do you spend knocking on doors?
19. Do you have a résumé with you?
20. What automation do you (not your office) have and use?
21. What is your average list to sales price ratio vs. the average for the market?
22. What is your average marketing time vs. the MLS average marketing time?
23. Do you do any radio and/or TV advertising?
24. Do you have a personal assistant? What is his or her job description?

As I said at the beginning of this chapter, for the next 30 days, I encourage you to go on as many listing presentations as possible—if not to increase production, then simply to raise your skill level. Bottom line: you need to have the integrity, the commitment, and the responsibility to keep your word and move forward to achieve your Next Level.

Before we conclude with this topic, I'd like to reiterate the two concepts that I feel are most important. First, when you're meeting with a seller, you want to look at yourself as a *coach*. You're there to coach that person and give the best advice based on what she or he is committed to. 99% of the time, the best thing for the seller to do is to hire you. Second, when you're there with that seller, you must truly *be present*. Be present to his or her situation; be present to what she or he is saying. Don't talk *at* the person, but talk *with* him or her.

And, remember, after each appointment—after you've given a dynamite presentation—as you're driving away in your car, ask yourself these two questions: "What did I do right?" and, more important, "What could I have done better?" It's by asking these questions that you become more skillful and a better real estate agent.

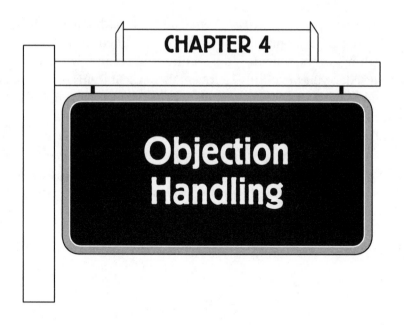

CHAPTER 4

Objection Handling

Power Fact

The art of objection handling lies in uncovering the real concern beneath the objection and addressing it in such a way that the sellers are once again focused squarely on their original commitment—why they are selling their home.

Overview

This chapter can make a tremendous difference for you in your career, especially in your listing presentations. How many listings have you lost in this last year alone because you didn't handle an objection effectively?

Often, we lose listings because we don't handle that key objection. You know the type: "I have a friend in the business" or "We want to try it on our own for a few weeks" or "We want to talk to other brokers," etc. In addition to sharing with you the 10 Commandments of Handling Objections, I'll also give you specific objection-handling techniques. These techniques have been time-tested and work incredibly well. I know they work, not only because I used them myself, but because agents who have tried them tell me the techniques helped increase their income without working harder—because now they lose fewer listings!

10 Commandments of Handling Objections

1. **Don't take objections personally.** Why would you take it personally? Because they're talking about you, right? But it really doesn't make sense. You've known these people for only, what, two hours? It's not about you personally—no matter what they say. Usually, when they're throwing an objection at you, they're really throwing one at the entire real estate industry.

2. **Handling objections is simply changing their perceptions.** Your vision and your prospect's vision of what's possible are what create your reality. When you receive an objection, that's coming from the seller's box of what's "Not Possible." Remember that outside of this box are "Possibilities." When they throw out an objection like "We have a friend in the business" or "We want to try it on our own" or "We'll give it to you for a lesser commission," yaddah, yaddah, yaddah, that's all coming from the "Not Possible" box. Keep focusing on what they're committed to. If you keep bringing them back to what they're committed to and you handle their concern or objection based on what they're committed to, you'll be fine.

3. **Look at objections as an opportunity to improve your skill.** I actually got to the point where I enjoyed handling objections. It became fun for me. I love the quote: "That which does not kill us makes us stronger." You may be so worried about handling possible objections that it distracts you from the presentation. It's as if during the presentation you're just waiting for their objections. When you're doing that, you're not being truly present mentally and you're not communicating effectively with them. And guess what? When you worry so much about objections that your presentation is horrible, you'll get even more objections! It's a self-fulfilling prophecy.

   You're going to have to let go of that. When you get an objection, look at it as an opportunity to become more skillful at coaching and communicating with somebody.

   The more objections you get early on in your career, the stronger you become because you learn from your mistakes. Warren Buffett (one of the richest people in the world) said in his autobiography, "Success is a terrible teacher, because you only learn from your failures."

   My son is five years old and I've been teaching him how to play checkers. The first few games he obviously lost (I'm a tough dad; I don't give him a handicap) and he got frustrated. So each time he lost I would tell him, "Michael, don't get frustrated because you learn from your mistakes." Well, I think it was game seven and, wouldn't you know it, he beat me! And you know what he said to me? "Daddy, that's OK, because you learn from your mistakes."

4. **Take your time when handling objections.** I've seen agents get an objection and become all weird and tongue-tied trying to rush with an answer. Take your time.

5. **Handle objections at the end.** What do I mean by this? Don't distract your focus; stay in control. If they give you an objection in the first part of your listing conversation, it may be answered by the time you're done with the presentation or it may not be an issue later on. I've had people who, from the moment I walked in, would say, "Darryl, we just want you to know that we're not listing tonight. We don't want to hear any long-winded presentation." "OK," I would answer, "well, let me just tell you a little bit about my background anyway." Two hours later, I'm leaving with the listing.

    Be clear and focused and committed to what they're committed to and you'll be all right.

6. **The better your presentation, the fewer objections you'll get.** If you go on a listing appointment and you're a powerful force—you feel good about yourself, you're confident in your abilities, you love this business, and you're well prepared—you'll give a dynamite presentation and get fewer objections.

7. **Use analogies.** When handling objections, tell stories—you know people think in pictures. When I say the word "horse," most of you will visualize an actual horse, not the letters h-o-r-s-e.

8. **Use subtle closes frequently.** Here's an example. When you're doing a presentation and you've got your yard sign, say, "Mr. and Mrs. So and So, one of the things we do is use this yard sign...." Then you talk about the benefits of the yard sign and how it relates to them, etc. When you're done explaining the yard sign, say something like this: "You know, Diana, as I was driving up I was thinking, would it look better on the right corner of your property or the left? What do you think? The right corner? I was kind of leaning towards that, too. OK." You see that? It's a subtle close. She's already thinking about the yard sign. These subtle closes make it a little easier when you're asking for that signature.

9. **Objections occur because you didn't effectively communicate.** Have you noticed that this is the third or fourth time I've made the same point ... in a slightly different fashion? You must be clear. Be confident and present them with a commitment to help them get what they want.

10. **To avoid objections, invite action for a listing agreement *assumptively*.** The worst thing you can do is go through your whole presentation and cramp up at the end. You say, "So, what do you folks think?" or "Should we get the ball rolling?" and you start doing the "Realtor shuffle," getting nervous and waiting for the objection. That's the worst thing you can do. There should not be two pieces, the presentation and the close. You should flow smoothly from presentation into close and you should be very assumptive. You should have the thought that, based on what they're committed to, it just makes sense that they hire you and put it on multiple and get a yard sign, etc. You have to *believe* that. So after your whole presentation, it's just another step that comes naturally.

Let's go through the process of the homeowner signing the listing agreement.

Step 1: Agree on price. As I said in Chapter 3, "The Listing Presentation," before you discuss price, make sure the sellers are ready to hire you regardless of the amount on your CMA. You would do this by asking the question, "Aside from price, based on what you've seen about me and my company, are you folks ready to go ahead and hire me?" If they don't say "yes," find out what's holding them back and handle that objection. If they do say "yes," present your CMA like we discussed in the previous chapter.

Step 2: Assumptively fill out the listing agreement. For some agents, the most difficult part is how to start writing on the listing agreement. Here is a great little technique. While holding your pen over the listing form, say this, "Let me just get some information. What's today's date?" When they answer you, it's like they're giving you permission to go ahead and start writing. If they're not ready to sign with you, this is when an objection will come up.

Step 3: Keep them involved. As you're filling out the paperwork, you don't want any silent pauses. If there's silence, they start thinking; if they start thinking, they'll probably throw out an objection. To prevent this, ask about what fixtures are staying with the house ... or have the couple follow along with you on the form.

Step 4: Hand them the pen and direct their signatures. If you lay it on the table, everyone will stare at it.

Step 5: Ask the spouse a question. We handled this exact topic in "The Listing Presentation." The key is to involve the spouse so the two can't communicate.

What's an Objection?

There's a difference between a *blow-off*, a *condition*, and an *objection*.

The *blow-off* is what they say to you so they don't have to make a decision. In other words, they are politely trying to get rid of you. It may sound like "We just need to sleep on it, because we never make any quick decisions; we promise to call you back" or "We'd like to list with you, but we're just the kind of people who need to think about it for a few days." Do you think when you leave that they're going to just sit there and think? No, when you leave they're going to talk about the *real* reason they didn't list with you.

Here's another example of a *blow-off*: "Give us a couple of weeks to try it on our own and then we'll call you." What are they going to do in a couple of weeks? Most likely, they're not going to call you. They're just blowing smoke at you, right? Now sometimes they *do* call you, but if you rely on this, you'll go broke.

What is your job when they give you the *blow-off*? Your job is to uncover the real objection that's holding them back. Later in the chapter, I'll show you some techniques for doing that.

Now, a *condition* is a *real reason* why they *can't* hire you at that moment. The condition might be that the job relocation hasn't come through yet. Or maybe there's not enough equity in the property and they can't make it work financially. Your job in this case is to follow up with them until they can list with you.

The *objection* is a concern *they believe to be real* as to why they shouldn't hire you or any other agent at that moment. For example, they want to try it on their own for a while to save the commission, they had a bad experience before, they have a friend in the business, etc. The *objection* is the only thing we can sink our teeth into and handle.

Recurring Concerns

Sometimes an agent will call and tell me that she or he keeps getting the same *objection*. If this rings true, that usually means there's something that you are doing (or not doing) in the presentation that keeps eliciting the same response. Let's go through what some of these recurring objections may be and why they are happening.

If you're getting the *blow-off*, you may not be creating urgency, the need for them to hire you now and not in a few weeks or a few days. It also could be, especially with FSBOs, that they still haven't bought into the real estate industry and they have no intention of calling you back.

By the way, here's a great way to create urgency. If homeowners think they have all summer, for example, two and a half months, let them know that most sales occur during the weekend, when people are off work. So, actually, they don't have the whole summer; they have only 10 weekends. And if they aren't going to call back for two weeks, we're now down to only eight weekends. Get my point?

If you keep getting the *commission* objection, my opinion is that it's because you're coming off as too "slick," you're not confident enough, or you're rushing your presentation and skipping a step. I remember a point in my career when I got a little too arrogant and I'd say, OK I'm here, sign right there. I started skipping steps, but one of the objections I kept getting was commission. So they'd hire me because they knew I was good, but they didn't respect me so they wanted to talk me down on my commission. Of course, in today's market, you might be getting this objection as a result of discount brokers. If that's the case, get clear about the difference between your fee and the other broker's fee. Whatever that difference is, let's say it's 2%, you simply have to show them how you are 2% better than your competition.

If you keep getting the *length of listing* objection, where people want to give you a shorter-term listing than what you need, then what you're not communicating is the process. The process of selling a home is this and this and this and this. And it takes as long as it takes.

If you keep getting the *price* objection, I believe you're not pre-validating the CMA. (I talk about how to present price in our chapter on the art of negotiating.)

Uncovering the Real Objection When You Get the Blow-Off

Your objective with the *blow-off* is to find out the real objection underneath. Here are three ways to do this.

Option 1: The Multiple Choice Technique

Seller: Wait a second, Darryl. I'm not ready to sign tonight. I need to give this some thought.

Darryl: Charles, I can appreciate that you want to give it some thought, because this is an important decision and I think if I were in your shoes I would want to think about any concerns I might have too. Just out of curiosity, what specific concerns do you want to think about?

Seller: I don't know.

Darryl: Well, is it something about the price we discussed and maybe even the net?

Seller: No.

Darryl: Is it something about the length of listing?

Seller: No, that's fine.

Darryl: OK, is there something about my company? Do you feel that we can do the job?

The point is that you feed each possible objection to the sellers, one at a time. How many should you feed them? Until you think enough is enough. If this doesn't work, you can then try the next option.

Option 2: The Key Concerns Technique

Here, instead of you feeding each possible concern one at a time, you share the ones you think it could be all at once and then ask them to pick one. It sounds like this:

Darryl: Well, Charles, I'm a little confused because, based on what you told me about why you're selling, I really believe I can help you. If I didn't think I could help you, then I wouldn't ask you to hire me. My batting average is pretty high and I like to keep it that way. So I feel good about us, that I can help you, but something is holding you back.

In my experience, when a seller is truly committed to selling, and I believe you are, and we don't go forward, it's usually because of one of *three key concerns*. It might be something about the *price*; for example, you think you may not net enough to make this move work. It could be the *length* of listing, that there's a concern making a commitment for the length of time we discussed. Or maybe it's *something about me or my company*—perhaps you think there's a better company out there or you don't feel my company has the knowledge or experience in this area. If you had to pick one of these as being one you had to think about, which would it be?

The next technique is radical, but it works really well.

Option 3: The Good Samaritan Technique—Referring Others

Let's say I do Options 1 and 2 with Charles and he still says, "Darryl, just give us a couple of weeks and then I'll call you." I would say, "Charles, I'm going to tell you this and I honestly believe it. Based on your situation, based on what's happening in the market, you need to hire someone to represent you and get you on multiple listing. Maybe I'm not the person to do it. I'd rather see you at least go with a broker—any broker—than not at all. So I'm going to give you the names and numbers of a couple of other brokers for you to talk to, because I'd rather see you hire an agent than try to do this on your own."

Now, if you say this, you *have* to believe what you're saying. It can't be a manipulation. The reason this works really well is because you're showing the sellers that you care more about them than yourself. If they are going to list with anyone, it definitely will be you after this unselfish act. And if they do list with one of the brokers you told them to call, guess what? You never had the listing to begin with. You've got nothing to lose and everything to gain with this technique.

By the way, I rarely got the listing the very moment I made this gesture. They usually would call me within a couple of days. So, when you use this technique, don't think they'll say, "Wow, give us your form." No, they'll take the names, maybe because they're calling your bluff, and you'll leave.

The Objection-Handling Process

Now that I've given you several ways to get past the blow-off, let's get into the objection-handling process. This process is what you actually use when you're clear on exactly what the objection is.

When we go through this process, I want you to concentrate on how I break down each step and what the objective is in each.

Step 1: Acknowledge. The first thing you want to do is say, "I don't blame you for feeling that. If I were in your shoes I would think the same thing." It doesn't have to be those exact words, but remember that one of the commandments in handling an objection is to take your time. So, let them know that it's OK that they feel that way.

And, while you're at it, here's a rule of thumb for you: never say in five words what you can say in 10. Let me explain.

If the objection is "I don't want to pay that commission," you might say, "Mr. Seller, I know how you feel." (That's the short answer.) Now, let's say the longer version. "Well, listen, Mr. Seller, I don't blame you for trying to see if you can get the most money for the house and you want to save on the commission. I think if I were in your shoes and I thought I could save on the commission, I'd want to do just that."

So, when they throw an objection at you, don't get weird. Just take your time. Now, go into Step 2.

Step 2: Ask Questions. Here, you want to get clear about their concern/issue/objection. The better you are with this step, the easier Step 3 will be, which is to actually handle their objection. For example: "Just out of curiosity, why do you feel that way?"

Let's say he says, "Well, we both know what the bottom line is and I'm with you on the pricing, but I'm really not comfortable with making the move to Florida with my bottom line being where it is. So if you can negotiate with me on your commission, then maybe we can go forward."

At this point, you might say, "So you do agree with me on the price?"

"Yeah, I can see where the market analysis shows where the price should be, and I agree with that."

"So it also sounds like you want to hire me, pending the commission question?"

"Yes."

"So, it's just a question of you wanting to see if you can make more money in your pocket?"

"I just want to be able to make the move comfortably to the next house. With my bottom line, it doesn't look like where I thought it should be."

"So you feel if we lowered the commission, then that would give you some more moving money?"

"You've got it."

I don't care how you do Step 2. Some trainers would say to ask open-ended questions, using the five W's and the H—Who, What, When, Where, Why, and How. But in Step 2, I do something else. I also confirm things that seem to be true, e.g., "I think I understand what you're saying, Mr. Seller, but I'm a little unclear. You do agree with the listing price, yes? And it sounds like you want to hire me, yes?" So I'm getting clear. That isn't an open-ended question. If anything, it's a tie-down.

Whatever questions you ask, your objective here is to get crystal clear about where they're coming from. Get clear about the box that they're in, the thoughts that are keeping them from going on.

Step 3: Confirm. Confirm that this is the *only* concern/issue/objection you need to handle. Some possible dialogue would be "Is that the only thing stopping us?" or "If I could show you…." These are called the "sharp-angled close."

"So, Mr. Seller, the only thing holding us back is that you want to see if you can get a few extra dollars?"

"Well, I'm concerned about how comfortable I'll be making a move with my bottom line where it's going to be."

"Let me ask you this: if we couldn't do any better than where your bottom line is now, are you still going to make this move?"

"Yes."

"Oh, OK. Well, if I could show you that by asking me to lower the brokerage fee you actually might lose money—that you'll get the best bottom line possible by leaving the brokerage fee where it is—could we then get the ball rolling?"

"You're saying I'll do better by leaving the commission where it is?"

"Yes, and therefore you'll get a higher bottom line."

"Well, if you could show me that, then OK."

"Alright…."

If he says "No," what do you do? Go back to the questions. Find out at Step 3 that this is it, that there aren't any other objections. And if there are other objections, find out now before you go on to Step 4.

Step 4: Handle Their Objection. Here you actually address their concern by using a visual and an analogy. Later in this chapter, I will give you several of these to use with different objections.

Step 5: Invite Action. Now that you've answered the objection to the customer's satisfaction, ask for action, either more questions and what you need to do to complete the transaction.

There's a whole process in handling an objection. In the next section, we will go through several visuals and demonstrate the dialogue. But, before we move on, let's just focus for a moment on Step 2 of the objection-handling process, where you probe to get clear about what's holding them back. It's a key step.

Where most agents are weak is in asking questions. Think about it: when you're on the phone prospecting, are you asking enough questions? When you're working with buyers, are you asking enough questions? When you're working on the presentation, trying to get clear about what the sellers are committed to, are you asking enough questions?

When you get an objection, you need to ask as many questions as it takes. Granted, in some cases when you get the objection you may already know what it is and you're pretty clear, so you may need to ask only one or two questions. But more times than not, you'll have to probe. Work at this area of asking questions. Get skillful.

22 Powerful Objection-Handling Dialogues

I want you to get a feel for the dialogue associated with each objection. So, in the pages that follow, I will "role-play" various objections that you may encounter and offer strategic replies to each. These 22 powerful techniques will definitely put more money in your pocket in the coming months.

THE ART OF NEGOTIATING TECHNIQUE: *"WE WANT TO SELL ON OUR OWN TO SAVE THE COMMISSION"* OR *"WE CAN DO A BETTER JOB"*

Darryl: Do you play cards?

Mr. Seller: I love playing cards.

Darryl: Let's say you're playing poker and in the middle of the table you've got $150,000.

Mr. Seller: Alright, I'm sweating bullets.

Darryl: Yes! So are you emotionally involved here? Of course. Let's say your hand has four aces and now you're wondering, "Should I ask for more? Should I raise?" Now, because you're emotionally involved, do you think that you could make a mistake?

Mr. Seller: Yeah. I would be more careful about everything.

Darryl: Let's use the same scenario. You're playing cards, but you're playing from another room. The same $150K is in the middle of the table, but this person you're playing with is in the other room. Now, I come into the room and I look at your hand and you're sweating bullets and are all excited, only now you don't have to worry about bluffing. I'm standing there and I say, "Alright, here's what I think you should do," and I give you some advice. Then you tell me, "Darryl, here's what I want you to tell them." Then I tell that person. Now they're sweating bullets too. But I'm not emotionally attached, so I can bluff better than you can. Would you agree with that? It's not my money on the table, but I'm still committed to us winning. My point is that because I'm the third-party negotiator, I can probably get us much more than you trying to sell it on your own. Do you follow?

THE DIRECTOR TECHNIQUE

Darryl: Mr. Seller, if you knew that by doing it on your own you could lose a sale or maybe lose thousands of dollars, would you then go ahead and let me represent you?

Mr. Seller: If you could convince me that you could do a better job, yes.

Darryl: I won't say that I could do a better job showing the home, because you've been living here for 10 years. Even I'm not arrogant enough to say that. But if you knew we would do a better job together because in partnership with me you'll actually save money vs. losing money doing it on your own, would you then hire me? [You don't want to insult him. Did you notice the way I phrased this?]

Mr. Seller: Yeah.

Darryl: OK, great. Let's say, Mr. Seller, that a buyer goes for a mortgage and the bank comes to look at the house and appraise it. You're selling it for, let's say, $140K and the bank appraises it for $130K. So now the bank tells the buyers, who then tell their attorney, who then tells your attorney, who then tells you. Did you ever play telephone in school? Did you ever notice that what comes out at the end is not the message that started out? That happens in real estate all the time. Because there are so many different elements involved in selling a house, there are lots of places for communication gaps. Have you noticed how many real estate offices are downtown? There wouldn't be so many of us if we didn't provide a valuable service.

I like to think that the service we provide is almost like we're the director of a Broadway show. The director talks to everybody—the stagehands, the lighting crew, the set designers, the costume designers. The costume designers, for instance, will never talk directly to the lighting crew. Yet both elements are critical to the show's success.

The real estate agent is the only person who speaks to everyone involved in selling your home. So if any problem occurs, I'm going to hear it directly from the horse's mouth and then you're going to hear it directly from me. I can't tell you how many home sales were on the verge of not closing and I was able to save them because I was hearing things firsthand. Can you now see the value of having a real estate agent?

You can also use the director technique when someone says, "Well, my attorney can do that for me."

Mr. Seller: I don't need an agent to qualify a buyer because my attorney will do that.

Darryl: Your attorney would never speak directly to the buyers, would he or she? Your attorney's going to talk to the buyers' attorney, who will then talk to the buyers. But your attorney would never talk directly to the bank appraiser. Remember, any time your attorney talks to anybody, he or she is going to charge you, too. The agent is the only one in a real estate transaction who talks to everybody. Therefore, we're in complete control of a transaction.

THE ONE-LINE FISHING TECHNIQUE

Darryl: So, Mr. Seller, let me ask you something. Is there anything else you're doing to advertise your house besides putting ads in the paper?

Mr. Seller: Yeah, I have a flier at work and I've just been talking to a lot of friends.

Darryl: You understand all the things I have—multiple listings, yard signs, relocation companies, referral systems. I explained all that to you, right?

Mr. Seller: Right.

Darryl: With you selling the house on your own, you might eventually succeed. But it may take forever. Let me just ask you this: if I could save you time and you knew it was better hiring me than just doing it on your own, would you then hire me?

Mr. Seller: Yeah.

Darryl: OK. Well, correct me if I'm wrong, but to sell the house we just need one buyer. We don't need 100, just one who's willing to pay our price. The only problem is to find that one we need, we may have to go through hundreds of prospective buyers. You said you put an ad in the paper and you've been putting up fliers. Well, if you were to go fishing and you wanted to find this one great fish, and you had a choice of throwing one line out there or a net, which do you think would give you better odds?

Mr. Seller: The net.

Darryl: Well, with you putting in ads and creating fliers, you're basically putting out one fishing line, hoping that you'll catch this one terrific fish. Whereas with what I do it's like throwing out one big net, so there's a lot more potential. Do you follow what I'm saying? So what's it going to be, the line or the net?

Mr. Seller: Well, I want to increase my odds of selling, so I guess the net.

Darryl: All right, let's get the ball rolling.

THE NINE DOTS TECHNIQUE

Figure 4-1. The nine dots puzzle

Darryl: Mr. Seller, I'm not saying that you can't sell the house on your own. You were doing some ads and fliers, and that's all good. But let me suggest something, because you've had some success selling several houses before with this method and this is good. What I'm going to suggest, Mr. Seller, is that because you sold some houses before and because you've had success with them, you have a certain system you use that works. But, like with anything else, you may have gotten into a routine that may not be in your best interests.

So, I don't want to be hokey with you, but I want to show you something that helps prove my point. Please take this pen. [This is good because you get the person writing.] What I'd like you to do is connect these nine dots with four straight lines without taking your pen off the paper. [Pause and let him or her try.] See, you can't do it. Most people can't. Let me show you how it works.

See, the reason you couldn't do it is because you were trying to stay in this box. In order to connect the nine dots, you have to go outside of the box. The only reason I illustrated this is because I'm suggesting that is how you sell homes—putting ads in the paper, putting up fliers, and talking to people—because it worked before, maybe you think that's the only way to sell a house. But you might not have gotten the price you deserved selling in this manner ... or you might have taken longer than you needed to. My

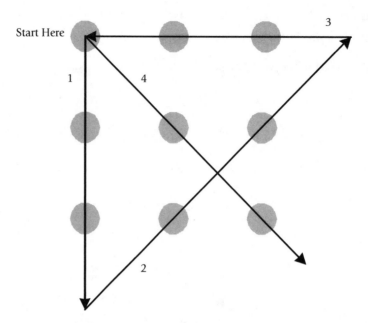

Figure 4-2. Solution to the nine dots puzzle

job as a real estate agent is to constantly think of new and innovative ways to market and give a house exposure. What used to work 10 years ago doesn't work as well now. So, I'm always trying to look outside of the box to see how I can get creative to get a house sold. Can you see that if we work together we're better off than you doing it on your own?

THE SIX BAKERS TECHNIQUE: *"BRING ME A BUYER AND I'LL PAY YOU A COMMISSION"*

Here's where they say that they want to sell it on their own, but if you bring them a buyer they'll pay you a commission.

Darryl: Are you doing that with other brokers, Mr. Seller?

Mr. Seller: Yes I am.

Darryl: If you knew that by hiring me you'd have more agents working for you to get your house sold than doing it this way, would you then hire me?

Mr. Seller: I would do it that way, but I still feel that any broker can come to my house and provide a buyer.

Darryl: Well, let me rephrase it. If you knew that by hiring me you're going to get the agents working *harder* for you than they would the other way, would you then list it with me?

Mr. Seller: Well, yes, if I knew they would work harder at getting it sold.

Darryl: Let's pretend. Do you have a daughter? If not, let's pretend you do and it's her 16th birthday. You're going to want a nice cake, right? So to get the best results on this cake, maybe you go to six bakers and you say, "My daughter's having a sweet 16 party and I want a gorgeous cake! Now, you six bakers, whoever bakes me the best, most beautiful cake, that's the baker I'm going to give my money to." How many bakers do you think are going to start rolling up their sleeves and start working for you?

Mr. Seller: None.

Darryl: It's the same thing here. You're saying, whoever does the best job, that's who I'm going to pay. So, therefore, no one is going to work for you. Especially when we have other people who have hired us and are committed to us and we want to keep our commitment to them.

THE CONFUSION TECHNIQUE

This continues the situation just above.

Darryl: So, Mr. Seller, you're doing this with other brokers, right?

Mr. Seller: Yes, I am. I'm notifying a lot of people.

Darryl: Mr. Seller, I recommend that you do one of two things: either hire a broker (and it doesn't have to be me, as long as you hire a broker) or don't work with any brokers, period. Don't do what you're doing.

Mr. Seller: Why?

Darryl: You're only going to make it worse. You see, imagine that you say to all the brokers, "Look, I want $100K for the house," right? So XYZ Realty looks at the house and says, "Alright, we're going to put it up for $107K." Then BSA Realty says, "We're going to put it up for $110K." Now ABC Realty says, "We're going to put it up for $109K." Are you following this scenario?

Mr. Seller: I think so.

Darryl: You see, you've already told them what you want, so they're going to charge different negotiation prices, different commissions. Now, here's a buyer. Funny thing about a serious buyer is that when they're looking at a house they say, "I want this, this, and this in a house," and then they go to another agent. (You know, serious buyers will work with a bunch of agents because they're interested in buying a home, not just being loyal to one agent.) That other agent may also show them your home. So now they see your house with one agent and it's $107K, with another agent it's $109K, and with another it's $110K. What would you feel?

Mr. Seller: That something's fishy here.

Darryl: Right. It's like "Would the real price please stand up?!" Now the buyer is confused. But let's take it back a second. Mr. Buyer and his wife are very interested in your house. They are considering it. They see it for $107K, and they say, "Oooh, I really like that house, but let me just look at a couple of others to compare before we get this one." Then, all of a sudden, they start getting different prices on this house. What would you do if you were that buyer?

Mr. Seller: I think I would get scared, as a buyer, seeing it for different prices with different agents.

Darryl: You'd say, what's wrong with this house? Then you'd stay away from it, right?

Mr. Seller: Well, as a buyer I might go with the agent who has the lowest price.

Darryl: Ahh. But, you know what, Mr. Seller? You really wouldn't. The reason is because you'll be thinking to yourself that there's probably an even better price that you don't yet know about. What's the real price? My point is that if you have all these prices on your home you're going to hurt your marketing effort rather than help. So I'm saying, do one of two things: either do it on your own and hope you get lucky, or hire one professional to manage all this for you.

You can tie down this concept with the following.

Darryl: Mr. Seller, do you think that not being committed to one agent works better for you?

Mr. Seller: Well, the agents are still able to get paid, but I only have to pay part of the brokerage fee, so I save money.

Darryl: Let me ask you a question, Mr. Seller. Based on everything we went over, my marketing plan and all of that, do you agree that the more marketing you have on a house the better your odds, because it has more exposure to more buyers who come through, which ultimately means the most amount of money?

Mr. Seller: More exposure is much better.

Darryl: OK, how many agents have you had through here looking at the house?

Mr. Seller: Four or five.

Darryl: Let's say each of those five offices has about 10 agents. Now, how many agents know your house is for sale? The five who have seen it or the other 45 in the offices?

Mr. Seller: All 50.

Darryl: No, that's the problem, because you haven't given a listing to one broker. It's called an open listing, and here's how it works. If I go into my office and tell everyone there, "Hey, Mr. Seller's house is for sale," if another agent in that office sells that house I get nothing.

Mr. Seller: So that would make you work harder to try to sell my house so the other agent won't.

Darryl: Well, maybe. But watch. You would get the original four or five working hard for you because they want to get the money in their pockets, but I'm saying that you could have 200 agents working for you if you list with a single broker, who then shares the commission with whoever sells your house. In your present scenario, if I were to tell anybody your house was for sale, I wouldn't get anything for it. So those four or five have nothing to gain by letting their fellow agents know it's for sale. Are you really going to get the exposure you need?

Mr. Seller: Not with this scenario, no.

THE PEN TECHNIQUE: "WE HAD A BAD EXPERIENCE BEFORE"

This next objection is they want to sell it on their own because they've hired a broker before and they've had a bad experience. How this works is that you have the seller take your pen and write the word "sold" and then you take the pen and write the word "sold," but differently. The point is same tool, different results.

Darryl: So, Mr. Seller, let me ask you a question. You had this bad experience about how long ago?

Mr. Seller: I had it for sale for six months and I dropped the listing just last month.

Darryl: So you don't want to go again with a broker because you had a bad experience?

Mr. Seller: Yeah, it was a tough one. [*Note:* I am not going through the entire process here, but I would ask several more questions about what happened, how it felt, etc.]

Darryl: So, Mr. Seller, I believe that you saw some value in multiple listing or you wouldn't have hired that broker six months ago, am I right?

Mr. Seller: I thought I saw some value in it.

Darryl: Yes, but the broker himself—obviously you're unhappy because that office didn't do the job for you. See, like anything else, multiple listing is a tool, and the tool itself does not get a house sold; it's all about how you use the tool. Just like a hammer can't build a deck without a skilled carpenter. The result you want is to get the house sold. See, here's how I like to demonstrate it. Do me a favor. Take my pen, Mr. Seller, and just write the word "sold" on this piece of paper anywhere. Now you see, I'm going to take the pen and write this same word in script. You see, Mr. Seller, we both used the same tool and got different results. What I'm saying is that if you hire me, I'm going to use many of the same tools, but I'll get a different result. I'm going to get the house sold.

THE AIRPLANE TECHNIQUE

Darryl: Mr. Seller, let's pretend here. Have you ever flown and had a bad experience on a flight?

Mr. Seller: Oh, yeah! I had a really bumpy flight to Chicago. It was really bad!

Darryl: Let's take a scenario like this. I'm going to purposely blow it out of proportion a little. You were flying to Chicago and you flew a particular airline. You were a few hours late. Your bags were a day late. The flight attendants went to a bad training program, "Arrogant 101," and you ran out of peanuts. Now, you need to go to California. Would you walk or would you still fly?

Mr. Seller: I'd take the plane

Darryl: Why? Because you know the plane is better than walking. You get there quicker and you won't pass out from muscle cramping and dehydration along the way. My point is, Mr. Seller, just because you had a bad experience, you aren't going to rule out flying all together. You may never work with that airline again, but you still see the value of flying. What I'm saying is, don't discount real estate agents just because you had a bad experience with that one. Just don't use that one again. Do you follow me?

Mr. Seller: Yeah, it makes sense.

THE CODE OF ETHICS TECHNIQUE

If you are a member of the National Association of Realtors, you should have a copy of the Realtor® Code of Ethics in your presentation book.

Darryl: Mr. Seller, if you knew that I was required to always look out for your best interests, would you hire me?

Mr. Seller: I'd give that consideration.

Darryl: Well, if there was no question in your mind that I'm always going to look out for your best interests, that I'll do my best to get your house sold, would you then hire me?

Mr. Seller: Sure.

Darryl: OK. I belong to the National Association of Realtors® as I mentioned earlier. As a member of this Association, there's a Code of Ethics I subscribe to and in Article 1 it says that I must always look out for your best interests. As a matter of fact, the State that licenses me takes this article quite seriously. They use this Code of Ethics to help regulate all real estate agents and their licensing. My point is this, because I'm a member of this Association and I subscribe to this Code of Ethics, if I didn't do everything in my power to look after your best interests, I'm breaking this Article and jeopardizing my license. I want you to know that I'd never do anything to jeopardize your trust or my license. So do you see that I could never do you wrong, even if I wanted to, because it's the law?

Mr. Seller: Yeah.

THE WINDOW SHOPPING TECHNIQUE: "WE WANT TO FIND A HOUSE FIRST, BEFORE WE SELL"

Mr. Seller: I don't want to wait to buy another house until I've already sold this one. I want to get another house under contract and then I'll worry about selling.

Darryl: I know from experience, after selling real estate for the past 20 years, that you're not going to be out in the street, and here's why I say that. When you look at a house before you've sold yours, you look at it differently. Maybe it's not as intently or as focused as when you are in the process of selling your home. It's the same as the difference between shopping and buying. Let's say you went to the store with no credit cards or money or anything. You couldn't walk out of that store with anything. You couldn't even put anything on layaway. Now let's say you walk into a department store with $150,000 cash in a bag, do you think just maybe you'll walk out of there with something?

Mr. Seller: Yeah.

Darryl: What I'm saying is that it's the same thing with buying and selling a house. Until you put this one on the market, you're window shopping—you're just looking—you can't make the commitment because you don't have the money that you'll have once you sell your current home. But once you've made the commitment that you're making the move and you put this house on the market, it's a whole other ballgame. Do you follow what I'm saying?

THE DRIVER'S SEAT TECHNIQUE

Darryl: So you want to find a house first before you put this one on the market. The only thing is you could lose money. Can I explain what I mean?

Mr. Seller: Yeah.

Darryl: OK. Two things are actually going to happen. Either you're going to have to end up paying top dollar for your new home or you're going to have to sell this one for less. Let me explain why that is. Let's say we go out and look at some houses, and you find a house you like. You go to the sellers and you want to negotiate them down from say $200K. Well, here's the thing: you haven't sold your house yet, so are the sellers for the new one going to be at some risk, since you haven't sold yours?

Mr. Seller: Sure.

Darryl: So what are the sellers going to do? They may sell it to you under some tough conditions. Do you think they'll be flexible on their price? Or do you think they'll stay firm, since they're taking a risk?

Mr. Seller: Well, they'd certainly be less apt to come down on their price.

Darryl: So we don't know how much money that could be. It could be a few thousand, right? Well, let's say you even do negotiate with the seller and work out a good deal. You're now under contract to buy that house. Now, what do you have to do with your house?

Mr. Seller: Get it up for sale.

Darryl: And sell it quickly. In order to sell your house quickly—you said you wanted $150K for your house—what would you have to do?

Mr. Seller: Discount it.

Darryl: See, the worst part about all of this is that you're not in the driver's seat. You've got to negotiate with this one, and you're not in a good position because you need the money quickly to pay for the other house. But here's the worst part. Whether it's contingent or not, if you don't sell your house in time and you have to drop the whole thing, you lose all around. Let's look at the flip side. Right now we're in the driver's seat, meaning you don't have any specific commitment to buying a particular house, right?

Mr. Seller: Right.

Darryl: That's beautiful, because here's what we do. We put your house on the market for the price that we want. We wait until we find a buyer. When one comes, we sell it—no pressure, we're in the driver's seat. We find a buyer and this person is willing to give us our price. Now we go and find the sellers of another house and say, "Look, I want to buy your home, and I've got $150K cash." Do you think that the sellers would be willing to listen to you?

Mr. Seller: Sure.

Darryl: And they might even do better on the price. Or maybe you can negotiate and say when you'd like to close based on your buyer. My point is that by selling your home first, you're in the driver's seat. If you go out and buy a house first, you're locked in because you've made a commitment. You're no longer in the driver's seat. You're a victim of everything you have to do.

THE BEWARE TECHNIQUE: "THE OTHER BROKER SAID SHE'LL DO IT FOR LESS COMMISSION"

This is when the seller says he's going to list with so-and-so because the agent said she'd do it for less commission.

Darryl: Well, Mr. Seller, I'd be really concerned and wary in that situation.

Mr. Seller: Why?

Darryl: Well, in this case she's saying she'll do it for 1% less, which is about $1,500, am I right?

Mr. Seller: Yes.

Darryl: So, what you're telling me is that this agent, without hesitation, is willing to give away $1,500 of her money?

Mr. Seller: That's right.

Darryl: The reason I'm saying to be wary is this: if she is so quick to give away her money just to get your listing, how quick do you think she is going to be to give away *your* money just to put the deal together?

The Three Ways to Travel Technique

Darryl: Mrs. Seller, let me show you something that I think will make a difference with this commission thing. You're not opposed to working with a broker, you're just shopping for the best commission, right?

Mrs. Seller: Yes.

Darryl: Let's say you're going to travel from here to California and you've got three ways to travel. You can drive, which will take more time, but will most likely be the cheapest way to go. A train will take a little less time, but cost a little more, too. But the fastest, smoothest, quickest ride is by plane, which is probably also the most ... what?

Mrs. Seller: Expensive.

Darryl: What's my point here, Mrs. Seller? It's that you get what you pay for. If you were to travel to California, which way would you choose?

Mrs. Seller: Plane.

Darryl: Sure, if you had to get there by a certain time. If this other agent is going to cut her commission, she's going to have to cut some services. Maybe she didn't explain that to you? But I'm sure that for an agent to work for that brokerage fee, she's not giving you the first-class service that I plan on giving you. So the choice is yours. Do you want to go with a professional? Or would you prefer to try the cut-rate model that may or may not ever get you to your destination?

THE BRAIN SURGERY SPECIAL TECHNIQUE

Darryl: So you want to save the commission and you're shopping around, right?

Mr. Seller: Yes.

Darryl: So, I know this isn't going to happen, but let's say you're going to need to have brain surgery done. Now I understand money is important. But you look in the paper and you see an ad like this: "This week's special—brain surgery: 20% off!" Would you call this doctor and have that done?

Mr. Seller: No.

Darryl: Why is that?

Mr. Seller: It's too important.

Darryl: Exactly. Some things are too important to discount. I'm assuming that selling your house and moving to where you want to move is one of the biggest investments and financial things you're managing in your life, right?

Mr. Seller: Right.

Darryl: So why would you want to go with somebody who discounts his or her service and maybe not get the quality that you need? Do you see what I'm saying?

Mr. Seller: Yeah.

THE RIGHT PLACE, WRONG BAIT TECHNIQUE: "WE WANT TO LIST IT AT A HIGHER PRICE"

This next objection is a price objection. They're willing to list with you, but at a higher price than you recommend.

Darryl: So Mr. Seller, let me ask you a question. Let's pretend you were going fishing and the fish were down here. Where would you want to place the bait?

Mr. Seller: Down here.

Darryl: Let's say that we place the bait up here. Are we going to get nibbles?

Mr. Seller: Doubtful.

Darryl: Yeah. We may get one dumb fish to stray from the pack. But the odds of catching the fish are not in our favor. Here's the reason I'm using this analogy. We'll do whatever you want, but I'm recommending that we should put the house on the market for $150K because, based on comparables, that's where the fish are. If we price it, though, at what you're suggesting, at $160K, I'm not saying that the house won't sell. It is possible that it will, but it's not probable. So the choice is yours. I'm coaching you here, but what do you want to do?

THE DOLLAR BILL TECHNIQUE

Darryl: Mr. Seller, let's pretend that I give you 100 one-dollar bills and I say, "Go to the mall and sell each one for 95 cents." This is hypothetical, obviously. For 95 cents, do you think you'd sell them?

Mr. Seller: Yes.

Darryl: In a couple of hours, who knows? Now let's say I give you 100 one-dollar bills and tell you to sell them for 85 cents each. You definitely would sell them in less time, right?

Mr. Seller: Sure.

Darryl: So let's take the same 100 one-dollar bills and I say to sell them for $1.10 each. How long do you think it would take you to sell them?

Mr. Seller: Forever.

Darryl: Probably a real long time. Mr. Seller, what I'm saying is by taking a house that's worth $150K and trying to get more for it than it's worth, it may take us an extremely long time.

Mr. Seller: I understand.

THE STAY FIRM TECHNIQUE

This is basically the same objection, but the sellers add, "We'll list with you, Darryl, but we want to keep it at a high price so we have haggling room."

Darryl: Mr. Seller, I can understand how you feel that we need to price the house higher so we have some negotiating room, because then we'll wind up at the price we actually want.

Mr. Seller: Everybody wants to negotiate.

Darryl: Yeah. But this is really important for you to understand. If I thought this would work in your best interest, I would say let's do it. After all, it would make me more money too, right? But as your coach, I say it's not in your best interests. Let me explain why. If we want $150K for the house, I'd rather that we ask $150K and say, "We're staying firm," rather than put it up at a higher price and then come down. Why? Because the higher we price the house the fewer the buyers that will come through the doors. Does that make sense?

Mr. Seller: I guess so.

Darryl: Now, where are you in a better position? To have one buyer who is interested in your house and you have to haggle with that one buyer or to have several and tell them you're staying firm?

Mr. Seller: With a lot more buyers.

Darryl: Definitely.

THE STALE BREAD TECHNIQUE

Darryl: Mr. Seller, based on the comps, the house is worth about $150K, is that right?

Mr. Seller: Yes.

Darryl: Now you want to try it for $160K?

Mr. Seller: Yes.

Darryl: OK, I don't have a problem with that, except for this. If we were to take your house that's valued at $150K and put it up on the market for $140K, do you think we would sell it quickly?

Mr. Seller: Definitely.

Darryl: Right. What would happen is tons of buyers would come out to see your house right away.

Mr. Seller: Well, we'd be giving it away.

Darryl: Right. Here, if we list it at $150K, we're going to get an average number of buyers to get the house sold in the time frame that I showed you, because that's fair market, comparable, etc. So if we go above fair market, we're going to have fewer potential buyers because of competition from other homes—it just weeds out more and more buyers. If we listed it for $200K, we'd have maybe one, if any, right? So the higher you go, the fewer buyers. The fewer buyers, the longer it takes. Well, my concern is that when a house stays on the market for too long, it gets stale. For example, let's use bread. You know, when bread stays on the shelf at a supermarket for too long, what happens?

Mr. Seller: They mark the price down.

Darryl: But it also gets stale, right? When a house is on the market for a while, in a sense it becomes stale. The agents don't show it as much; they start to lose interest. It becomes back-burner stuff because it's stale. When is the best time to sell? As soon as you put it on the market. You want to package the house in its best light—the price, its appearance, everything.

This is a good technique, especially when sellers say they want to try it at a higher price for 30 days or something and then they'll lower it.

Darryl: If we already know, Mr. Seller, that in 30 days we're going to come down to the price that the CMA is now saying, we're better off starting out that way because a house is never hotter than when it first comes on the market.

THE PRESENTATION TECHNIQUE

Here is where they say, "We'll list it at a higher price, and we don't feel we need to fix it up."

Darryl: Do you want to get the most for the house?

Mr. Seller: Of course.

Darryl: Well, if we don't do anything different to the house, we should go with the price that I've recommended. If you want to go with the higher price, then there is something else you need to do.

Mr. Seller: What's that?

Darryl: Have you ever heard the expression "It's all in the presentation"?

Mr. Seller: Yes, I have.

Darryl: Mr. Seller, let's say that you want a steak. At a fine restaurant, they might charge somewhere around $35.00 for a standard cut of meat. If we go to a local, fast food-type steakhouse chain we're going to pay about $9.95. Same steak. What's the difference? The atmosphere, the decor, the building, the location, the service, the presentation. So, as an analogy, if we want to take our $9.95 steak and get $35 for it, we're going to have to make some adjustments in the presentation of the home. Either you've got to invest several thousand dollars to fix the house up to get that price or just leave it the way it is and go with the price I'm suggesting.

THE CONTRACTOR TECHNIQUE: *"WE'LL LIST BUT FOR A SHORTER TIME"*

Darryl: Ms. Seller, let me ask you a question. Imagine that you were a contractor and I came up to you and said I wanted to add an extension onto my house, so I wanted to know how much and how long. You tell me how much and you say that it would take approximately six months. I say to you, "OK, Ms. Seller, price is no problem, but I want you to do it in three months." Would you take the job?

Ms. Seller: I'd charge more.

Darryl: You're going to charge more? OK, that's a good point. But, if you couldn't charge more, would you take the job?

Ms. Seller: Probably not.

Darryl: Right. Why, because it takes as long as it takes. If you add an extension, you know it takes six months and the only way to do it in three is to hire more people to help you get it done quicker .... Which means you have to pay more. Which means that the only way I can get the house sold in less time than what I'm asking is if you paid me more. But I don't want you to pay me more.

Ms. Seller: I don't want to pay you more either.

Darryl: Fine. So let's keep it at six months.

Ms. Seller: OK.

THE RIGHT RECIPE TECHNIQUE

Darryl: Mr. Seller, I'm not saying that it's impossible, but I don't know for sure. The only thing I know for sure is that I'm going to get as much exposure as I can for the house and increase our probabilities so it does happen. But I need six months as a cushion, just in case. Here's why I say that. Let's say you were going to bake a cake and the recipe says you need four eggs, how many would you buy?

Mr. Seller: A dozen.

Darryl: Exactly, or at least half a dozen, why?

Mr. Seller: Because you'd use them for something else, and they are generally sold that way.

Darryl: You buy products like that because that's how they're sold, and maybe one of those eggs is bad or you break one, you have a spare. Or you know you'll probably need them for something else. You get more than you need immediately, just in case. I'm saying the same thing. I need those extra months just in case. I don't want to start a job and not be able to finish it.

THE CONTRACT OR SETTLEMENT TECHNIQUE

Here, you know that the house will sell in about three or four months, but you want a six-month listing because it's safer for you or because the broker will only do six-month contracts, etc. The sellers don't want to wait six months; they're urgent to sell it in three to four months.

Darryl: Mr. Seller, the reason I need six months is because when I find a buyer who's willing to pay the price you want and we go to contract, legally I've earned my commission. Legally I could collect the commission then, but what I do is defer my brokerage fee until settlement, in case anything should happen. So I want the listing agreement in effect until settlement. But now, if you want to pay me at contract instead, then I can do a shorter listing. The choice is yours.

Mr. Seller: No. I have to wait to get my money to pay you.

Darryl: Fair enough. You win.

Well, there you have it—a very extensive chapter with lots of goodies to consider. I want to again impress upon you that your primary commitment has to be to help the sellers achieve what they're committed to. That's why you ask so many probing questions during the listing presentation process—you need to clearly understand where they're coming from. Similarly, when sellers have an objection, your mission is to view this as something that's stopping them from achieving their goals and to help them through it.

Remember, don't ever take an objection personally! It's not about you, no matter what was said. Your job is to uncover the true concern beneath the objection and to coach the sellers through it as gently as possible. Of course, you won't use verbatim the dialogues that we've just reviewed. But with the information contained in this chapter, you'll be well-prepared to handle most objections thrown at you and to confidently capture more of the sellers who have been getting away.

Bonus Section on Handling Commission Objections

This essay came from one of my top Power Agents in a recent Power Program. She took a lot of the concepts and dialogue that we teach in the course and summarized them here. It has some great concepts you can pull from it. Enjoy.

As an industry, I believe we think of a commission in the wrong terms. I think that most of us, as Realtors, think a commission benefits us, but in fact, it really benefits the seller. I never call it a *commission,* by the way, but rather a *marketing fee,* because I feel a seller is hiring me to *market* his or her castle. Professionals who receive commissions are hired to *sell* something, where we as listing agents are hired to market properties to other agents, buyers, neighbors, appraisers, etc.

In my listing presentation I strongly stress the fact that a seller basically has to sell his or her home three times. First to agents, because if agents don't think it's a good value, they will *never* show it to their buyers, then to buyers, and lastly to appraisers. According to the National Association of Realtors, 51% of all real estate sold is sold as a direct result of an agent. Because of this fact, it is extremely important that we market the home to agents and make it appealing for them to show buyers.

First and foremost, you have to believe that the marketing fee (whether it's 6% or some other figure) is in the best interest of the seller—and do I believe that, absolutely! Next to price, it's the most important thing a seller can do to get his or her house sold. Consumers are willing to pay top dollar for goods or services when you can show them how it benefits them.

Second, you have to maintain control from the very beginning. If you let a seller dictate your salary, you might as well put a collar around your neck and give the seller the leash, because throughout the entire transaction the seller is going to drag you around and the seller will be in charge. This doesn't mean that I think you should make decisions for your seller, but I truly believe *most* buyers and sellers do as they are directed.

I see three things when I find an agent accepting less than a 6% marketing fee. First, an agent who doesn't understand how a 6% marketing fee benefits a seller or simply doesn't know how to justify it. Second, an agent who is incapable of explaining the benefits of a 6% marketing fee. And third, an uneducated and unmotivated seller.

Working as a buyer's agent, I do not want to expose buyers to an unmotivated seller. What if problems come up, repairs need to be made, etc.? That buyer is going to have money invested, money that he or she might not have to reinvest in another property. When I am working with a buyer and pulling up available listings in his or her price range and desired areas, I'll sort through them and throw away the listings that are not paying a 6% marketing fee. I do this because it shows me the level of motivation a seller has and I only want to work with motivated buyers and sellers. It doesn't mean I won't at some point show those listings, but I truly believe it's in the buyer's best interest to work with a seller who really wants to sell.

I try to explain it to sellers in simple terms.

It doesn't make any difference what you sell your house for. It doesn't make any difference if you pay points for the buyer. It doesn't make any difference if you have to make repairs. It doesn't make any difference if you buy the Home Protection Plan. And it doesn't make any difference what marketing fee you pay. *The only thing that matters is what you put in your pocket at the end of the day!*

As we all know, these are expenses that are passed along to the buyer and are reflected in what you'll sell your house for. It's the same when you buy a loaf of bread for $1.00. It didn't cost $1.00 to bake that loaf of bread—what you as the consumer are paying for, in addition to the ingredients to bake that bread, are the packaging, the advertising, the truck that brought the bread to the store, the stock clerk, etc. These are expenses that are always passed along to the consumer. The same principle applies to selling real estate. In simple terms, it's a cost of doing business.

As agents, we know this to be true, because if we write a contract and ask the seller to pay closing costs for a buyer, we tell the buyer that anything we ask the seller to do has to be reflected in the offering price. Because the bottom line is what the seller will *net*.

The difference between a 6% commission and 7% marketing fee [these are examples only] is a 14% cut in pay. (I then show them a MLS printout sheet that has the commissions and explain the 45%-55% split between brokers.) Just like in any other profession, real estate agents are in this business for one reason and one reason only—to put food on the table for their family. If your boss came up to you and said, "I have two jobs here and you can choose the one you want. They both require the same expertise and same amount of time at the same distance from home—in other words, the same basic job. *But* Job A is going to pay 14% *more* than Job B." Which job would you try to get? And it's the same with real estate agents.

If an agent comes in and almost immediately offers to take a listing at a reduced commission (and please understand, there is a big difference between a *commission* and a *marketing fee*), it's like an upfront apology, because that's all they have to offer you. And, if they can't even negotiate their own salary, the amount of money they are going to put in their own pocket, what are they going to do with the price of your house and the money you hope to put in your pocket?

Some agents will even come in and offer a 5% commission … and the difference between a 5% and a 7% marketing fee is a 29% cut in pay! Certain agents can do this because they receive all the commissions and just pay a monthly office fee. How it's going to show up in the computer is, let's say for example purposes, 2.25% versus 3.15%.

These agents are betting on the fact that no other agents in their right mind will take a 29% pay cut, so they are going to be the only agents showing that property to *sell* that property. So, instead of having thousands of agents working for you, you'll have just one. Other agents might show it, but they'll use it as a means to sell other properties that pay a higher percentage. Also, if that same agent has two properties that are similar, in the same subdivision, same price range, same style, etc., but one seller is willing to pay a higher marketing fee, which property do *you* think that agent is going to try to sell—one where he or she makes 29% less money for the same amount of work? I don't think so.

Please remember that I don't get paid until the deal closes. If I thought for a moment that a smaller fee would get your house sold faster and for more money, I'd do it in a heartbeat because I want to get paid as soon as possible. But, the fact of the matter is, it doesn't. And doesn't it make good sense that, because you are offering a X% marketing fee, more agents are going to show your property? Therefore, doesn't greater exposure equal higher price? It's the same with nationally known products versus plain-label generic products. The nationally known products can command and bring a higher price because of a larger marketing audience.

If one of your family members needed surgery, would you hire a doctor based on his expertise, knowledge, experience, follow-up care—in other words, what he or she can offer you? Or, would you hire a surgeon based on what it's going to cost you? The sellers will probably say, "Yes, but this is selling real estate, not brain surgery." I tell the sellers, "No, this isn't brain surgery, but this is the single most important investment that you can make, not only for yourself, but also your family. So don't make a decision on this investment based on what it's going to cost you, but instead on what you'll put in your pocket."

If you won the lottery and received, for instance, $100,000, you would more than likely contact an investment broker to help you invest and put this money to the best possible use. Would you choose an investment broker based on his or her experience, area of expertise, knowledge, education, follow-up service, company he or she is associated with, reputation, and his or her plan for you *or* would you place all this money in the hands of an investment broker who would immediately say to you, "I'll do it cheaper"? Because in the big picture, it doesn't really matter what it's going to cost, but instead what is the return on your investment. And this principle clearly applies to real estate as well.

I was talking to a seller who had also talked to another agent, who offered a lower commission. This seller owned a really nice Italian restaurant downtown, so I used this analogy. I said, "If someone came to your restaurant for dinner, say a pasta entree, salad, and drink, do you think that would cost $15 or $20?" And he said, "Yes, they could probably get dinner for $20." I then said, "Well, isn't it true that someone could go to Fazoli's and get a pasta entree, salad, and drink for $5 or $6?" And he said, "Yes, they probably could." I then said, "Well, if they can go to Fazoli's and get dinner for $5 or $6, why would they ever want to pay $20 at your restaurant?" He got very indignant and said, "We provide really good service, we have an excellent atmosphere, we use the finest ingredients," etc. And I said, "So what you're telling me is you get what you pay for."

I had another instance where a seller wanted me to list the house from January through March and then he would take the listing back in the good selling months of April and May. His wife did nails for a living and I used this analogy. "What does it cost for someone to have Angie do their nails, $25?" He replied that it was around that. I said, "Well, isn't it true that someone could go to Wal-Mart and buy the supplies for approximately $5-$6?" And he replied, "Probably." I said, "Well, if that's the case, why would anyone want to pay Angie $25 when they could do the job themselves for a fourth of the cost?" He said, "Because she is really good, talented, etc." And I said, "So, when you want a job done right, you hire a professional?" I listed the house at top commission for six months.

Most consumers are willing to pay as long as they can see the benefits. Most people will pay Cadillac prices *but* they expect and deserve Cadillac service. And keep this in mind: we have only one thing to offer sellers, that Cadillac marketing service that only our company can provide.

New agents are told that the amount of money we make is limited only by ourselves. We are told to set a goal for the amount of money we want to make and to work to achieve that monetary goal. We immediately go out and start working to achieve that goal by taking listings for less money. So now, in order to meet this goal we have set for ourselves, we are going to have to work harder. We need to take more listings at less money, so we are working longer and harder and in essence we are spreading ourselves too thin. If we are spreading ourselves too thin, can we really give the level of service sellers expect and desire? If you are able to take fewer listings for the same amount of money, you will have less stress and more time. It will show in your attitude and sellers will naturally want to refer business your way.

In closing, we need to remember that we are only guidance counselors, not decision makers. Buyers and sellers are looking to us for guidance, for our expertise and, most important, our honesty. We need to bring back integrity. If all agents had as their personal goal to do a good job first and foremost, they would never want for another deal, because the business would come to them. There is enough business out there for everyone; there is more than enough business for agents with high levels of integrity.

Final Thoughts on Commissions

It is unwise to pay too much. But it is worse to pay too little.

When you pay too much, you lose a little money, that is all. When you pay too little, you sometimes lose everything, because the thing you bought was incapable of doing the thing it was bought to do.

The common law of business balance prohibits paying a little and getting a lot. It can't be done.

—John Ruskin (1819-1900)

No matter what fee you charge, there will always be someone who will charge less than you. Your mission is to sell a net *gain* that equals the difference. First ask the sellers, "If our fees weren't different, who would you hire?" They should prefer you to the other agent. Ask them why they would choose you. They will cite benefits you offer over the competitor. Say to them, "If you prefer us because of the additional benefits we offer, then wouldn't you expect to pay more?" If they don't see a difference, then you have not established your value-added benefit.

CHAPTER 5

Servicing Listings to Sell

Power Fact

As agents, we know that listings are the backbone of what we do and we know that it's important to build our inventory, but most agents don't do enough with their listings once they get them.

Overview

In this chapter, I'm going to provide useful concepts to help you get your inventory sold and a bunch of ideas about how to service your sellers. I honestly don't care if you use the ideas that I share with you. What's important is that you put a system in place that helps you achieve these important goals. My purpose throughout this chapter is to expand your thinking about how to service your sellers and to help you put your system in place. That's it. This system will free you up mentally and enable you to build a larger listing inventory.

Five Crucial Concepts of Servicing

Concept #1: Sellers want communication. Most agents think the only thing homeowners want when they list with an agent is to sell their house.

Of course this is important, but from the time they list with you to the time it sells, the number-one thing homeowners want from their listing agent is communication.

Here's a typical scenario. You've listed a home and it's been a month or two months and you've lost touch with the sellers. The activity has been poor and you don't want to call them because they're going to yell at you, so you avoid them like the plague. However, what you have to understand is that the major complaint that sellers have about agents is that *"they listed my house and I never heard from them or saw them again."* In this chapter, I'm going to give you a system to stay in communication with your sellers without having to call them all the time.

Concept #2: The more committed they are, the easier it is to sell. A seller can't be committed both to price and to moving. This is important. You have some sellers who are totally committed to price. In fact, they may say, "Well, if we get our price, then we'll sell." You may have listings where you're more committed to selling the house than the sellers are! You've beaten your head against the wall wondering what to do to make the house sell and they're stressing you out. *Stop that!* There's nothing wrong with taking an overpriced listing—as long as you communicate up front in the listing presentation that the house is overpriced.

I've had agents say point-blank in the listing presentation, "Mr. and Mrs. Seller, we can't be committed to price and be committed to moving at the same time. It's one or the other. If you're more committed to price than to moving, that's OK with me. I just want to make sure that we're both clear that by being more committed to price, you may never sell."

Concept #3: Don't make promises you can't keep. Some of you think that your job on the listing presentation is to out-promise your competition in order to get the listing. For example, "I'm going to advertise this house every day until it sells." Now, if you don't do that, you're probably going to get a phone call. In Chapter 3, we outlined everything you *can* do to market a home without promising that you're going to do any one single item on the list. You just say to the seller, "Here's what we do to market homes—multiple listing, yard sign, etc." But you're not saying directly, "I'm going to do every one of these things every single day."

Concept #4: Sell the agents, not the buyers. If you want to get your property sold, you want to get more agents through the door, which means more showings. The more showings, the better chance you're going to have a sale.

When I was listing and selling real estate, my focus was not to get buyers through the door. My focus was to get the agents excited and thinking about the house, so that of all the homes on the market in this particular price range, they remembered my listing.

How many buyers do you have? For any given house, you may personally have about five buyers. Now let's say there are 100 agents in your market. Those 100 agents, assuming they have an equal number of buyers, represent a total of 500 buyers. Which is better, for you and your five buyers to be excited or for 100 agents and their 500 buyers to be excited about this house? The agents! If you start thinking that your job as a marketing agent is not to sell the home, but to motivate the other agents in your market, you're going to relate to your marketing efforts and technique a whole different way.

When I did brokers' open houses, I looked at myself as the director of my agent community. It was important to me that all the other agents liked me. They had to respect me, too. It's almost like when you're talking to a seller on the listing presentation. You know how you say, "Here's where our buyers come from—a certain number from ads, a certain number from yard signs, etc." Well, this is a similar concept, but the key fact is that over 80% of our sales are from agents, not from buyers. On the listing presentation, you might say, "So our job, Mr. Seller, is to sell agents, not buyers. Now, what have you done to sell agents? You've got a FSBO ad and a yard sign. You can't sell to that 80% until you hire an agent like me to represent you to the other agents."

Concept #5: Price it right. The very best technique to service the seller is to price your inventory correctly. There was an agent in one of my *Power Program* classes who came up to me and said she had a house that wasn't selling. In fact, she had a lot of inventory that wasn't selling. I asked her what she was doing. She rattled off all the marketing steps she was taking. I said it was probably the price then. She said she thought it was priced really well. I said, "Well, if you're doing all the marketing you say you are, I can't give you any other suggestions on it. That's all I know: it's either the price or the marketing."

19 Tips and Techniques for Marketing Your Listings

1. **Have an individual folder for each listing.** Even if you're computerized, there are still papers and forms you must keep. This tip may sound kind of basic, but I know some agents whose desks are one big folder.

2. **Place your listings by your phone with the price and expiration date.** Why is this important? It's a constant motivator and keeps you focused.

3. **Get a higher commission.** Remember that one of your tasks is to sell other agents to help you sell this home. Would a higher commission help you sell the agents? You bet. There are several ideas on how to get a higher commission in Chapter 4.

4. **Brokers' open houses.** Agents tell me that brokers' open houses really don't work. They do them, but the attendance is sometimes low, and they have all the typical reasons why brokers' open houses can't succeed. I believe that brokers' open houses are one of the best techniques to service your listings. I say that because one of the most important concepts is to *sell the agents and not the buyers.* If that's true, then a brokers' open house is one of the best tools to use.

   I want you to picture the brokers' open house in this way. It's not just something for you to do to show the seller that you're servicing him or her; rather, it's an opportunity for you to introduce this product.

   You know, if you look at any industry, when a business has a new product that it's going to roll out, it makes it a huge event and invites a bunch of people and a lot of press. It's very much like a party. And it's exactly the same concept here. A brokers' open house should be done in the first one to two weeks that a house goes to multiple listing, because a house is never at a better point than when it first hits the market.

   Now, I'm going to give you some tips on how to make this brokers' open house successful. One of the things, obviously, is to have food. I say *obviously* because we know agents love free food. But when I say "food," I don't mean just bagels and cream cheese. I mean *real food.* When I used to do my brokers' open houses, I served, at one time, chicken, mashed potatoes, rolls, salad, soda, coffee, and dessert. Or spaghetti and meatballs with salad and garlic bread and soda, so on and so forth. I mean a *huge* spread. It should only cost between $30 and $50, unless you have it catered, which you may want to do, depending on the list price.

   Let me just stop here because you may be thinking, "Darryl, I tried that before. I had a lot of food and almost no one showed up and I had leftovers for the next week." But the key when you do these brokers' open houses is to start a reputation for yourself that you have the best food. To develop that reputation is going to take some time. So the first time you do this, maybe a handful of people will show up. Then the next time a few more, and then some more. Eventually you will get that reputation and will begin to get huge turnouts.

My tip for you in doing these open houses is to promote them. You can do the flier and the fax and put it on the multiple listing. But the morning of your open house, you should be getting on the phone and calling all the surrounding offices. So, if your open house is 12-2 or 1:30-2:30, you call in the morning and say, "Hi, I'm Darryl Davis from Power Realty and I'm calling to *personally invite you* to a brokers' open house." Now that phrase, *"personally invite you,"* is very important. There is something magic about those words that seems to have some kind of impact. "It's being held from 12 to 2, there are three bedrooms, two baths at X price, and here's what we will be serving." Give them the menu and make it a party, an invitation, an event. Make it special.

By the way, in addition to the feature sheets you have on that particular property, make sure you have some with you about your other listings, especially the ones that are not getting a lot of activity. The brokers' open house is a great vehicle for you to promote those listings as well.

I know there's one major drawback to these open houses: they take some time. You're going to have to take an hour before to prepare and an hour afterwards to clean up. But there are a lot of benefits. We're showing the homeowners that we're working for them. It's great for you, because if you're selling yourself to your colleagues, it's an opportunity for you to say "thank you" for what they do for you. But most important, it gives you that quick exposure and spotlights that house.

5. **Opinion sheets.** I find most agents around the country have and use opinion sheets. That said, all the questions on those opinion sheets are not as important as the last one, "What price do you think the house is going to sell for?"

After the open house, you sit down with the seller and you go over these sheets. You show the seller, "Here's what the brokers are telling us this house should sell for." So, let's say we have a house listed for $299K, and two brokers say it will sell for $299 and five say the high $290s and 20 say $280s and a few $278s. So the bottom line is that most of the agents are telling you the house will sell in the high $280s. You can now say to Mr. and Mrs. Seller that the price they decided to go with is a little bit higher than most of the agents in the area believe it is actually going to sell for. "So, either we can leave the price the way it is and hope we'll get the activity or we can adjust the price so we can make sure we'll get the activity that we need to get it sold so you can move on with your life."

These opinion sheets were very valuable to me. I seldom failed to get

---

PROPERTY _____

LIST PRICE _____

1. Your opinion of the outside is
   Excellent _____
   Average _____
   Poor _____

2. Your opinion of the inside is
   Excellent _____
   Average _____
   Poor _____

3. How long do you think it will take to sell?
   60-120 days _____
   121-180 days _____
   181-270 days _____

4. Your opinion of the price is:
   Too high _____
   Average _____
   Too low _____

5. What price do you think this house should sell for?

NAME _____

COMPANY _____

Figure 5-1. A property opinion sheet

price reductions within the first couple of weeks the house was on the market. I didn't succeed all the time, but if you have price reductions 50% of the time, that's probably a whole lot more than you're getting right now.

You may say, "Darryl, yeah, that's a great idea, opinion sheets. But agents don't fill them out. Their comment is 'Why should I help you sell your listing?'"

Here's what to do. After an agent previews the house, she or he will come into the kitchen to eat. I would then say, "Before you sit down, do me a favor, please just fill out this form." Most of the time the agent will. But if he or she says something like "Darryl, why should I help you sell your listing?" I would answer, "Because you're a nice person and because I would do the same for you." Now if he takes the form and places it on the table and starts to make his dish without filling the form out first, I would take the plate out of his hand and say, "Here, let me do that for you while you fill out the opinion sheet."

By the way, I encourage you to make sure you support other agents from other companies and attend their open houses. You should check them out because you want the same support from them. If you're complaining that no one shows up for your brokers' open houses, ask yourself if you go to theirs. When you go to theirs, don't go just to sit down and eat. Go through that house and fill out an opinion sheet, give them your card, shake hands with the other agents who are previewing the home, and leave. Use it as a networking opportunity to promote yourself. You want to create this perception with your colleagues that you're too busy—you're successful—to sit down and eat. People want to be around people who are successful.

6. **Public open houses.** Public open houses have some positives and negatives. The one major drawback is that it takes some time. But the major plus is that it promotes you and highlights your listing, it shows the sellers you're servicing them, and, most important, you'll get listing leads. What I recommend you do with these is make sure you have *backup houses*. Here's what I mean.

If we had a really hot listing for which we were doing a public open house and we knew we were going to get a lot of traffic, we'd have two agents handle the public open house. So let's say our open house was for a colonial priced at $250K. Because of the price, style, and location, we knew we were going to get a great turnout. From the listings in our office, we'd pull any similar homes in a similar price range and bring them with us to the open house. Then, when buyers were coming through, if we found an "A" buyer, rather than let that person go to another brokers' open house or another company, I'd take her or him to see some of those backup houses while the second agent finished the open house. When I got back, if the other agent had found an "A" buyer, we would alternate. It was very effective and in some cases we actually sold homes from public open houses. You and I both know that it's very rare to do this. But by using this backup house concept and teamwork, it's very possible that you might sell a home that weekend.

7. **Showcase your listings.** Take a larger-than-usual ad out in one of the local papers and, instead of promoting a public open house on just one

listing, promote four, five, or six at one time. Put all the information about these houses into the ad and announce open houses that one weekend.

"But Darryl, how am I going to run six houses all at once?" Very simple, you don't run them all. Here's how you work it out. You tell the homeowners that one of the things you do to market homes is this thing called "showcasing your listings." You explain the concept, how you do it, and how it creates a lot of interest and activity in the market, but you impress upon the owners that they have to be there to run the open house. All they have to do is take names and phone numbers—that's it.

Now, you tell them, they don't have to participate in this. You can do an open house just for them, but you find that having six at once creates more synergy, more excitement, and more promotion. You ask the homeowners, "Would you be interested in your house being one of the select few?" You emphasize that you don't do this for every home. If there are 20 listings in your inventory, you don't showcase all 20 at once; you showcase just a handful. Most of the time, the homeowners say they'd be happy to do it.

8. **"Just listed" letters.** We all know about "just sold" cards. I'm not crazy about cards, because they're too easy to throw out. When I get a postcard, I quickly glance at it and very quickly throw it into the garbage. With a letter, I have to take the time to open up an envelope. If it's from a real estate agent, I'll still read it because it has a photo. As a matter of fact, I've seen a lot of these "just listed" letters, and I think they're effective. If you're going to do these, don't do postcards. When you get computerized, it's a lot easier to do the letters (see Figure 5-2 on next page).

9. **Call 100 neighbors.** Sit down at your desk and call 100 neighbors around a house you just listed. You do this for four reasons: 1) to tell them about the listing, 2) to ask if they know anyone else who might be selling in the area, 3) to ask if they themselves might be thinking of selling, and 4) to find out if they know anyone who they'd like to make their new neighbor. Now, I know this is kind of basic, but some of you just hate to pick up the phone. So, if you listed only one house in one month, you've now called 100 more people than you did the previous month. These are not cold calls, because you are giving them valuable information, topical news, and an opportunity to choose their new neighbor. If you include this as part of your servicing campaign for sellers, it won't seem like cold calls; it will seem like "just listed" calls. It's just a psychological difference.

Dear Neighbor,

I am pleased to announce that I have just **LISTED** a fine home in your neighborhood.

I am professionally marketing the property above and would be pleased to provide more information if you know someone who may be interested in this home.

I will have inquiries from buyers who desire this area and for one reason or another, this home may not work for them. If you, or someone in the area, are anticipating a move, I would be pleased to be of service.

Sincerely,

John Doe

Professional Real Estate Agent

Office: 123-4569

Pager: 321-7654

If your home is currently listed for sale with another broker, this is not intended as a solicitation of that listing.

Figure 5-2. Example of new listing letter.

10. **Do the 10-10-20 Rule.** This is for those people, like me, who aren't crazy about door knocking. When I was an agent, I would hear speakers say, "When you've just listed a home, you should knock on 100 doors." Not me. I'm not into door knocking. I know it works, but it takes a lot of time and energy. I feel it's useful to knock on 10 doors to the left and 10 to the right, and 20 doors across the street. You're hitting just that immediate area. The reason to do this is that the people in these homes are the most likely to know the listing family personally and therefore are most likely to want to help them find a buyer.

11. **Advertise in specialized papers.** Let's say you've just listed a waterfront property. People who are going to buy waterfront property are a special type of buyer. These people also own boats or want to own boats. So I recommend, for example, that you look in boating magazines and other publications that people who like water tend to read and then advertise in those publications. Or if you've listed a farm, there are certain farm or equestrian magazines you can advertise in. There are even some properties that would be used by a professional, like a doctor. Start focusing on specific industries to draw from.

12. **Give a gift to the selling agent.** Let me clarify. When one of your listings sells, give a gift to the selling agent. Not necessarily to the seller, but

for sure to the agent. The reason you want to do this is because we're talking about servicing listings. You want to start creating a reputation for yourself so that all the agents know whenever they sell one of your listings they're going to get this great gift from you. That's a terrific way to help you get your existing listings serviced and get a lot of activity. Remember, your job is to focus on selling agents on your inventory versus selling buyers. If you give gifts, you're going to have a good reputation.

Now, I'm *not* talking about flowers or alcohol or wine. Let me give you an example of a great gift. What one of my students in California would do every time another agent sold one of her listings is give that agent *a color TV*. Now, I know what you're thinking: "Darryl, I can't even afford a new color TV for myself." You can get a nice color TV for $225, so you might want to consider taking $225 away from one of your other marketing tools and putting it toward this. Another question you might have is "What happens if the same agent sells more than one of your listings? Does that mean you're going to give him or her more than one color TV?" Absolutely, that's the key—consistency. Don't keep changing the gifts or customizing them. It's the same one over and over again.

That repetition helps create consistency and build reputation. I think this is a very powerful suggestion, regardless of the average sales price in your market. Here's what you do. You don't promote this TV, because then it wouldn't be a gift—"Sell my listing and I'll give you a TV." You want to make it a surprise. So, you don't promote it. Also, you don't give it at the closing. You give it to the selling agent on the day of her or his office meeting. If you know the office meeting is at 9 a.m., you go in at 9:20 with this huge package, wrapped up, bow on top, and you make a big commotion—"Is Mary here? Excuse me. Excuse me. Mary, this is a big 'thank you' for selling my listing on XYZ Street. I'm sorry for interrupting everybody." Then you wave goodbye and walk out. Now, you have 20 agents in an office meeting all excited about what Mary got. They open it up and they see this color TV. Do you think you just won Mary over? Absolutely! Do you think you did some great PR with the other 19 agents in the office? Absolutely! Do you think that that color TV is going to give you future business, not only with Mary but with the other 19 agents in that company? Absolutely! So ask me if it's worth that investment. I think it is.

Now let's say you don't want to give a color TV and you want to get more creative … or perhaps a TV is too expensive. As a rule of thumb, bigger is better. It doesn't have to cost a lot, as long as it's in a big box. (But please don't take a pen set and put it in a huge box. That would only disappoint them!) Something like a microwave oven, a DVD player, automatic coffee maker, etc. The problem with these items is people don't usually need more than one of these things. Once again, the key is to use the same item for the next few years.

13. **Fax your hot listings to other agents.** I suggest creating a form that you can use to showcase your hot listings for other agents to see. It says "Hot Fax" and gives you room to put your listings. You put a little note to the other agents saying, "Here are some of the hot listings that I have—of all my listings, these are the best of the best" (see Figure 5-3).

14. **Use report cards.** You may have a system in your office that already serves this purpose. If not, see Figure 5-4. This form helps you track the activity of other agents calling on your listings. Whenever an agent wants to preview your listing, show it, or simply know the status, you log the information on this form. You should use this form with the sellers every so often and show them the activity. If you have a listing that's been on the market for 30 days and the report card shows that you've gotten very few calls from other agents, then you know something is wrong. You've got to communicate that with the sellers. It's just another tool to keep you in communication and help you get an adjustment of either price or terms with the sellers.

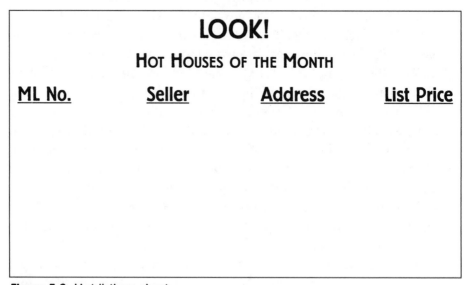

LOOK!
HOT HOUSES OF THE MONTH

<u>ML No.</u>	<u>Seller</u>	<u>Address</u>	<u>List Price</u>

Figure 5-3. Hot listings sheet

Report Card

Owner _____

List Price _____

Address _____

Home Phone _____ Work Phone _____

Show Instructions _____

Date	Agent	Office	Notes

Figure 5-4. Example of a report card form

15. **30- and 60-day reviews.** I know some agents who religiously sit down with their sellers at a 30-day and a 60-day mark and have a conversation about any of three things: a price adjustment, a terms adjustment, or the marketing tools. Maybe a homeowner wasn't open to seller's financing, but might be now, if you suggest it again. Maybe a homeowner wouldn't let you do a yard sign, but at a 30- or 60-day review, you revisit the idea.

16. **Semimonthly calls.** Stay in touch with the seller every two weeks. When you call her or him, you can have a conversation about what the competition has sold. "The reason I'm calling is that a house similar in price range to yours just sold, by the way, for $10K less than what we're listed for." You could also let the seller know when you'll be running an ad in the paper about the house or what kind of responses you're getting from the agents. It's very important that sellers hear from us every two weeks. The number-one complaint about agents is that they list homes and the sellers don't ever hear from them again.

17. **Agent evaluation cards.** This is a card that you send out to agents every time they show your home. Let's say that you know that an agent has shown your property (because you have a tracking device). You send this cover letter (Figure 5-5) with a postage-paid postcard, asking the agent to evaluate the home and include what the buyers thought as well. Now, not all agents will take the time to return this card, but follow this: if you mail out, say, 50 in a month, and only 10 agents mail it back, that's still 10 more than you would have gotten if you hadn't sent it out. The letter you send with the postcards is worded in such a way that it creates respect among your colleagues, so I think they'll take the two minutes it takes to fill this out and mail it back to you (see Figure 5-6).

    Again, this agent response card is based on the assumption that you've created a good reputation for yourself. If agents don't like you because you're unfair or manipulative, it won't work. But if you create that positive relationship and cultivate respect from other agents, they will send the cards back to you. Even if they don't respond, it's another contact with agents who showed interest in your listing. This mailing, if nothing else, will remind that agent and perhaps it will generate another showing or two. *Note:* To help improve your response rate, you might consider e-mailing or phoning an agent to ask the questions and then fill out the forms yourself.

18. **Farming agents.** You may have some powerhouse agents in your area who are very successful. You should create a separate mailing list and perhaps personalize any kind of mailing you send to these agents, utilizing a computerized mail-merge function with a letter template. Let's say you're sending a mailing to all the offices about a brokers' open

---

Thanks, I appreciate your help!!

Dear Fellow Agent,

Thank you for taking the time to show and/or preview my listing. As you know, cooperation between agents is a necessary ingredient for success, and our success is enhanced by people like you!

Would you please take a moment to tell me what you think of my listing. Just fill out the enclosed evaluation card and drop it in the mail. I have also included an information brochure to help remind you of the property.

Again, thank you! I look forward to working with you in the near future!

Sincerely,

John Doe

Figure 5-65 Cover letter for agent evaluation card

Agent Evaluation Card

Seller _____

Address _____

Agent _____

Company _____

Circle whichever applies: Previewing the house / Showed to buyers

Price _____

Condition _____

Additional Comments _____

_____

Figure 5-6. Example of an agent evaluation card

house and you'll be sending a general flier to each office. If one of the top-producing agents in your market is in that office, make sure he or she gets his or her own individual flier. This way, top agents get this personal attention they deserve because they are successful.

19. **Commonsense pricing.** If a house is going to be listed for $200,000, most agents will put it on MLS for—how much?—$199,990. Now watch what happens. If you have a buyer who wants to buy a house for $190,000, you may do a search of homes from $185,000 to $200,000. If you have another buyer who wants to pay around $210,000, you may do a search from $200,000 to $220,000. That house listed for $199,990 will show up on only one search result. But if it were listed for $200,000, it would show up on both searches, which means more exposure. Not to mention the fact that when you look at all these houses, which will be more memorable: $199,990 like the other houses or $200,000?

■   ■   ■

We've reviewed a lot of material about how to service your listings and how to truly take care of your clients. I hope that you picked up some useful ideas out of this. Staying in communication and deepening your relationship with your sellers will enhance your reputation, build your sales, and set you up in your career.

CHAPTER 6

Working with Buyers:
How to Work with Fewer Buyers, Make More Sales, and Have More Fun in the Process

Power Fact

The more you try to sell a house, the more you unsell it. The best way to sell a house is to open up the door.

Overview

The purpose of this chapter is to help you fulfill the promise of the sub-title! I know what it's like to take buyers out and the frustration of showing them house after house and they don't purchase or (worse) purchase from somebody else. Working with buyers can really drain your enthusiasm and get you down. So I promise that if you really, truly apply the material in this chapter, you will be able to take a buyer out, show her or him just a handful of homes, and make a sale. Power Agents tell us that this is one of their favorite sessions of The Power Program.

10 Keys to Working with Buyers

1. **Buyers can be a drain on your income ... if you're not careful.** I have the opportunity to talk to top producers throughout the country on a regular basis and I've asked them what is the source of their income. As I've said previously in this book, they've all told me basical-

ly the same thing: 75% of their income comes from listings sold and 25% from working with buyers. I want you to keep that 75/25 rule in mind. Take it to heart—75% of your energy should be focused on building your listing inventory and 25% on working with buyers.

2. **Have the right attitude.** What is the attitude of most agents when working with a buyer? That they have to make the sale, right? When you're working with buyers and your attitude is "I need to make a sale" and you're showing them house after house, you are not going to be effective. Buyers can sense this attitude of desperation. This is the wrong attitude to take. Here's the right attitude: "I don't need a sale because I've got plenty of listings."

When I was showing houses, I was most effective when my attitude shifted to "Hey, I've got plenty of listings, so whether you buy or you don't, I don't care, because I know my inventory will eventually sell." When you have this attitude, you're not trying to sell them and they pick up on this. Now, they are free to make their own decision to buy a house or not, without feeling the pressure of being "sold." This is another reason why top agents do so well, because they have so much business, their careers are not dependent on any one buyer buying a house.

Have you ever gone to a car dealership and tried to buy a car? Do you like it when they're trying to sell you a car? It is frustrating and it is awful, right? People don't like to be sold anything. What they like to do is buy. There is a difference.

3. **There are two reasons to work with buyers.**
   A. **THEY'RE EASY AND QUICK MONEY.** If this is not true for you, you're probably not working with them correctly. Now, let me share something interesting about my background. I hated working with buyers. I really did. I enjoyed working with listings. But now I believe that working with buyers is a necessary evil, so to speak. So, when you do not like doing something, but you need to do it, you learn how to do it in less time and be more effective. If you do what I'm going to teach you in this chapter, you will be able to take a buyer out, show him or her maybe three, five, or eight homes at most, and make a sale.
   B. **THEY'RE A BREAK FROM LISTINGS.** Here is what I recommend, as I've said in the chapter on time management: focus on building your listing inventory. Go on a listing campaign and list as many as you possibly can, until you get tired of hearing your own dialogue. When you get to that point, take a break from listings and go "play with buyers."

Just take them out, show them some houses, and maintain the attitude, "Hey, I don't care if you buy or don't buy, because I've built my inventory." Working with buyers can be fun. When it's not fun, it's because you are too committed to making a sale. Then it's not fun at all; it's stressful.

4. **There are three types of buyers.** This is pretty basic. There are "A" buyers, "B" buyers, and "C" buyers. Let's highlight this a little bit.
   - "A" buyers are those who have to buy. There is no question: they are going to buy. Maybe they sold their house and they are going to be homeless in a couple of months. You get the picture.
   - "B" buyers are those who want to buy. They do not have to, but they want to. It's something that they've wanted to do for a while. They've seen some homes and now they are ready.
   - "C" buyers are those who would like to buy. They do not have to, they do not want to, they would like to. There's no real commitment here, but they might be thinking, "Gosh, if we bought a new house, our lives would just be better."

   Now, here is what I want to highlight about "A," "B," and "C" buyers: "A" buyers you should always work with—always—because there is not a question about them buying or not. The questions are: are they buying from you or another agent ... and when are they going to buy?

   I would work with "B" buyers when I'm taking a break from listings. They are motivated and ready to move forward in their lives.

   As for "C" buyers, never take them out. Instead, refer them out. I know, some of you are thinking, "But, Darryl, they are going to buy someday." Yeah, but you need money today. Otherwise, you won't have a someday. If you're working with these "someday" buyers, you're wasting a lot of time.

   If you want to keep earning what you've been earning, then keep doing what you've been doing. But, if you want to get to that Next Level, you need to start being more effective. How you will be more effective is to always work with the "A" buyers, work with "B" buyers only when you are not listing, and refer "C" buyers to other agents. There's an additional positive to doing this, by the way. If "C" buyers eventually do buy, you'll get a referral fee just for answering the telephone. Not a bad deal, right?

5. **Know your inventory.** I am talking about your in-house inventory. This may sound very basic, but there are many agents who haven't pre-

viewed all of their office listings. It is important that you know your inventory. Even if it is not your listing, it is the office's listing. It's important because when a buyer calls in on that ad or that sign, you should know that you have that listing. Sometimes, during The Power Program, I'll call off an ad live in front of the room. Here is what often happens.

"Uh, which house?

"It was a three-bedroom Tudor."

"What paper?"

"The Times."

"Let me see." (Paper crumpling.) "I can't seem to find…." (More paper crumpling.)

"It sounds like you're having trouble."

"Well, yeah, we have a lot in our office."

This is not a good answer. I don't want you doing that—ever. So, that's why it's important that you know your inventory, so that you sound professional at all times.

6. **Do not sell a house over the phone.** Do not try. Let me ask you a question. What is the purpose of an ad … or a sign … or any of the other promotions that you might do? To make the phone ring. I bet that if I called your office on one of your ads and asked a typical agent, "Well, does it have big bedrooms?" I would hear, "Oh yes, it has large bedrooms and huge closets and the windows are situated in such a way that when the sun rises in the morning, it beats on your face, and it's truly beautiful." Because you're trying to get this buyer to come in for the purpose of seeing that home and some agents think that you get people to come into the office by seducing them with words about how wonderful this house is. That is not the best avenue to pursue, as you will see when we move on.

7. **They are calling to eliminate your ad.** What do you think buyers are committed to when they call you? To scheduling an appointment? No. Picture this. Mrs. Hunna Hunna sits down on the weekend with the newspaper and her red pen. She circles all these ads that look like the house she wants to buy. Now, Mr. Hunna Hunna has nothing to do with this. He says, "Just get the appointments and maybe I will go with you." So, now she pulls out these half-dozen ads and she starts calling. Her objective is to find that one perfect, extraordinary home that she is going

to see with her husband. The point is to just recognize that they are not calling to make an appointment with you. You have to do some work in order to get them to want an appointment with you.

8. **They may be loyal to another agent.** This is something you should be aware of. One thing you should never do is give out the address of the property, because you may just be helping the other agent. The point of the ad is to make the phone ring and then for you to get the buyer into the office. If you give out the address, it will be nearly impossible to get buyers to come into the office.

9. **Don't pay too much attention to what they say they want.** Should you ask them what they want on the telephone? Should you ask them when you see them? Of course. But just don't pay too much attention to their response. I say that because they expect you to ask and they want to share that with you—but, as you know, they really, truly don't know what they want, because if they really did know, they would have found it already. They may have a concept of what they want. They may have an idea about it. But they really don't know. Just keep this in the back of your mind. So, when buyers say that they want all these things in a home, don't think that your job is to focus on finding that precise home.

10. **There are four keys to listen for when working with buyers.** You should find these out on the telephone, when they come into the office, or whenever you can.

    A. **WHY ARE YOU MOVING?** What's the motivation? Is their present house too small or too big? Was there a divorce? Did they sell their home?

    B. **WHEN DO YOU NEED TO MOVE?** What is the time frame we are working with—30 days, 60 days, six months, six years?

    C. **WHY THIS AREA?** This is really an important key. Think about it. Of all the places that they can buy in the United States and Canada, why are they choosing not only your state, but your neighborhood?

    D. **WHAT ELSE HAVE YOU SEEN?** If you're familiar with what they've already seen, it can tell you a lot about their likes and dislikes. Besides, you may discover a FSBO you were unaware of.

■　　■　　■

When working with buyers, it's imperative that you focus on two things, which I'll address throughout the rest of this chapter:

■ **CREATE URGENCY.** The majority of buyers like to drag out the buying process. They look at as many homes as possible and then they have to go home and think about it before they make an offer, etc. So, keep in mind that, as soon as you're in contact with a buyer, you should create this urgency that it is better for her or him to buy today than tomorrow. You'll see later on how I start to create this buying urgency.

■ **MANAGE THE EMOTIONAL ROLLER COASTER OF THE BUYER.** I believe that when it comes time for buyers, even experienced buyers, to actually make a commitment, they mentally get in the presence of mortgage, monthly payments, debt, and so on—and these things can stop them from moving forward. A good part of what we do is to manage the emotional roller coaster the buyers will go through. We do this by constantly reminding them of their commitment to their next level of home ownership.

The Phone Inquiry

Let's now go over the process of handling a phone inquiry.

Part 1: Introduction

The introduction sounds like this: "Hi, this is Margaret. Who am I speaking to? Your phone number, please? How may I help you?"

Why is it important to get a phone number up front? To take control, so you can get back to them, to see if they're serious with you, etc. But it's really not important that you get their name and telephone number up front. Even though I have it in the dialogue right here, it's not vital that you get it. Here's an example.

"Hi, this is Darryl Davis. Who am I speaking to?"

(Let them answer.)

"May I have your phone number, please?"

"We don't want to give it to you."

"OK. That's fine. And how may I help you?"

You see, what's important is that they come into the office so you can sit down and have a face-to-face meeting with them. After you finish the five-part process and you're closing for the appointment, that's when you need their telephone number and name, because that's when you've established a relationship with them. So ask, but do not be attached to getting it.

Part 2: Available

"Yes, I am familiar with the house. Can I ask you to hold for a moment, while I see if the house is still available?"

That does two things: it puts you in control and, if they're "A" buyers and if they've been sitting there making call after call and eliminating ad after ad after ad, it creates a little buyer urgency. So, maybe they will not be as cavalier or arrogant about eliminating ads. They'll be thinking, "Wow, maybe this house is not available. I hope it is." Now, once you come back from hold, Part 3 is to qualify.

Part 3: Qualify

In the qualifying stage, you start asking questions to find out what they're committed to: what is their motivation? This is very important.

"Mr. Johnson, thank you for holding. The house is still available. Let me ask you, are you looking for yourself or someone else?" Is that an important question? It is, because you could spend several minutes on the phone with these people and then they throw out that objection that they learned in "buying school"—"Oh, this isn't for me; it's for my daughter. I'm just calling to get some information." And you just wasted some of your time.

Here are some other qualifying questions you might ask:

- What price range are you in?
- How long have you been looking? Or did you just start?
- How long have you looked in this area?
- Any particular reason for wanting to buy in this town?
- Have you seen any houses that you like?
- Why didn't you buy one of those?
- When were you thinking of making the move?
- Are you renting now or do you own?
- How much money are you working with to purchase this home? Does this include the monies needed for closing, which would be about _____, or do you have that separately?
- Are you working with another agent?
- May I have your e-mail address?

Keep in mind that there is no particular order for these qualifying questions. You can do whatever works best for you. As a matter of fact, you don't even have to ask these exact questions. You can use your own.

So, what's the main purpose of Part 3? To find out if they are "A" buyers, "B" buyers, or "C" buyers. Got it? That's the whole purpose, to find out how motivated they are.

Once you have asked enough questions and you feel like you have it handled, you move on to Part 4, fair exchange.

Part 4: Fair Exchange

The pattern for fair exchange is question, answer, question, answer, question, and answer. The concept is that if I am going to answer your question, then I am going to ask you to answer one of mine. It may sound something like this:

Darryl: So, what would you folks like to know about the house?

Caller: How many bedrooms does it have?

Darryl: The house has three bedrooms. Is that what you need or are you looking for more?"

Caller: Three bedrooms are fine.

Darryl: What else would you like to know?

Caller: Well, does it have a full basement?

Darryl: Yes. By the way, what style are you folks looking at?

Caller: We're looking for Tudors.

Darryl: Oh, I see. Anything else I can tell you about this home?

They ask you a question; you answer them. You ask a question; they answer you. After they answer you, then invite them to ask you other questions about the ad. You keep doing this until you feel you are ready to schedule an appointment.

By the way, there may be some overlap between Parts 3 and 4. Be flexible. You don't want to come across like you're doing a survey.

Part 5: Schedule Appointment

There are four parts to scheduling the appointment. Let's go through them.

Step 1. Confirm. You want to confirm that the callers are interested in the house they called in about. You might say, "It sounds like this house may work for you" or "So, this house doesn't work, but let me ask you, are you folks serious about buying a house?"

Step 2. Validate your company. Here's where you want to convey that they have stumbled onto the best company to help them accomplish their commitment of finding a home. You do this to gain loyalty, have them stop calling other ads, and encourage them to come into the office to meet with you. The dialogue may sound like this:

> "Let me tell you how I work. My company is very active in the neighborhood. As a matter of fact, regardless of how a seller is selling, whether it is privately through us or with another company, we have access to all of these homes. You can say that we're a one-stop real estate office. I'm sharing this with you because I know you probably have other ads circled. Instead of spending all your time calling each one, I can help you narrow down your list and find the best houses for you."

Step 3. Get them excited about the Six-Step Buying Process.

> "In addition, we have in my office what's called the 'Six-Step Buying Process.' This is designed to help buyers like you find the right house with the least amount of aggravation. Buyers who are familiar with this process are at a real advantage."

Step 4. Invite action.

> "So let's find a time when you and your significant other can come into the office, I'll show you the Six-Step Buying Process. In addition, we can go through all the homes that are currently in your price range, show you everything that is out there, and together pick the best of the best and even go look at them.... OK, I'll see you at 3:00. And I just want to be sure I am clear with you folks: you'll need to set aside two hours for me, because it's going to take that long at our first meeting."

The Face-to-Face Presentation

Earlier in this chapter, we said that there are two things you should focus on when working with buyers: to create urgency and to manage the emotional roller coaster. So when buyers come in for a face-to-face meeting, sort of like a buyer consultation, you want to start to set the stage immediately as to what they can expect in working with you.

I promise you that if you use this system the way I created it, you will be able to show buyers—the first time you meet them—a handful of homes and make a sale. Agents who take my yearlong training course, The Power Program, double their production, on average, over their previous year. They say this is one of the most valuable things they learn.

Now, in order to set the stage, you need to give the buyers an overview of what your appointment with them is going to look like, what you're going to do with them, when, how you'll do it, etc.

Dentists and doctors are great at this. If, for instance, you were going to the dentist to have a root canal done, the dentist would speak to you before doing any work. He might say, "Alright, Debbie, here is what we are going to do. You know you've got this bad molar over here, so what I need to do is give you a shot of Novocaine to numb the area. Then, we are going to drill away some of the bad parts. If you start to feel anything, just raise your hand." And so on. The point is, before the dentist gets started, he explains what he's about to do so you'll feel more at ease and have less stress.

With a buyer, it's the same thing. What I want you to do is create a Buyer Presentation Book, which is basically like a listing presentation you might conduct. The first page in the Buyer Presentation Book is the Six-Step Buying Process:

Step 1: Inform
Step 2: Ask questions
Step 3: Select Houses
Step 4: Inspect
Step 5: Paperwork
Step 6: Ongoing Service

You will go over each step with the buyer before you actually start showing property, explaining what you are going to accomplish during your meeting. You won't actually start doing the steps until after you've explained all six (just like the dentist first explains everything, then starts taking action). This whole conversation will take about an hour before you even start showing property. You might think that this is a long time, but keep in mind that I'm showing you how to take buyers out for the first time, show a handful of homes, and make a sale. This meeting in the office is essential to making this happen. Let's now go through the dialogue that explains each step.

The Six-Step Buying Process

They come into the office and you greet them. "How are you doing? ... Nice to see you .... Take a seat .... Have some coffee. I'll be with you folks in a second...."

Then, you sit down and say, "Charles and Debbie, before we actually get started looking at houses, I'd like to sit and talk with you for a little bit. I have been in this business for a long time and I have learned that there is a process to help you folks find the right house at the best possible price and in the least amount of time. As a matter of fact, if any agent has to physically show you more than five to seven houses, they are not doing their job."

Now, you've just prepared them for the fact you're not making a career out of showing them property and you've let them know that any agent who does so is not serving them. Now, here are the six steps in the process, with dialogue so you'll see how this all goes together.

Step 1. Inform

"The first thing I would like to do is inform you about myself and about my company. The reason I want to do that is because when you folks buy a house, I feel it's important that you trust the credentials of the agent and the company that agent works for. So I want to let you know what those credentials are and I mean this sincerely. If, after going through my credentials and those of my company, you don't believe that I am a qualified agent to help you in getting that house today, I give you permission to tell me. Fair enough? Now, assuming I pass the interview, the next thing I would like to do is ask some questions."

Step 2. Ask Questions

"I'm going to ask you some more detailed questions than when we were on the phone, so I can get a better picture in my mind of what type of home you are looking for. See, the better idea I can get, the better I can help you folks. Do you mind if I ask you questions later on? … OK, great."

Step 3. Select Houses

"The third thing we will do is select the houses we're going to look at. Now, what I'm going to do is show you all of the houses that are currently on the market. Not physically, but through the multiple listing service, our in-house inventory, etc. The reason I want to do that is because, Charles and Debbie, assuming we find the right house today, I don't want you to procrastinate, thinking, "Is there something better out there for me?" So, this way you know I have already shown them all to you. Does that make sense? … Great."

Step 4. Inspect

"After we select our houses, we'll physically go take a look at then. When we do, I'm not going to bring any of the technical aspects of the home—taxes, yard size, all that stuff. My experience has taught me that what's important is if the house talks to you when you first walk in, does it feel like it is a place you can call home? In other words, if you don't like it, all of the other information is not important. I want you to just look at the house, get the overall feeling of it. As a matter of fact, I encourage you to write down the things that you find that stand out about the house. Did you folks bring a pen and paper? … OK, great. So take that with you."

Step 5. Paperwork

"Assuming we find the right house today, we'll come back to the office and go over the paperwork. The first set of papers is all the detailed information I didn't bring with me when we looked at the house—taxes, yard size, etc. The second is a review of the financial aspect of buying the home and putting together an offer that works for everyone."

Step 6. Ongoing Service

"When the seller accepts our offer, we move onto Step 6, Ongoing Service. I want you folks to know that I am not committed to just selling you a house, if we come that far, but I am committed to building a relationship with you, so that even after you move into this new home, if you ever need anything real estate-related, I want you to feel free to call me.

"So do you have any questions about this process?"

Got it? Let me explain a very important point about the buying process. Have you done anything yet? No. All you've done is explain what you're going to do. You've outlined it. You don't start doing anything yet. You don't talk about your buyer agency and you're not qualifying their finances. You're just explaining, in a general outline, what you're going to do during this appointment. Then, once you've explained it, you start doing each step.

Now, let's go through the steps, one at a time.

Implementing the Six-Step Buying Process

Step 1. Inform. Now, the Buyer Presentation Book is what you would use to inform them about your credentials.

Section one of your Buyer Presentation Book should validate you. In this section, you should have accomplishments, awards, testimonial letters, pictures of satisfied buyers, training that you've gone through, etc. Similar to what you would have for a seller, but not as much.

Section two validates your company. Here you should have statistics, such as your office market share, and office or company accolades or awards. Have a picture of your broker or manager and her or his background. You may even want to take your buyers for a tour of your office. You should talk about additional services your office provides, like referrals for termite companies, engineers, insurance, etc. You need to think about these things and put them in your Buyer Presentation Book.

Section three has information about your neighborhood, almost like a relocation packet.

So, the Buyer Presentation Book is how we deal with Step 1 in the buying process.

Step 2. Ask Questions. Let's briefly talk about the importance of asking questions.

- It helps you find out what the buyers' motivation is. In other words, it helps distinguish "A" buyers, "B" buyers, and "C" buyers.
- It helps establish a relationship of control. It saves a lot of time and energy. The more questions you ask, the easier it will be for you.
- It helps eliminate objections. If one of your questions is "When we find the right house today, is there anybody else you need to check with before you make your final decision?" that would help eliminate objections, right?
- Most important, it helps stimulate their desire, which is one of your main goals when you work with buyers. From the time they call in to the time you fill out that contract, you want to keep stimulating desire. Get them mentally in the presence of the joy of owning a home.

Here are some questions you might ask:

- Where are you folks from?
- How many people will be living in the home?
- Where are you employed? How long? What is your position? Income?
- How long have you been looking for a home?
- How many houses have you seen?
- Did you see anything you liked? Why didn't you buy one of those?
- Once you find a house that you want to buy, do you need to check with anyone before making a decision?
- How soon were you thinking of making this move?

- What is the total initial investment we're working with?
- What is the price range you're looking in? What monthly payments do you feel comfortable with?
- Please tell me about the house you want to buy.
- When we find you the right house today, are you ready to go ahead and buy it today?

Now that we've reviewed the questions, let me tell you something. It actually doesn't matter which questions you ask. You can use mine or you can use yours, as long as the questions you use help accomplish what you need at this point in the face-to-face meeting with the buyers.

■   ■   ■

Of all the questions we just reviewed, the most important is "When we find you the right house today, are you ready to go ahead and buy it today?" I first heard this question in an interview on Real Estate Today, where a highly successful agent said that she always asks her buyers that question: "Once we find the right house, are you ready to buy it today?" And if they say, "No," she finds out what is holding them back—and if it's something she cannot resolve, she reschedules and tells them to call her when they are ready to buy.

"But, Darryl, wait a second. These buyers came in, they scheduled their time, and you're telling me that if they are not going to buy today I shouldn't even take them out?"

That's right.

"But, Darryl, they'll get upset with me because they'll feel like they're wasting their time."

Listen, they absolutely did not waste their time. And here's how you present it:

Charles, Debbie, isn't it great that we found out now that you're not ready to buy? Imagine if we had spent hours and hours looking at houses. I mean, this was a blessing in disguise. And if nothing else, you were able to learn about me and how I work, so when you are ready to buy, you know this is the place to come.

Or you can simply take Charles and Debbie and refer them to somebody else.

Step 3. Select Houses. If buyers are buying a house for whatever price—$50,000, $100,000, or $500,000—don't you think that they should be part of the process of picking the houses they may want to go look at? If you were in their shoes, wouldn't you want to? By not having them be part of the process, you're really shooting yourself in the foot. That is when you usually get "This is really nice, but we want to see some other houses because we're not sure this is the one for us." How you totally eliminate that reaction is by showing them all the houses that are on the market. Not physically, but with the multiple listing printout, in-house inventory, etc.

So let's say Debbie and Charles are looking for homes in the area of about $200,000. You knew that already because you asked them when they called in. So you say, "I took the liberty of printing out all the houses in our price range, and here is what I came up with."

Earlier in the book, I taught you about the shiny penny list. Now, in the printout, let's say there are 30 homes and five of them are shiny pennies. The shiny pennies are the ones you want the buyers to pick from. So, before they come in, you call these five shiny pennies and set tentative appointments.

Now, when you give Debbie and Charles this long printout, you don't say, "Alright, here are all the houses. Debbie and Charles, go to work. Here's a pen; pick out the ones you want to see."

Why not? Because out of 30 homes, how many will they pick? Probably 30. That's why you have to help them in the selection process. How you do this is by "unselling" the 25 that are not shiny pennies and really pushing the five that are.

> So, Debbie and Charles, let's go through them and see what we have. Now, here's a house that does not have that full basement. You guys said you definitely want a full basement, right? Over here, this house only has two bedrooms; you said you definitely need three. Here is another one, only 1.5 baths. Here's one with three bedrooms; this is a possibility, yes? OK, great. Now over here, this does not work … and this does not work … and this does not work. Oh, here's one. Out of all of this, we only found five.

Now, what's real important is that, as you're eliminating those 25 non-shiny pennies, you need to add a little drama. For example, either cross them off your list with a big marker or crumple each one up or throw it on the floor. What you want is to create this mindset in the buyers: "Oh my gosh, out of all these homes, there are only five that work for us. If we don't buy one of these, we won't have a new home."

This process creates a tremendous amount of urgency. Then, when the buyers go to look at those five, they're not looking at them to see if they like any. They're looking at each one to see which is the best one out of the five; they're looking at them with more of a commitment to picking one that works best. It's an awesome technique!

One note of caution. It's very important that you don't let them take the printout away from you. You need to stay in control of this, because if they were to get that printout in their hands, they would wind up picking all the homes to look at.

Let's briefly discuss the importance of selecting together:

- They feel a part of the process. This way, it's not like they come in and you throw a bunch of houses in their face and just chauffeur them around.
- It stimulates their desire to buy. You have all those homes on the list, you narrowed them down, and then you crossed off, crossed off, and crossed off some more. Their mindset will now be that, if they don't buy one of these five that they picked, the only ones that met all of their criteria, then there is nothing else out there in this market. That's it. They've seen them all.
- It creates urgency. "If you don't like one of these, Charles and Debbie, then I have nothing more to show you." Obviously, if they don't like the homes, you will put them in your files and when the next shiny penny comes on the market, you will call them and the other buyers in that price range.
- The process builds commitment. As you go through each one of these and they say, "No, that's not it … no, that's not it … yeah, let's take a look at that one," they're actually building buying momentum every time they, not you, select that shiny penny.

Now, there's one other thing I want to re-emphasize. The reason you set tentative appointments up front is because if you don't you're setting yourself up for failure.

Let's say that you go through this selection process, they pick the five shiny pennies, and then you go to the phone, but only three shiny pennies are home. So, you take the buyers and you show them these three. They like one of the three—I mean, they really like it. But they tell you that they have to see the other two, because maybe they are better.

But look what you can do. If you have these five shiny pennies, but you get hold of only four of them to set up the tentative appointments before the buyers come in, how many homes are you going to make sure the buyers pick off that list? Four.

As for "A" buyers, you "marry those people"—you're inseparable from them until they buy. You show "A" buyers everything and anything—shiny pennies, dogs, the whole nine yards, because they're definitely going to buy. So, you don't worry so much about this process. You still do it with them, but you have a lot more flexibility there.

Step 4. Inspect Now, this is the step where you actually start showing property to the buyers. Some of these tips that I am going to give you are little things; some are a bit bigger. But here's the bottom line: the more you try to sell a house, the more you unsell it. The best way to sell a house is to just open up the door and let them see if they like it. So, don't put too much stock in these precise techniques. The key really is your attitude.

I used to say to buyers, "You folks know what you're looking for. If you like it, tell me." And that was it. If they liked it, they bought it. If they didn't, that was fine too. The trouble comes when you're too attached to making a sale, like it's something you absolutely must do. Interestingly, when you're not attached to it, because you've built your listing inventory and you aren't financially dependent upon any one sale, you feel in control of your career and your buyers will sense, that around you, they're free to buy a home, as opposed to being sold one.

So, start with your attitude and focus on having fun with your buyers. Then, with that perspective, the following pointers will help.

19 Expert Tips for Showing Property

1. **Do a daily update.** To stay fresh on the market, first thing in the morning do a printout to look at all the new houses on the market and look for those shiny pennies.

2. **Ask sellers why they are moving.** When you're previewing other agents' inventory, especially when it's not in-house inventory, ask the sellers why they're moving. You do this to find out how motivated they are.

   Here's an example. When you're previewing, you may find a house that, based on its price, location, and square footage, is not a shiny penny. It's average. It's fair market. You're going through, however, and you ask the sellers, "Where you folks moving to?" "Well, we're moving to Florida because I have a sick aunt; we need to get there in the next 30 days." Is this now a shiny penny? You betcha. Things like that are not going to be printed on the listing sheet.

   By the way, I'm always amazed that when I teach this, there are always a few agents who think it's against the law to ask another agent's sellers this question when previewing. I'm not going to get into teaching law, but just for the record, you absolutely can ask sellers any question when you are previewing their house.

3. **Work the house and not the buyer.** What's another way of saying that? The shiny penny list. I can't stress this enough. If you want to work with fewer buyers and make more sales, you need to put together a shiny penny list. If your company gets involved, great; if not, you can do it yourself. Take the best of the best in all the price ranges and make your own separate list and focus on showing those properties. Power Agents in my program have a saying: "Less stress, income higher, work the house and not the buyer."

4. **Set tentative appointments.** As we've mentioned, before your buyers come, make sure you set tentative appointments with the shiny pennies that you want to lead them to.

5. **Explain the sellers' job.** When you make the appointment with the sellers, the sellers' job is to basically do two things: get the house ready ... and leave. Clean the house, straighten up the clutter, maybe get a nice aroma wafting through, keep the heat up in the winter and the AC cooling it in the summer, turn the lights on, and leave. Make certain your sellers know this when you're showing your listings.

6. **Take the scenic route when first showing the property.** This applies to houses that might have some kind of flaw. So, let's say you're going to show a house that's by the sewer plant. If you can take the buyers to the house without passing the plant, that would be better. Obviously you'll need to show it to them eventually, but you don't want to do it before they go into the house; otherwise, they'll never give the house a chance.

7. **Lower their expectations.** This is very useful. Let's say you're in the car and the house you're going to show them is a real beauty. Don't tell them this, because that would just make their expectations higher. Instead, try this: "You know what, Deb, Charles, this house I can't remember too well, but I think it needs a little bit of work. Be a little open-minded. I think you might like it." Now, you go into the house and what are they going to say? "Ah, Darryl, this isn't too bad. Wow, it has a new kitchen!" They're pleasantly surprised because you lowered their expectations. It's much better than talking it up and having them be disappointed because they were expecting so much. Unfortunately, a lot of agents raise expectations because they're excited about the possi-

bility of a getting a contract. They say, "You're going to love this house!" And that only hurts them.

8. **Park across the street, when possible.** My Power Agents tell me this silly little item makes a big difference. When you park across the street and the buyers get out of the car, they can see a broad view of the house and kind of soak it all in. It's called enjoying the "curb appeal" of the home. When you park in the driveway, the house feels too close to them and they can't soak it all in.

9. **Take only a pad and a pen with you**. Do not take any of that MLS information. (Of course, you should take the directions, the address, and the phone number in case you get lost!) The reason you don't carry all of the details with you is because every time buyers ask a question and you answer it, you are giving them a reason to eliminate this house and to keep giving you objections. What you want is for them to walk into the house and forget all of this, to just soak it in. "Do you like it or don't you? Don't worry about the refrigerator stain or the taxes or the yard or the square footage of the living room. Do you like it? Now, do you have a question for me? Ask me, I'll jot it down, and then, when we go back to the office, I'll sit down and we'll answer all your questions." That's the other purpose of this approach: it gives you a reason to go back to the office.

10. **Use one car.** You want to use one car because you can use that opportunity to have conversations and build rapport. What if a buyer insists on taking two cars because "we have an appointment right after we finish with you"? You say, "Oh, I thought I mentioned that we needed two hours." "Well, we couldn't give it to you today." "Alright, that's no problem. Let's reschedule for when you do have two hours, because this is important and I'm not going to rush it."

11. **Do not share the price until you are outside.** Do not share the price of the home that you're showing them until after you've shown it to them. This is the biggest mistake that some agents make. As they're driving up to the house, they say, "There it is. Now that one is $209,000." When they say that, what they are doing is making this whole process of buying a home become mainly about money. They say, "This one is $209, this one is $219, and this one is $205." But it's not about price; it's about the house and whether the buyers like it or not. As soon as you point out the price, they'll walk into the house judging the house to see if it's worth as much as these greedy sellers are asking. They will judge it

rather than be in the presence of "Do we or don't we like it?"

12. **Encourage them to write down the positives.** This will have them focus on what works for them about each home.

13. **Show the best feature last.** Let's say you know that they're really going to love this finished basement. Do not show that first. Have that be the icing on the cake. This is smarter than ending the tour by showing them the smelly, greasy garage! It's a little thing and it's common sense, but again, our job is to manage their emotions.

14. **Watch for buying signals.** Here, I'll give you an example of what not to do. There are some trainers out there who tell you precisely how to show the house. They say, "You should always go in front of the buyer so you control the buying mood." Then some others say, "Do not do that because you get in the way of the rooms; walk behind them." And there's another speaker out there—I don't think he's going to last too long on the speaking circuit—who says you should always walk in front of the buyers, but backwards. ("Here, let me show you folks the basement. It's right over here … aaaaaaahhhhhhh!") I think you should forget all of this garbage and just watch for buying signals. For example, you might find the buyers whispering in the corner or they'll start asking about what stays with the house or they'll start jumping for joy. All of these are buying signals.

15. **Acknowledge and capitalize on the buying signals.** When they ask, "Do the drapes stay?" you can respond with "Would you like them to leave the drapes? You would? Let me jot that down: 'buyer wants drapes.'" Be subtle about tying those down. Just walk around with a little pad and note those buying signals. Another great technique is to call the listing company and let the buyers feel the anxiety of asking if there are other offers: "I'll call the listing company to see if there are other offers.... I sure hope there aren't yet." Then ask them, "If there's another offer, what do you want to do?"

16. **Appeal to their emotions, not their logic.** Remember that there are two types of selling—emotional and logical. When you are working with a seller, you should use a lot of logic: "We have a marketing plan," "I'm a marketing agent," etc. When you are working with buyers, it's more emotional. This is so because buying a home is about the "dream" of the new life that comes with that house.

17. **Focus on payments, not price.** When it comes time to actually do the paperwork, you know that buyers focus on price: "Let's offer $200K." "Where did you get that number? You can afford $215K." "Well let's offer $200, because they're asking $209."

   Instead of getting into this, assume a full price offer and share with them what monthly payments would be. "This house comes to $1800 a month. Based on what you shared with me earlier, that's right in line with what you feel comfortable with, right?"
   "Yes." "OK, great. Let's write it up." And then you proceed to write a full-price offer.

   Now, I know what you're thinking. "But Darryl, as a buyer's agent, I have an obligation to get the buyer the house at the best possible price." Well, unless your state is different from most states, nowhere in the buyer's agency agreement does it say that. What it probably says is that it's your fiduciary responsibility to look out for their best interests.

   Is it in their best interest for you to coach them to try and negotiate the price with the sellers so they can save $50, or $75, or even $100 a month and in doing so cause them to risk losing the house? How can they lose the house? Well, while they're trying to save $2 a day, a better offer comes in or perhaps the sellers become offended and tempers flare and now the buyers don't like the sellers and to spite them the buyers say, "The heck with them—let them keep the house." But more important, when you have the focus on saving money, it's no longer about buying a home. I could go on and on but I think I've made my point.

18. **Show their favorite house a second time.** So you have five houses to show; in which order should you show them? Well, some training programs say that you should always show the cream puff first and the dog last. Some say to show the dog first and the cream puff last. I'm not so complicated. I believe you show based on geography. You go in order and watch for buying signals.

   Let's say you show the first house. "Oh this is nice." You show the next house. "It's not bad." You show house #3 and it's "Ding, ding, ding! When can we move in? Do the drapes stay? We love the floor." Now, do you show them houses 4 and 5? Yes, absolutely. Watch what happens.

   You show them house #4 and they say, "Yeah. It's OK, but we really like the third one." "Well, come on. Let's go see house #5." "No, we don't want to." "Come on, we promised the seller. She's waiting for us. Let's just show up, and we'll breeze through." "OK."

You show them house #5. "You guys still love that third one, don't you?" "Yes."

See, showing the last two houses reaffirms for them how much they like house #3. Besides, if they put an offer in without seeing those last two, they may start to have second thoughts later on.

OK now, what do you have to do? "Hey, let us go back to house #3. We don't have an appointment, but I don't think the seller will mind. Let's run on through it again."

So, show them all the houses, but whatever house they love out of all the homes you showed them, bring them back a second time that same day. (Obviously, if they love the last house you show them, you don't need to do that!)

19. **Let houses sell houses.** Like I said before we began with these tips, it's best thing not to be so attached to each technique. After all, they're just ideas. Open up the doors and let them buy it or not.

Step 5: Paperwork. This is the step where the buyers come back and actually write their offer. We cover this in the next chapter, "The Art of Negotiating."

Step 6: Ongoing Service. This, essentially, is you staying in touch with your past clients. This is covered in great detail in Chapter 11, "Building a Referral Business."

■   ■   ■

Working with buyers is a lot easier than you and I make it out to be. The only way we can have more fun and not get so anxious about working with buyers is to build our inventory. When we have a good amount of listings in our inventory, we feel a sense of accomplishment. We know that our listings are working for us and our income is secure. I said it before and I'll say it again—you need to focus your energy on building your inventory. And once you have that, then you can take buyers out and you can have fun with them. You show them property: if they buy something, great, and if they don't, that's fine too.

There's a big difference between taking buyers out because you want to and taking buyers out because you need to make a sale. When you have the attitude that you have to sell them a house because you must make a commission and it is all about you, you're not going to be nearly as effective as when you're doing it just for the joy of being with them and trying to contribute to their lives by finding them a great home.

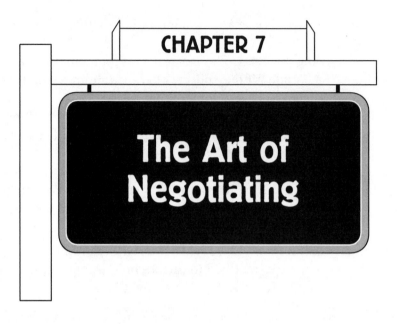

CHAPTER 7

The Art of Negotiating

Power Fact

Negotiating is like a dance. The movement, the unspoken communication, the partnership. As real estate agents, our responsibility is to introduce these two partners, the buyer and the seller, who are sometimes reluctant at first, and to choreograph a beautiful performance that leaves each partner better off than before.

Overview

Every buyer and seller, every human being, brings a certain *listening* into any situation. You do this yourself. It's that little voice inside your head that comments on everything you do and see. It's your expectations, your opinions, your feelings. Negotiation is all about successful communication. And successful communication stems from getting in touch with your own listening and the listening of those around you.

In this chapter, I'll offer you an array of practical tips and techniques that you can put to use immediately. Some of it will be real-estate-specific and some of it will deal with your mental outlook. All of it will help you excel at the art of negotiating.

Before You Present an Offer

It's obviously a lot easier to present offers if you are the listing *and* selling agent. However, to provide you with maximum benefit, I'll assume for the purpose of this chapter that you are the selling agent only and *not* the listing agent. This is the harder route to travel, so the following tips and techniques are vital to your success.

In most parts of the country, I find that selling agents *believe* that they are *legally required* to take their offer and present it to the listing agent and have that agent present it to the sellers. I'm sure you would agree that it makes absolutely no sense to give your offer to the listing agent and hope and pray that she or he will be able to convey all that needs to be conveyed about your buyers. Of course he or she can't; in most cases the listing agent hasn't even met the buyers. So, I can't stress enough that it's an absolute *must* that you be there in person to present your offer to the seller. (Of course, if the homeowner lives in Florida and you are in California, this would be impractical.)

There are several reasons why you should present the offer directly:

1. If you give the offer to the listing agent, it may be days before she or he gives it to the seller.
2. If the listing agent has his or her own offer, he or she will obviously present it in a better light than yours.
3. There might be questions that a seller has about these buyers that only you, the selling agent, can answer. And it's best to do this face-to-face.
4. If the seller counters your offer, you don't have to go back and forth with telephone calls. You can simply call your buyers from the seller's house, get the verbal from the buyers, and walk out of the house with an accepted offer or move on.

You might be thinking, "But, Darryl, that's not how it's done in my market." Once again, I can guarantee you that it's not an issue of legality; it's just a cultural issue or a tradition. Later, I will show you how the listing agent *must* let you present your offer directly to the sellers.

Now, might this technique cause a listing agent to be uncomfortable? Perhaps. But the only time that a listing agent would get upset with a selling agent for doing it this way is when she doesn't understand how this benefits her seller or because he has his own agenda and wants to be in control. For these agents, the entire process is about them, and not their clients.

What's the benefit to the listing agent for having the selling agent present the offer?

First, the benefit is that the listing agent will have better odds of getting this offer accepted if it's presented in this manner, which means that the house will get sold and everyone gets paid.

My second response is that the question is actually irrelevant. Remember, this process is not supposed to be about what's better for the listing agent. The listing agent has a fiduciary responsibility to do what's best for the homeowners. And what's best for the homeowners is to hear all the details about the buyers directly from the selling agent's mouth. Quite simply, this technique is beneficial to both the homeowners and the buyers.

"What if I still encounter resistance from the listing agent?" Here's a technique to use in case the listing agent really gives you a hard time.

Check your local Board/MLS rules. Most likely, there is a rule that says that you as the selling agent have a right to be there when presenting the offer. Of course, this doesn't ensure that the listing agent will actually let you in, so let me share with you how to guarantee that this happens. Very simply, on your offer that the buyer signs, you should write, "This offer is subject to [Your Name] presenting this offer directly to the homeowners."

Now, legally, the listing agent must let you in to present the offer. The only way that he or she wouldn't have to do this is if the homeowners told the listing agent, upon hearing that the offer is contingent upon you presenting it, "Well, then I don't want to hear the offer." Now let me ask you, how many homeowners will understand that there's an offer waiting out there but will decline to hear it because they would have to meet with the selling agent? I never met one.

That said, don't be surprised if, when you call the listing agent to set the appointment to present the offer, the listing agent tells you that the homeowner said she or he doesn't want to hear the offer. Of course, this might not be the homeowner's actual wishes; it could just be the listing agent being a control freak. So, to protect yourself in this scenario, tell the listing agent, "As you know, our obligation to the seller is that all offers must be presented. To protect ourselves from a legal standpoint, let's get a letter from the seller stating that she understands there's an offer out there from my buyers, but she's choosing not to hear it. That's the safest thing to do." If the listing agent is bluffing, this technique will call his bluff; otherwise he'll produce the letter.

Now that you understand why you must present the offer personally, the rest of this chapter will help you do this and will enable you to get more offers accepted in far less time.

Have the Buyers Write a Letter to the Sellers

When presenting offers, agents too often focus the conversation on price. They incorrectly assume that this is the most important thing to the seller. While this might be true in some cases, there are two things that may be equally if not more important to most sellers.

1. **The commitment of the sellers to move on with their life.** There were many times that I went in to present an offer and the conversation was initially all about price, price, price—"How much money am I making?" But when I talked to the homeowners about their Next Level, what they were committed to, that all shifted.

   "We want to get to Florida to be with the kids," they would tell me.

   In this context, I would ask them, "Is it worth holding out for an extra few thousand dollars that you may never see and sacrifice getting to Florida when you want to?"

   Though my offers may have been less than what the homeowners wanted, they were often accepted because I reminded the sellers of their initial commitment. Selling their house was about moving on in their life.

2. **Whether the sellers like the buyers.** For some homeowners, this isn't too important. But for most, it is. How many times have you seen an offer that wasn't quite what the sellers wanted but they made the exception because they really liked the buyers who were going to live in their home? You see, there's a psychological element in selling a house. After all, it's more than a house; it's a *home*. And most homeowners want to transfer their deed to someone who will appreciate their home as much as they have.

   Our task, then, is to "humanize" the buyers, to make them look like a real flesh-and-blood family who are going to appreciate the home. We do this by having the buyers write a letter to the sellers.

How to Get the Letter

After the buyers write the offer and while they are still in your office, you give them a blank sheet of paper and tell them, "Write a letter to the Johnsons telling them why you're so excited about the possibility of owning this home. Let it rip; whatever comes out will be perfect."

Here are a few samples (Figure 7-1) of real letters my *Power Agents* had their buyers write to the seller. I've changed the names and addresses to keep identities private.

This came from a Power Agent in Wisconsin

To [Seller],

I am enclosing this letter with my offer because I want you to know something about my boys and myself.

Both times that I went through your home I saw a great deal of potential. I saw a place where two boys could grow up and learn responsibility. I firmly believe the best place for a boy (kids) is on a farm where they have room to run and healthy things to do.

I grew up in the country with horses, dogs, cats, etc., and I dearly love the country. I am a single parent trying to give my kids the best home life and preparation for their future that I can.

The offer is what I know I can handle and still be able to finish the upstairs for the boys. My oldest is almost 13 and very much an early bird. My youngest is 8 and a night owl. The age and difference between the two boys makes it necessary to have their own rooms as soon as possible in a new home.

As a single parent I do what I can to provide the best for my boys and I see a great foundation for my kids and their future there. I thank you for opening your home for us to see. I truly hope that we can work something out.

Sincerely

Krista Lewandowski

■　　■　　■

This was written by a couple in Minneapolis

Dear Mr. Ringwelsky,

We are writing hoping to find you in the best of health and to introduce our family and myself. We have four small children in need of a home—hopefully your home.

We resides at 3341 4th Avenue. I don't know if you're familiar with 4th Avenue, but it's not a street where you want your children to grow up. We live among drugs, guns, and even murder. We noticed your fenced yard, the kind of place I'd like to see my children playing in. While we can't offer you a whole lot of money for your home, we can promise you that we will love and take care of it if given the chance.

Thank you,

Mr. and Mrs. Greer

P S. The kids will love the little playhouse in the backyard.

Figure 7-1. Example letters from buyers to sellers (continued on next page)

Long Island, New York: The asking price was $215,000, and the listing agent said the homeowners would take nothing less than $210,000 because they had already rejected that.

Dear Mrs. O'Keefe,

My children and I visited your house yesterday and were very impressed with your home. I am a recent widow and wanted a home that the children and I would love and will make our transition to New York an easier process. I hope we will be able to negotiate the sale so we can be settled as soon as possible.

Thank you,

Maureen Sweeney

■   ■   ■

Dear Mr. and Mrs. DeWare,

As we present this offer, we'd like to thank you for considering us as buyers for your home. We have looked at many houses, but none of them had the same feeling yours has. Along with meeting our needs as a large family, your home is filled with the love of 27 years. We all had the sensation that we were being "hugged" when we walked in. The children, who obviously don't understand the negotiation process, have all chosen their bedrooms already! We have, of course, told friends and family about your home, and they are keeping all of us in their prayers. For this reason, we feel confident that we can reach an agreement that everyone is comfortable with. No matter what the outcome, we are grateful to be considered as the possible next family to take residence in the warmth of your home.

Sincerely,

The Robinson Family

■   ■   ■

Since we haven't met face to face I thought you may want to know a little about the family interested in your home. We are a young couple looking to buy our first home. We have a 4-year-old daughter and a little girl on the way in two weeks. We've been looking to buy a home for about two years and have even thought about making a few offers, but for various reasons each time something just didn't seem right, and we chose to continue renting. We drove past your house and fell in love with the beautiful green yard. We knew that this was the home for us even though we had not yet seen the inside. Once we were able to see the inside and the beautiful backyard, we felt that this house was custom made for our family. The wallpaper is everything that I would have picked myself, and the backyard is the perfect place for my girls to play with friends. For the first time we feel we've found

Figure 7-1. Example letters from buyers to sellers (continued on next page)

a house that's right for us, and buying a home may not be such a scary thing. So while you are considering our offer please keep in mind that your home will be going to a family who will love it and care for it the way that you have.

Brad and Wendy Turner

Figure 7-1. Example letters from buyers to sellers (concluded)

This technique is so powerful that I have actually seen some homeowners, after reading the letter, accept the offer without even countering. What's also so great about this technique is that, while the buyers are writing the letter, they resell themselves on why they want the house. This helps you reduce potential buyer's remorse ... and if the buyers are asked to come up with a few thousand dollars from their original offer, it's easier because they're that much more committed.

By the way, as the buyers are writing the letter, this is a good time to call the listing agent to schedule a time to present the offer to the sellers. Why? Because when you call the listing agent to schedule this appointment and she or he asks you how much the offer is, you can respond with "I still have the buyers in the office and we're not finished putting the deal together; I just wanted to call to set up the appointment before they left." You see, if you tell the listing agent any details about the offer, he or she will mess it up by telling the homeowners what the offer is before you get there. You must not let that happen.

Meet with the Listing Agent Before the Presentation

If you're not the listing agent, you should meet with the listing agent prior to going into the sellers' house or before the sellers come to your office. You do this to join forces with the agent and link together to produce a positive result. What you *don't* want is for this listing agent to take the attitude "OK, I'm representing the sellers. You're representing the buyers. I'm going to check you out and keep an eye on you." It should be "We both get this accepted or we both don't. And if we both do, we get paid for our efforts."

So you want to call the listing agent and set up a meeting right away. Again, she or he will likely ask you on the phone how much the offer is. Just say that you'll be happy to tell him or her when you meet face to face. "The reason is we are still working out some of the final details."

Find out the Sellers' Motivation

If it's not your listing, you want to find out from the listing agent the where, when, and why of these sellers. *Where* are the sellers moving? *When* do they want to get there? And *why* are they moving there?

Is this important for you to know? Absolutely. Just as we said above, we want to know what they're committed to, because that's what we're going to focus on during our conversation. Our job is more than to sell their house; it's to help them meet their objectives. The more you know about their goals, the better you can help structure a deal that works for everyone.

Review the Listing Agreement

If it's not your listing, you won't have the agreement, but you'll have the printout. You should look at how long the property has been on the market. Also, if the listing agent will tell you, find out whether they've had any offers and, if so, for how much, etc. Why do we want to know this? Sellers who have had a lot of offers may realize they lost some opportunities to sell their house and may be more motivated. Or this might tell you that they are "tough cookies." If they've been on the market for only a few days, you ought to know that too.

Review the Market Conditions

Get clear about the number of houses that are on the market. Also, review the number of houses sold.

A Six-Step Process for Presenting the Offer

Are you ready for the best way to present an offer? It's a six-part process. But before I share this with you, let me say two more things about creating a partnership with the listing agent and the homeowners.

First, you should compliment the listing agent in front of the sellers. You can say something like "Mr. and Mrs. Seller, before we begin, I just want to say that you made the right choice in hiring Hunna to market your house. He/she is well respected in the market and it's because of his/her efforts that I'm here." You just scored some points with the listing agent and she or he may be more cooperative with you.

Second, let the homeowners know that, even though you represent the buyers in this case (if you have a buyer agency relationship), you have an obligation to be fair to all parties. Let them know it's important to you that they, as homeowners, also meet their goals and objectives.

Step 1: Talk about the sellers' motivation. We discussed this above, so this is just a brief recap. After you let the homeowners know that you are committed to helping them achieve their goals, it's only natural for you to discuss what they are committed to (where are they moving, when they need to get there, etc.). If the listing agent told you this information before, you simply review it now, with the sellers elaborating on it. You want to bring to the surface what they're committed to, so that this forms the context of your discussion. Otherwise, they'll be listening to you like they would to any other salesperson and be focusing only on the money.

Some agents have asked me if it is legal to ask the homeowners these types of questions. Unless something has changed from the time I wrote this book, it's *absolutely* legal to ask. Of course, the homeowners don't have to answer you if they don't want to.

Step 2: Humanize the buyers. After you share some of the facts about the buyers—how long they've been married, where they work, the names of the kids, etc.—you read the letter out loud to the sellers. Don't give it to them, but read it out loud. You will be amazed at the reaction you'll get. Like I said earlier, I've seen some sellers start to cry and not even counter after hearing the letter. Of course, there also will be times where sellers will say, "That's nice, but how much?" But that's the exception, not the rule.

Step 3: Manage their listening. Here's what I mean. Most homeowners will naturally listen to your offer with a certain amount of arrogance. "If this offer isn't what we want, we'll wait for a better one," they might think. But we want them to listen more with an attitude of "We're fortunate to have an offer." In a hot market, this is a little more difficult to do, but it still helps if you frame the discussion in this manner. To do this, bring along the single-line printout of all the homes in your market. Not just for their town, but for your whole market, with all the styles.

Say, "Mr. and Mrs. Seller, here is an updated list of all the homes that are currently on the market." (Feverishly flip through all the pages.) "Now, out of all these homes, these buyers picked yours. I feel very happy for you." See how that creates some urgency?

The second aspect to managing their listening is to *explain the difference between* terms *and* price. Here's how the explanation might go.

"Mr. and Mrs. Seller, there are two things to look at with any offer—price and terms. Although price is important, I believe terms are just as important, if not more so. Here's why I say that. Let's say some buyers gave you full price, or even more than you're asking, but they're putting down only 1%

… they have terrible credit … they want you to hold a note … they want you to pay closing costs … and they couldn't afford the house if it were free. Chances are you would never see a penny of that great *price* they offered you. So you want to make sure that when you go to contract, you will make it to settlement."

The point here, once again, is to continue to lessen the focus on price.

Step 4: Present the terms first. Next, you put the sellers' minds at ease and really push the positives of these particular buyers. Mention items like the deposit, if it's a large one. If they own and the house is sold, that's a positive. If they rent, it's a positive. Even if they're putting down just 10%, you can make this a positive too. You might say, "I have a pre-commitment letter from one of the mortgage companies I work with. They qualify for a 90% loan, so there shouldn't be any problem with them obtaining finance." And so forth. Let the sellers know that they can close and go to contract as soon as possible.

Step 5: Present price. Now is when you present price. One of the best techniques is to first do a little research. Let's say, based on your MLS stats, that homeowners on average get 97.2% of their asking price in your area.

If your buyers' offer is better than that percentage, include that fact. For example, "Mr. and Mrs. Seller, for your information, the average homeowner sells his or her house for 97.2% of their asking price; in this case, these buyers' offer represents 98.3 %, which comes to $300,000."

Now, if the offer is for less than the average, try narrowing your focus by just looking at the MLS averages for their development or their style of home. You can usually tweak the information to come out to what you need. Of course, if the buyers are really off course, all I can say is "You can't win them all."

Step 6: Invite action. Here's what this looks like: A) recap the positives, B) hand them the pen, C) direct the signature, D) ask the spouse a question.

When you do this, it's important to make sure that you're mentally "present." There should be nothing else on your mind, no hidden agenda, no personal issues clouding your thoughts—nothing except 100% concentration on the sellers and a sincere commitment to help them achieve what they are committed to.

Sample Dialogue

Let me demonstrate what presenting an offer may sound like when you're the selling agent and the listing agent is named Donna Lister:

Darryl: Mr. and Mrs. Seller, before we begin, let me say something. When you hired Donna, you made the right decision. She is considered one of the best agents in the market and it's because of her efforts that I'm even here today with an offer.

Sellers: Well, that is very nice of you to say.

Darryl: Also, even though I represent the buyers in this sale, I still have a responsibility to be fair and to operate with a high level of integrity. If I can help you folks achieve your goals and help the buyers with theirs, we've created a win-win.

Sellers: We agree.

Darryl: So tell me, where are you folks moving to?

Sellers: Texas.

Darryl: Oh, that's great.

And you continue to ask them when they need to be there, etc. For example purposes, let's say they have to be in Texas in four months.

Darryl: Four months. So I feel we might have made it in the nick of time. Well, let me tell you a little about these buyers. They are a lovely couple. They have two children, Brad and Chelsea, and they've been looking for a long time. The reason they're interested in this house is because they want to be in this neighborhood. They have some friends here, it's close to where she works, they like the access to the parkways, and they were raving about the school district. As a matter of fact, they were so excited that they did something kind of cute. They wrote a letter to you and I want to read it to you now.

Dear Mr. and Mrs. Seller,

We're so excited that you are considering our offer to purchase your home because we've been looking in your neighborhood for quite a while. Your house is really wonderful; we can see how much pride you take in it. Our family has already fallen in love with the home.... And so on.

Isn't that cute?

Sellers: Yeah.

Darryl: So, these are really nice people. And the other reason why I'm really excited about being here—I don't know if Donna has had a chance to show you this—is because of what's happened on the market recently. There's been an increase in activity. Let me show you. This list represents all the houses that are currently on the market in our town. Can you believe this? There are over 100 houses. And I feel so glad that I'm here with these buyers and they like this house because out of all of these houses they chose yours. So, I feel a little lucky, if you will. Are you with me?

Now, I want to tell you what they're offering. Let me explain one important point. There are two things we have to look at. There's price—how much we're going to walk away with. And, more important, we have terms. Here's the reason I say "more important." Let's say we're asking $179K and these buyers are willing to pay $179K. Initially, we might think, "That's great!" But let's say, hypothetically, that they're putting down only 10%, they've got iffy credit, and they want you to hold a promissory note. Plus, they wouldn't be able to close for six months and you want to be in Texas in four. Can you see how that wouldn't work?

Sellers: Right.

Darryl: See, we can have the best price, but the terms might not work. And, on the flip side, we can have great terms and a poor price. So there are two areas we need to look at closely. Is this making sense?

Sellers: Yeah.

Darryl: So, let me first go through the terms with you, because I believe that's more important and I'm really excited about their terms. First off, they've sold a house from where they're moving and the time frame works out perfectly. Four months is when they'd like to be here. And that's what works for you. Right?

Sellers: Right.

Darryl: It gets better. They're also putting down 20%, which will make it extremely easy for them to qualify. And if for some reason we had challenges with the house appraising, there's still room for them to obtain the mortgage.

Oh, and there is another thing. They're buying the house "as is," meaning we don't have to do any improvements to the house. Some buyers will move in only if you do this and that. But with these buyers, as long as the house is not falling down, you don't have to spend any money.

Sellers: This sounds great.

Darryl: All right now. Let's look at price. Mr. and Mrs. Seller, for your information, the average homeowner in this area sells his or her house for 97.2% of the asking price. In our case, these buyers' offer represents

98.3%, which comes to $200,000.

Sellers: Well, we would have liked to get more money. You don't suppose they would come up just a couple of thousand more?

At this point, we would have to deal with their objection. (I cover dealing with objections next.) But there you have it—the essence of the six-step process for presenting the offer.

Handling Sellers' Objections

I can't address every possible objection you may receive when you're talking with sellers, but here are some of the most common ones.

"We want to counter."

Remember the very beginning of this chapter, where I described negotiating as a dance? Well, here's where that analogy really comes into play. In most negotiations, it always seems as if buyers and sellers compromise toward each other's positions to some extent, but there remains a sticking point of a few thousand dollars at the end. At this point, some lesser skilled agents will cut their commission to put the contract together. Here's a technique to handle this issue.

It begins when the buyers first make their offer. Let's say the asking price is $200,000 and the buyers offer $185,000.

You have a gut feeling, based on experience, that the sellers will actually accept $192,000. So you add a few thousand to that figure and say to the buyers, "If you had to go to $195,000—if it was a choice between owning this home or not—could that work for you?" They might say "no," but they may be thinking, "There's no way we'll go to $195,000, no way. Maybe $192,000."

Now, with the sellers, you do the same technique in reverse. You present them with the offer of $185,000 and they say that they'll counter with $195,000. You have a feeling that the buyers will come up to $192,000, so you subtract a few thousand from that figure and ask, "If you had to go to $190,000—if it was a choice between you moving to Florida or not—could that work for you?"

You see what we've done? Now, if the buyers come up to $192,000, it looks to the sellers like the buyers have given us $2,000 *more* than we anticipated. Likewise, from the buyers' point of view, if the sellers accept $192,000, it looks like they've accepted an offer for $3,000 *less* than we anticipated. This is what I call the "negotiating dance." This works most of the time.

"We won't accept because the price is too low."

Here's exactly what to say to deal with this objection:

We have a choice: either accept what the buyers are offering or wait several months for a new buyer who may never materialize. I have no problem if you folks decide not to accept this offer, but my concern for you is how long it might take. If the terms were really bad, my advice would be to stay firm. But because these particular buyers have really great terms, my advice is to go for it. If I thought you were giving your house away, I wouldn't even bring you this offer because I would buy it myself.

Once again, you're focusing more on the terms and less on the price. You could also add this: "Mr. and Mrs. Seller, would you buy your house for $200,000?" (Don't let them answer; but I can tell you they will probably think: "No, that's why we're selling.")

"The reason why I ask this is because if you don't take this offer, it's like you are buying your house back for $200,000—because right now it's sold." (I call this the "buy-back" technique.)

"Will you cut your commission?"

Before I share with you how to address this question, please keep this in mind. Negotiating a sale is a two-way negotiation, not a three-way, meaning you should *never* discuss with the seller *or* the buyer how much you're getting paid. That was discussed and decided when the homeowners signed the listing agreement and/or when the buyers signed the buyer agency agreement. This is not the time to renegotiate that.

So, what do we do? Bring the discussion back to their *net*. Here's a way to do this.

Sellers: Will you cut your commission?

Darryl: Are you asking me because what the buyers are offering doesn't work for you?

Sellers: Well, we would like to net a little bit more.

Darryl: How much more?

Sellers: Another $2,000.

Darryl: If I couldn't get you another $2,000, but I could get you, let's say, another $1,000, would that work for you?

Sellers: Yes.

Darryl: OK. Let me go back to the buyers and see if they can come up to that price.

So what you've done here is taken the focus off cutting your commission and brought it back to the sellers' net.

These next two dialogues assume that you are the listing agent *and* the selling agent.

Sellers: Darryl, because you're getting both the listing sold side and the buyer sold side, that's a lot of money. We should get a discount on the commission.

Darryl: Well, here's the fact. Yeah, I am getting from both sides, because I'm doing double the work.

Sellers: You put our house on the market and it sold in just a week. You're making thousands of dollars for just seven days of work.

Here's what I used to say: "You should actually pay me more because I did such a good job." (Of course, you'd say this smiling, not with an arrogant tone.) If that didn't work, you could say, "Tell me if you would feel better about my commission if we did this: not accept this offer and drag it out a few months."

The best way to handle this one is on the listing appointment, when they sign with you. Let them know as you're leaving the house with the listing that, as soon as it hits MLS, there are hundreds of potential buyers for their home and you've seen houses sell in the first two weeks. Be sure to tell them, "If this should happen, don't think we priced it too low."

Here's the most important thing about the topic of commission: *don't talk about it.* Because if you talk about it, it just calls attention to the money you earned and to the percentages, etc.

"Do you want to sell this house to these buyers?"

"Yeah, but that commission bothers me."

"I totally understand, but do you want to move?"

Just keep bringing it back to this. The focus should always be on them moving on with their life and not on how much money you're getting paid.

Conclusion

I believe that you can have all the techniques in the world on how to negotiate with buyers and sellers, but unless you know how to communicate effectively, it'll make no difference. We've talked about the listening that buyers and sellers bring to the table. Well, that's common with all people. It's just part of being human. In case you haven't noticed, we're not exactly blank slates, seeing the world each day with innocent eyes. We go into situations and we bring with us expectations, opinions, or point of views.

So, the more you can get tuned into the listening that buyers and sellers and other people around you may bring to a certain situation, the more effective you'll be as a negotiator. That's why part of your success assignment these next 30 days is to be aware of your own listening and the listening of the people around you. Please focus on that.

Clear your mind. Recognize the voice in your own head and understand that other people have their own listening as well. Do this and it won't be long before you find yourself being much more powerful at the art of negotiation.

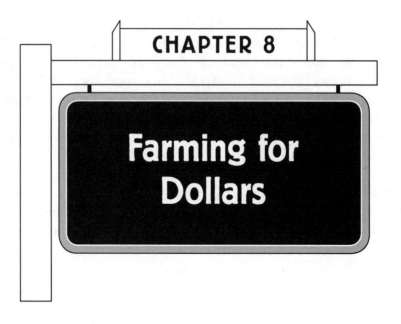

CHAPTER 8

Farming for Dollars

Power Fact

Farming in real estate, like agriculture, is an art. It's about planting seeds, cultivating leads, and seeing what will develop. The key, of course, is to consistently nourish your real estate farm with mailings and events.

Overview

The concept of farming is very basic: we take a bunch of people, mail them a bunch of stuff, and see what sticks. But why aren't enough agents doing it? Why do some agents start and never finish it? And why do others do it but never see results?

The main reason most farming efforts fail is *lack of consistency.* The worst thing you can do is start a farming program and then give up, whether it's because you're not seeing results soon enough or you don't have the money any more to work the farm or you get confused or stressed out. Being consistent and working it persistently is the key. This means you've got to make a commitment that you're going to work it for the next several years. So you've got to ask yourself the question, "Am I ready to make that kind of commitment?" If you do, I promise you there's a tremendous amount of benefit to working a farm.

This chapter will explain the advantages to working a farm, the overall concepts of farming, the steps in putting it together, and how to work it. I'll show you how simple it is to get it started.

Farming vs. Door Knocking

When most agents hear *farming*, they think *door knocking*. Although door knocking may be part of it, to me farming is more focused on doing direct mail. I am not against door knocking. I know and you know that door knocking does work. And if it works for you, you should keep doing it.

But I want you to consider this. If you have 500 people in your farm and you're giving them the personal touch of door knocking, you're going to get some results. Now, if you're not door knocking and you're just doing mailings and phone calls to your farm, well, you might need 1,000 people to get the same results as with that personal touch.

Which is better for you? Personally, I would rather sit in my office and delegate to someone the job of mailing 1,000 pieces a month than personally go out there every week knocking on doors. Although there are some top producers who regularly use door knocking, most do not. They farm, but they don't door knock. When you're making that kind of income, you don't have the time to be knocking on doors. (*Note:* Those at this level who do door knock typically have a team of people doing this for them.) So, I want you to think like a top producer. Think how an agent with a six-figure income would work a farm. That's what I'm going to cover with you in this chapter.

By the way, there are three basic types of farms:

- People whom you don't know and with whom you've never done business
- People who know you (your sphere of influence) but with whom you haven't done business
- People who know you and with whom you've done business (your past clients)

For the purpose of this book, when I discuss farming, I'm referring to the first type.

Advantages of Farming

There are certain advantages that I strongly believe you'll achieve once you make a commitment to farming.

1. **Business comes to you.** One of the great things about farming on a consistent basis is that eventually business comes to you. In response to your ads and your mailings and the events you might host (all explained later in this chapter), you will begin to get business.

2. **You won't have to do as much *cold* calling.** If you want to generate some listing appointments, you don't need to open up the phone book and call complete strangers. In addition to calling FSBOs and expireds, you can call your farm. Because these people have received pieces from you before, they're considered warm calls, not cold calls.

3. **It's a non-threatening way to prospect.** It's non-threatening for you (some agents find it difficult calling FSBOs and expireds) and it's non-threatening to the homeowners because you are mailing them things of value.

4. **Farming creates a steady flow of income.** Eventually, after about a year or so, you'll start to get a steady flow of business from your farm. The key, though, is to work it consistently. To have a farm is one thing; to have it succeed is another—you've got to work the farm. It's not like you mail one month, you mail the next month, and then you skip a month. Once you skip a month, you're just starting over.

Five Fundamental Concepts of Farming

1. **Your objective is to have a specific group of people know your name, face, and what you do for a living.** You want to become a local celebrity to this specific group. You want to program the mind of the homeowners so that whenever they think of real estate, they think of you. You will do this through mailings, advertising, etc.

2. **Be great at other basic real estate skills before you start to farm.** You get into business and somebody—maybe your broker, maybe your manager, maybe another agent—tells you that you need to "list to last" in this business. So, you ask, "How do I do that?" First, they tell you, "You need to call all your relatives." So you call all your relatives and you send them a letter: "I'm in real estate." Then, after that they say, "Now you need to farm." What do you do? You go knock on a bunch of doors, you mail a bunch of stuff out, …and then a lot of agents stop—because either they run out of money or they run out of mailing ideas.

   But the underlying problem is that agents really should not start to farm until they've mastered the other areas needed to generate listings.

Farming isn't the solution to your problems; farming isn't the answer to getting to your Next Level. Calling FSBOs, expireds, cold calling—those are the answers. After you master the art of prospecting, then farming is the next step, the Next Level, because farming is clearly a long-term investment of money and time. Farming is designed to generate *future* business, but most agents need *now* business.

You have to know this about farming: you won't see a return on your money and time for a year or two. The first year, you might see nothing. You can't start to farm thinking, "I'm going to make a killing this year by getting a bunch of people and mailing them a bunch of stuff and they're going to start calling me." It doesn't happen that way. You farm to invest in your career long term.

3. **Create a hook.** Tell me which sounds better: mailing to people as just Joe Schmoe, real estate agent from XYZ Company, or mailing to people as a unique agent with your own slogan, your own hook? Your hook may be the type of houses you work, your previous profession, or the fact you sell a house every seven days. In the next chapter, "The Art of Self-Promotion," there's a worksheet to help you create your hook and your slogan.

4. **Have a narrow focus.** What's the most common narrow focus for farming? Focusing on a geographic location. But there are other ways you could go. It could be a certain type of property, like waterfront property.

   One broker I worked with had great success with this technique. Mac became familiar with the certain jargon that they use, like "bulkhead" and "dredging," and so on. Mac even had a tide table. For the whole year, he could tell you when it was high tide and when it was low tide for different areas, so he'd show property only during the high tide periods. Waterfront was his focus and he was very effective at it.

   So you may want to start thinking of areas where you can focus your farming efforts. You could zero in on types of houses—colonials and Tudors, for example. If I were getting back into sales, my focus would be colonials and Tudors, because they're my favorites and I know a lot about those types of homes. You could also farm to people in a club, group, or fraternal organization or who share similar interests or hobbies as you do.

5. **Have six months of mailings and money before you start.** This is an extremely important concept. Why? Because when you run out of ideas or money, you quit. I've seen it happen so many times. The first

time an agent mails out something, it's usually the introduction letter: "Hi, my name is. ... I'm going to be your area specialist." Now, for the next 30 days, what is that agent going to be thinking about? *What the heck am I going to mail out next?* And every 30 days it's the same story. And it becomes so stressful, they stop. So, before you start, I want you to make sure you've got your pieces together. I'm going to give you some great ideas on this later. It's so easy, it's ridiculous. And, please, be certain to have the money before you start.

Developing Your Farm

There are six steps in developing and maintaining a farm from which you might regularly draw clients.

Step 1: Select Your Target Market

Here are some categories you might choose from.

A. Style of home. Tudors, colonials, capes, etc.

B. Uniqueness. Waterfront homes, two families, condos. You could say these are styles, but I call it "uniqueness" because when you're dealing with waterfront homes or legal two families or condos, there are whole other aspects of that property that you need to know about. With waterfront, you're dealing with the things like bulkheads and dredging; with legal multiple families, there's zoning and whether it pays for itself; with condos, there's the board; and so on.

C. Profession. You may have been in a profession before real estate. If you were a teacher, for instance, there's a possibility you could create a farm of just teachers. Or you might just choose to focus on doctors, for example.

D. Geography. It's possible that if you pick a style of home, that style may fall into a specific geographic location.

Step 2: Determine the Size

Whether you decide you're going to focus on geography, profession, style of home, etc., determine how many people you're ultimately going to have in this farm. I'm of the belief that you should not start farming unless you have at least 500 people, because farming is a pure numbers game. If you started with only 20 people in your farm, you might not get a lead for 20 years.

For you to determine the exact number for your farm, you should work it backwards. Figure how much money you can commit to your farm for a year, then divide it by 12 months. That's how much you can put toward your mailings each month. Then, simply figure the cost of printing and mailing for a few different quantities. This will tell you how many people you can have in your farm.

Step 3: Pick Your Location

Location tip #1: Choose a location within the influence or service area of your office. Why? Because your office is known there. Whenever I teach this, it never fails that I have agents whose office is in one town and who live in another and they want their farm to be where they live. Here's an extreme example to show why this doesn't work. Let's say your office is in Texas and you live in North Carolina. Now, does that mean your farm is in North Carolina? It doesn't make a lot of sense. The same concept is sound even if you look at towns. If the town that you live in is not where your office has influence, you're going to have an uphill battle.

Location tip #2: Pick a high-turnover area. For years I lived in a town called East Rockaway. It was the type of town where people are born, live, get married, and give birth. Then they grow old, die, and leave their house to their children. That means there is no turnover of property. It would have been easy to become the area celebrity because no one else was work-ing it, but there would have been nothing to be had. Instead, you should look in your MLS, find a printout of all the sold properties in a certain vicinity, and see if turnover is high.

Here's another thought. When a new subdivision is built, we know some things in general. In five to seven years, some people will move because that's life. In 10 to 12 years, some will move because they want a new home and theirs will need a roof, boiler etc. In 16-20 years, some will move because the kids are gone.

Location tip #3: Pick an area that doesn't have too much competi-tion. Remember Mac, my previous broker? Mac listed and sold about 80% of all the waterfront properties in our area. So, if you came to work in my neighborhood and you wanted to break into waterfront property, you'd be competing with Mac. Could you succeed and take the market away from him? Maybe. But it would be a real battle for you, because he had that cat-egory and that location locked up. Now, I understand that you might not be able to find an area that hasn't been locked up. But if you can, it's bet-ter than going head to head with a competitor. What if your office has so many agents and every agent has a farm in that market area, so there's nothing left for you? Well, then you may have to resort to the outer perimeters of the service area or to where you live.

Step #4: Get Computerized

In the old days, BC (before computers), we would tell you to put together a three-ring binder. But this is outdated. Can you imaging having a three-ring binder and an individual page for each person in a thousand-person farm? It'd be hard to manage all that paperwork. That's why getting computerized in today's real estate industry is no longer a luxury; it's a necessity. Before you get farming, you must have database software—such as Top Producer, which is specific to real estate. This software will enable you to effectively manage your farm. For instance, all of your letters can be customized— "Dear Stu" instead of "Dear Neighbor"—and an alarm can go off each month telling you when to mail what to your farm. You can point and click and your mailing is mostly done.

Step #5: Develop a Mailing List of Names

If your target market is geographic, it's pretty easy to develop your mailing list. You can probably download the information from your MLS. If your target market is a profession, you can buy this list from a mailing list service, such as Polk. To find more companies, look in the Yellow Pages under "mailing services." You can purchase a mailing list with many different criteria, such as income, occupation, number of children, etc.

Step #6: Mail Out Your Intro Letter

Here is a sample first mailing. Use this when you're ready to start working your farm consistently.

Dear Mr. and Mrs. _____:

My name is [your name], and I am the manager of [company and office name] right here in [your town]. It's my pleasure to let you know that [agent's name] is the new real estate marketing specialist for your area and [she/he] is qualified to help you and your family with all of your real estate needs.

[Agent] has been with our office for [years/months] and has an established track record of superior performance. [Her/His] customers and clients have praised [her/his] dedication, diligence, and ability to get the most money in the sale of their homes in the least amount of time with the minimum disruption to their family and life. [She/He] has earned various awards, including [list awards here].

There have been numerous changes in real estate regulations and policies since you bought your home, and [agent] continues to educate [herself/himself] to stay current and competitive. So, if you or any of your family members or friends have any thoughts about selling your home, you can be confident that [agent] will provide you with superior service in a professional manner.

You will be hearing from [agent] in the next few days to introduce [herself/himself] and offer [her/his] assistance if you have any questions about any real estate related manner. I also invite and encourage you to call me personally.

We look forward to the opportunity to serve your real estate needs.

Sincerely,

Broker/Manager's Name

Well, there you have it, the foundation for starting a farm. Now, I'm going to go through some tips on how to work your farm.

There are many great ways to do it, but I want you to keep it simple. You don't have to do all of these. As a matter of fact, if you just did one of them, your farm would work. The one I suggest you focus on is mailing out "just listed / just sold" fliers or letters. If you just mailed out "just listed / just sold" flyers once a month with a photo on each of these flyers and you did that consistently, that would be all you really needed to work your farm. But I'm going to give you a slew of ideas and if you want to do some other things to break up the monotony, you can.

Tips for Working Your Farm

1. **Mail "just listed/just sold" fliers.** You can do a series of letters. Here's one simple and very effective example. "Dear Mr. and Mrs. Martin, I just wanted to keep you up to date on what's been happening in your neighborhood." Show a chart of properties sold during the previous month and new houses listed for sale during this same period.

   This is great because all you have to do is send out one of these letters every time you list or sell something. You might also want to send this out on a monthly basis. You don't have to do any other fancy, schmancy mailings. Very simple!

   Now, hopefully, you're either listing or selling one property a month. If you're not, you can say, "Here are all the properties that have sold in your neighborhood from this date to this date." Does it say that *you* sold all those properties? No. But if your face is on the stationery, what does it suggest?

Here are samples of letters you can mail out each month:

Re: Another home sold by Darryl Davis

Dear [Name],

I am delighted to announce that I have sold the home located at:

5 Las Lomas Drive, Power City

We still have many qualified buyers looking to own a home in your neighborhood. If you are contemplating a move or know of someone who is, please contact us.

If you would like to find out if you qualify for a *FREE Over-the-Phone Market Analysis* on your home, simply call me at (631) 929-5555. There is no obligation.

Sincerely,

Darryl Davis

Farm Letter No. 1

Dear [Name[,

I thought you might like to know the following homes have sold in your subdivision.

2367 Powell Avenue

3099 Power Court

2479 Christopher Lane

If you would ever like your home SOLD instead of JUST LISTED, give me a call. I have a marketing program that works very well in getting homes sold in your neighborhood.

If you would like a FREE Over-the-Phone Market Analysis on your home, simply call me at (631) 929-5555. There is no obligation.

Sincerely,

Darryl Davis

P.S. If your home is currently listed for sale with another broker, this is not intended as a solicitation of that listing.

Farm Letter No. 2

Dear [Name],

I just wanted to keep you up to date as to what has been happening in your neighborhood.

Properties sold from January 1 to January 31:

2367 Powell Avenue

3099 Power Court

2479 Christopher Lane

New Houses listed for sale during January:

4568 Jennifer Way

2755 Easy Avenue

1379 Concord Lane

If you would ever like your home SOLD instead of JUST LISTED, give me a call. I have a proven marketing program for getting homes sold in your neighborhood.

If you would like a *FREE Over-the-Phone Market Analysis* on your home, simply call me at (631) 929-5555. There is no obligation.

Sincerely,

Darryl Davis

P.S. If your home is currently listed for sale with another broker, this is not intended as a solicitation of that listing.

Farm Letter No. 3

I've just made farming extremely easy for you. Each month, you could have your computer "spit out" these letters and all you would have to change is the property information. I would rotate among the types of letters each month. Quite frankly, if you didn't do anything else that I teach in the book from this point forward, you could still see some great results just from doing these letters (if you have at least 500 people in your farm).

2. Survey calls. After you've been doing mailings for a few months, you call everybody in your farm. Instead of saying, "Have you thought about selling or do you know anybody who is selling?" it would go like this:

Darryl: Hi, this is Darryl Davis from Power Realty. Oh, you've been getting my mailings? Great. The reason I'm calling is we're doing a survey. How long have you lived in the neighborhood? What do you like best about it? What do you think the most attractive feature is about the neighborhood?

Watch this one:

Darryl: If you were to think of moving, where would you move? Oh, when would you do that?

Homeowner: Oh, we were thinking about moving in maybe six months.

Darryl: Good thing I called when I did. If you were thinking about hiring an agent in the future, what would you be looking for in that agent?

Great technique! A different type of survey call would ask what changes they would like to see in their neighborhood. I know some agents who have had stop signs, lights, and speed bumps installed in a community because they asked for suggestions in the survey and residents responded. What a great way to get your picture in the paper, "saving the lives of our local children"!

3. **Find bird dogs.** That's a polite way of saying "nosy neighbors." There are certain nosy neighbors who listen to everybody and talk to everybody and would love to tell you about it. So these are good people who can find out for you if somebody is thinking of listing or selling. And, of course, if they give you several leads, you should consider giving them a thank-you gift.

4. **Sponsor a children's sports team.** You can work the crowd by showing up at the games and being in the stands, furnishing the refreshments that the parents normally furnish each game, and networking. Plus, you get your name on their uniform and an ad in the local paper that supports them. (Usually they put out a booklet for the organization.) Also, whether your team does well or not, you can mail a "Congratulations!" letter to all of the parents involved. They say the best way to a man's heart is through his stomach. I don't know how true that is, but what *is* true is the best way to parents' hearts is through their children.

5. **Car magnets.** When driving through your farm, have those suckers on. When you go to your supermarket, have them on. This is also true for open houses, previewing, showing, the children's sports games, etc. And don't forget about using unique vanity plates too.

6. **Deliver a buyer or seller seminar.** I have two tips for you about a buyer or seller seminar. One idea is you should not do it alone; you should do it with one or two other agents. The reason is that it's better to have others there working with you. Plus, when you combine your farm with other farms, it's more numbers for your mailing. The other tip is to have three or four guest speakers. Consider mortgage brokers, attor-

neys, home inspectors, remodeling companies, roofers, landscapers, title companies, movers, pest control people, and home food delivery businesses. Anyone who can help buyers or sellers to save money in any way. The guest speakers should pay a few dollars to help offset your promotional expenses. You should promote the seminar with an ad in the paper with their photos and their titles, so it's worth it to them. Now, if you have four guest speakers and each one talks for 15 minutes, that's an hour. You could lead into the session for 15 minutes and then conduct a 15-minute question-and-answer segment at the end. That's a one-and-a-half-hour seminar.

7. **Welcome new neighbors.** Here's how you welcome new neighbors:
   - **DINNER**. When people move in, they don't have the time or the food. You can bring dinner over or give them a coupon to a restaurant.
   - **A WELCOME PACKAGE.** Put together a package with a basket of cleaning stuff, light bulbs, change of address cards, and so on.
   - **A COMBINATION.** Along the same lines, you might buy an aluminum pan, pasta, sauce, cheese, so it's a welcome package … but it's dinner. All they have to do is cook it.

8. **Use mailings.** Remember, these are for cold mailings—people you've never done business with before. Mail once a month, the letters I mentioned earlier or any of the following:
   - **TESTIMONIALS.** You might send a letter to a prospect with a copy of a testimonial letter on the back. To get testimonials, you can call up your client who just closed on the house and say, "Debbie, can I ask you a question? Were you happy with my service? Great. And would you recommend me to other people? Would you mind doing me a favor? I'd like for you to write a short testimonial letter saying how great I am to work with and so on, because I'd like to mail it to the neighbors and let them know." The letter should begin with "Dear Neighbor" rather than "Dear Darryl." Then you take this letter and use it as a testimonial in a mailing.
   - **NOTE PADS.** Make sure you put your number on it to encourage people to call you for more when they run out.
   - **MAGNETS.** An oldie, but a goodie. You should see my refrigerator: *Power Program* students galore. I don't feel right throwing them out.
   - **ARTICLES.** For example, if you're specializing in waterfront property and you see an article on boating, cut it out and send it to everybody. Or if you're specializing in colonials and Tudors and you see some-

thing about these types of homes, clip it and send it out. Also, if you see anyone in your farm in the papers (local or otherwise) for some accomplishment (making the dean's list, winning a trophy, or whatever), with a photo, make copies of the article and send it as a warm congratulation to that person's family (in your farm). Send it to the whole farm so they know that "one of their own" made good.

- **A NEIGHBORHOOD DIRECTORY.** To generate a sense of community, create a directory of all the neighbors and what their jobs are. Call people in your farm telling them you're putting together a directory of the neighborhood and everyone's profession, so whenever residents need a particular service, they can keep the business in the neighborhood. Then ask them if they would like to be listed in this directory. Of course, make sure you include yourself and be very visible. If your farm is geographic, this is a great one.

- **CALENDARS.** You can buy the yearly calendar, but one of my student *Power Groups* came up with the idea to do monthly calendars. It's a foldout piece with a month on one side. Every month, they mail out this calendar. That's one way to make sure you stick to a schedule! What's awesome about this is you could have your whole year's worth of mailings already printed and give them to a mailing house to mail out for you. You now are mailing to your farm once a month consistently and you only had to set it up once for the whole year.

- **SEEDS.** I know these top producers who mail out seeds with a slogan, "Come grow with me."

- **POST-IT® NOTES.** You can have Post-it® notes made up with your company name and logo.

- **PENS.** Another oldie, but a goodie.

- **BROCHURES.** Make sure these are written and designed professionally.

- **THE CMA MAILING.** Instead of the traditional comparative market analysis, there are a couple of unique things you can do.

- **ADD ON THE CMA, "SEE IF YOU QUALIFY FOR A FREE MARKET ANALYSIS."** The qualification is whether the homeowners are selling in six months or less; otherwise, prices would change dramatically and not be worth their time. This approach creates perceived value, as it's not giving away something for free.

- **OFFER A "FREE OVER-THE-PHONE MARKET ANALYSIS,"** which I covered in great detail in the Chapter 2, "The Art of Prospecting." My students get tons of listings because of this. If people know they don't have to sit through a long-winded sales pitch, they'll be more apt to call you. So it makes the phone ring. Remember, the trick is to make sure you tell them a wide range—"based on this information, I would estimate that your house is worth between $300K and $350K." The only way to narrow it down is to physically see their house, which inevitably would turn into a listing conversation.

- **USE THE LINE, "YOU'D BE AMAZED AT HOW MUCH YOUR HOME IS WORTH!"** It's a simple line, but very effective. Of course, use this in a hot market only!

Seven Tips for Effective Mailings

1. **Do shared-cost mailings.** Take a business related to real estate—gardeners, plumbers, electricians, painters—services that homeowners would order directly. With your mailing, you do an insert for that company. It could be a flyer with a little P.S. that says, "This is someone I know that I recommend to you," and their business card. Of course, you ask the business to share some of the cost; that's why it's called a shared-cost mailing.

2. **Package stuffers.** These are the value-pack cards, such as the "entertainment book," filled with businesses offering "buy one, get one free" deals. Direct mail experts have proven that these work. Most businesses would be happy to let you put one of their coupons in your mailing and would even be happy to pay for a small portion of the cost.

3. **Personalized envelopes.** A student of mine started a farm and in just one year she generated $4,000,000 in sales with fewer than 500 families in this farm. How did she do this? She used personal envelopes and stationery, not company envelopes or company stationery, and she addressed each envelope by hand. (Her letters were typed.) That's what I call the personal touch.

4. **Use real stamps, not Pitney Bowes stamps.** Pitney Bowes is metered. A metered symbol on the envelope suggests junk mail. Real stamps work better. And you can even get real stamps that are for bulk mailings.

5. **Put teasers on the envelope.** For example, "Free Offer," "Act Now," "Announcing…," "Refrigerate after Opening" for something they'll keep on the fridge, "Dated Material Inside." These are all little enticements for the prospect to open the envelope.

6. Different sizes of envelopes. Instead of mailing in a regular business envelope, you may want to consider an odd size every few months.

7. Use mailing houses. You give them the pieces and the envelopes, and they stuff, seal, and send them for you.

"Eventful" Ideas

Let me give you a few ideas about possible events. Of course, you don't have to do *all* of these. However, anything you can do to motivate your farm will make a difference.

Holiday mailings or giveaways. For many of the following tips (particularly Easter, Halloween, Thanksgiving, and Christmas), consider getting media involvement. Let the local paper know what you're doing; maybe radio or TV stations would be interested. Also, be sure to take photos (digital is preferred) and send or e-mail them to the media ... and to participants. Always have your logo sign as a backdrop for the photos with the year prominently displayed. This way, you can do it each year and it becomes a natural for your scrapbook.

On *Valentine's Day* you could give away chocolate roses. For *St. Patrick's Day* you could do some kind of pin.

For *Easter* consider an Easter egg hunt for your farm. Here's how you can do this. Do a mailing to your farm and say, "We're having an Easter egg hunt. If you're interested in participating, just come to my office on this day and pick up your Easter egg." The families come to your office and pick up these plastic Easter eggs that are empty. Then you'd tell the families to get some jellybeans or other candy and fill these empty eggs. And Easter morning, all of the fathers come to this empty field and plant the eggs. Then, in the afternoon, all of the mothers and children come and hunt for the eggs. It's a great idea because all you're doing is providing plastic Easter eggs. Now, if you want to fill them yourself, that's fine, but it's all about getting the people involved. Get them to contribute the candy. Get them to plant the eggs. And, if you've got 500 people in your farm but only 50 families show up in the fields, it still works, and you've mailed out to the 500 people in your farm to keep your name in front of them.

For *Mother's Day* you can do something with flowers, seeds, forget-me-nots, etc.

On the *Fourth of July* you could have flags on the lawn. But beware: don't do what one of my students did. She put out nearly 1,000 flags and a lot of people called to complain because on the flags it said "Made in Taiwan."

For *Labor Day* you can do back-to-school coupons. Go to local vendors, tell them you're doing this big mailing, and ask if they would like to participate by providing a 10% off coupon. Visit stationery stores, clothing stores, dry cleaners, and so on.

On *Halloween* you could do a contest for the kid who draws the best pumpkin or cuts out the best face. Or you might mail a coupon out to your whole farm to come pick up a free pumpkin at your office, from a huge tractor of pumpkins in your parking lot. In addition, instead of just giving out loose candy, you could place it in a bag that has your company information on it. This is a great idea because Halloween is the only time of year your farm comes to you. Check out Amsterdam Printing in Amsterdam, NY (800 833-6231, www.amsterdamprinting.com). At the time I wrote this book, you could order Halloween bags customized with your company information.

For *Thanksgiving* you can do a raffle for a turkey or something, but I think it's nice to do a food drive for families that don't have food.

Around *Christmas* you can participate in the "Toys for Tots" program. You call the U.S. Marine Corps or the local "Toys for Tots" coordinator (www.toysfortots.org) and have your office designated as a location for dropping off toys for disadvantaged kids.

■ ■ ■

That's it for farming. I really hope that you got some ideas and expanded your thinking on how to work your farm. If there's only one thing that has really sunk into your mind, it should be to focus on creating a systematic approach to identifying and staying in touch with your farm. Plant the seeds now and water them regularly. You'll be pleased with how your business grows.

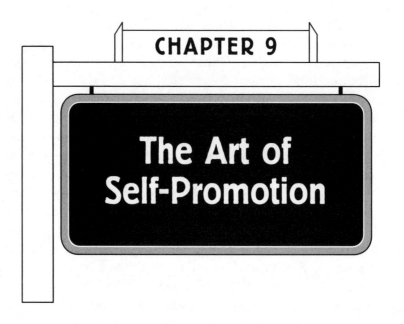

CHAPTER 9

The Art of Self-Promotion

Power Fact

Your office will give you certain building blocks to get you started—a phone, some important policies and procedures, maybe a bit of advertising. But it's up to you to build your business and take your career to the Next Level.

Overview

Throughout this book, we've discussed the skills you need to build your career and become good at what you do—such as listing presentations, prospecting, working with buyers, etc. If you're truly a "business within a business" in your office (I'll explain this concept in just a moment), then as a business you need to focus on managing yourself effectively. This includes servicing your client base and farming. It also means that you must focus on self-promotion.

As you read this chapter, consider what you can do to distinguish yourself from all the other agents out there. You may be doing some self-promotion now. If so, read this chapter with an awareness of how effective your current efforts are and be open to the possibilities of taking your self-promotion to the Next Level.

One last thought. In Chapter 8, "Farming for Dollars," we covered a *lot* of items that could apply to self-promotion. So I encourage you to reread that chapter after you finish this one and look to pull ideas from both in your promotional efforts.

Eight Essential Concepts of Self-Promotion

1. **You are a business within a business.** Here's what I mean. There's your company and then there's you. The company structure is similar to the McDonald's Corporation, for instance, compared with an individual McDonald's restaurant. The franchiser, McDonald's, provides the franchisee with the name, national advertising, training on procedures and policies, and a manual on how to run the business. It's up to the franchisee to generate revenue, to staff, to do local advertising. In the same way, your company office provides you with an infrastructure and history to boost credibility, an office, a phone, and perhaps some advertising to back up the name, but it's up to you to build the sales, to generate the revenue, to promote yourself, to create supportive business relationships, and, in some cases, to hire people to work for you, such as an assistant. The bottom line is, you are responsible for your career—so start thinking of yourself less as a salesperson and more as a businessperson.

2. **Your objective should be to become a local celebrity.** In the farming chapter, I said that being a celebrity means that people in a specific area know your face, your name, and what you do for a living. Again, this area doesn't have to be based on geography; it could be style of home, waterfront property, clubs, organizations, etc. What are you doing to stand out from every other agent out there?

3. **You must be the center of your marketing.** *You* should be the focus of your self-promotion, but at the same time, don't diminish your company. Does your company have a lot of area clout? Is your broker spending money to promote the office? You want to ride the coattails of those efforts. With this in mind, an effective promotional piece or ad should have the company colors, logo, and name and might have big lettering of your name along with your photo.

4. **You need to be unique.** In show business lingo, you've got to have a gimmick or a hook. The same concept is true in sales and real estate. What makes you unique and different? You might embody this in your logo and slogan, as we will discuss later in this chapter.

5. **Think** *perceived value.* When I got into speaking many years ago, I knew I had to have a brochure. So I spent $3,000 for 1,000 brochures; that's $3 apiece. Full color, several photos—it was gorgeous. If you looked at it, you would have thought, "This guy's been around for a while." But that was the first thing I came up with and that was the only thing I had. I didn't have demo tapes or a video; I didn't have cassette programs. As a matter of fact, I hadn't even delivered a seminar yet. But that brochure was my foot in the door to some major companies and the efforts paid off.

   I've promoted a lot of things in my life, and what I've learned is this concept of *perceived value*: people have to *think* you're very successful. You may not be yet, but you have to send out that image. It's better to have one expensive-looking brochure than five shoddy ones.

   Here's another example. I know an agent in Texas who got into the business about 10 years ago. When she started, she had no listings, but she knew that listings were important to a new agent. So, she went to everyone in her office and asked, "Would you like me to advertise your listings for you?" They'd say, "Sure, less money out of my pocket." Then, she'd take out a full-page ad in the local newspaper every week with her name, so in advertising the listings she was promoting herself. So everybody reading the ads said, "Wow! She must be a great agent because everybody is hiring her." And that's how she got all her business, just by doing that. She closed over $2,000,000 worth of real estate in her first year, back in 1993. Not bad, right? That's the power of perceived value.

6. **Expect to wait one year for results.** All your marketing and promotional efforts—slogans, logos, ads, fliers, etc.—need time to sink into the public's mind. It might take up to a year. That's why you should first master the basics, like prospecting. Prospecting is a short-term method of creating inventory and it requires many hours of direct effort. Self-promotion takes fewer hours of direct effort, yet provides phenomenal results in the long run. The next point ties into this.

7. **The key to success is repetition.** If you are going to start doing some kind of self-promotion campaign, you've got to stick with it. You need to be consistent and persistent to make it work. Remember that your goal is to be the first agent to come to mind when people in your service area think of real estate in any way. You want to be their resource, which means that they must see your name and face so often that they think of you when they see or hear anything real estate-related.

Let's play a game now. I'll ask you about the first thoughts that come to your mind as you read the next few lines. Ready?

"Golden Arches."

Did you think McDonald's? I'll bet most people would. Let's try another one.

"Things go better with _____."

Did you say Coke?

The point is that you know these names and products because you've seen them over and over for years. The good news is that you don't have to market to the entire world like these companies, just to the people in your immediate service area.

8. **Focus on building a client base.** If you do your job to build your client base—prospecting, servicing listings, etc.—and you're getting *great* testimonials for the work you did, within five years you should be in a position where your "machine" (the procedures and systems you put in place to work for you) will provide you with 80% of your income or more. That's having eight out of 10 closings provided by "low direct effort" activities like farming and self-promotion. Nice!

Preparing for a Self-Promotion Campaign

Here are some techniques for preparing your self-promotion campaign.

- **ESTABLISH A TARGET MARKET.** Just as we discussed in our chapter on farming, you need to determine who you want to attract and why. What's the market that you want to become a local celebrity in? For example, it could be based on geography, price range, style of home, etc.

- **IDENTIFY YOUR MARKET POSITION.** Your market position is what makes you different from other agents. Your market position could be the type of houses you work or, if you're a top agent, your level of production. (Later in this chapter, I'll provide a detailed exercise to help you distinguish your market position.)

- **CREATE A LOGO AND A SLOGAN.** (Don't do this until you are clear about your market position!) For instance, if you focus on land development, you can have a photo of you standing in an open field, with a slogan that says, "Howard Realtor—Outstanding in His Field." There are companies that will do this for you. (I suggest You, Inc., Provo, UT, 888 233-5554.) Or you can sit down with some other agents and brainstorm. (More on slogans later in this chapter.)

■ **LOOK FOR AN AREA THAT HASN'T BEEN SATURATED, IF POSSIBLE.** Remember my previous broker, Mac, who focused on waterfront properties? If you tried to get into waterfront properties in the towns he was in, you'd have an uphill battle because he had it locked up. So you want to look for an area that hasn't been exploited.

■ **IDENTIFY YOUR COMPETITION'S STRENGTHS AND WEAKNESS.** When you're in a listing presentation, your competitors may come up in the conversation, so it's good to know their strengths and weaknesses. If you look at their strengths, it may give you some ideas that you can emulate and some tips on what to avoid. Consider these questions for each competitor. What's his reputation in the community? What's her reputation with other agents? What's his current inventory? What's her marketing presence? What kind of advertising promotion does he use? Does she have a logo? Does he use fliers? And so on (see Figure 9-1).

■ **DESIGN A MARKETING PLAN.** Make sure you *avoid* the "*shotgun approach.*" In other words, have a master plan before you start. Some agents do things on the spur of the moment, without any overall plan.

For instance, you might go to a seminar and hear about an idea like a double-eraser pencil. "Isn't that a neat idea?" you think. So, you buy these pencils and you put a slogan on them: "Don't make any mistakes—buy your home from Darryl Davis." Then, you mail these pencils to a bunch of people. A couple of months later, you put an ad in a real estate magazine. Then you mail out some packets of seeds with "Come grow with me" printed on them. And you sit back and see what works. But there's no cohesive "branding" message. No system. No clear sense of what comes next.

With the shotgun approach, you try an idea that excites you … and then you switch tactics with another idea … and then another … and so on. Don't keep changing your message, because *repetition and consistency are the keys to success in self-promotion.*

So, I suggest that you read this next section, get some good ideas, set aside the money, and prepare the pieces to promote yourself. Have these pieces ready to go in your office. And carefully target who you are trying to reach and when. I've included a simple chart to help you plan out your promotional campaign (see Figure 9-2).

■ **GET A PROFESSIONAL PHOTO.** This is very important. Make sure it's not one of those glamour shot photos; it should look like you. Once

Competition Analysis

Agent _____ Company _____

Address _____ Office Phone _____

City _____ Age _____

Years of Experience _____ Yearly Volume _____ Credentials _____

Farm Area_____ Years in Farm _____ # of Houses _____

Current # of Listings _____ # of Yard Signs _____

Reputation in Community _____

Reputation with Other Agents _____

Personality Type _____ Specialty _____

Assistants _____

	POOR	FAIR	GOOD	EXCELLENT
Institutional Advertising				
Classified Advertising				
Direct Mail				
Cable Television				
Listing Expired Listings				
Listing FSBOs				
Agent Referrals				
	YES	**NO**		
Uses Personal Brochures				
Video Brochure				
Uses Flyers				
Just Listed/Sold Postcards				
Promotional Postcards				
Promotional Give-A-Ways				
Has a Slogan				
Has a Logo				
Bus Bench Advertising				
Prices List Accurately				
Listings Frequently Expire				
Advertising Is Creative				

Figure 9-1. Form for competition analysis

you've done this, you'll want to start to incorporate it in as much of your promotional materials as possible. Also, it's not expensive at all to get your own personalized stationery.

ACTIVITY	JAN	FEB	MAR	APR	MAY	JUN	JUL	AUG	SEP	OCT	NOV	DEC

Figure 9-2. Self-Promotion Campaign Chart

- **SAVE MONEY BEFORE YOU START PROMOTING.** You should open separate bank accounts and start funding your promotional efforts *now*. Have money for at least six months of promotion before you begin. Studies show that people must see your message five to six times before they'll remember it. Repetition is the key and you need the funds to go the distance.

Identifying Your Market Position

The following is designed to help you come up with your unique market position. I encourage you to write down your answers.

- **WHAT IS MY MISSION STATEMENT?** I think it's really useful to have a mission statement that declares what you're about in the area of real estate. A mission statement is usually one or two sentences that sum up your business strategy.

   I did some training for other sales industries a few years ago and we did research on the Disney Corporation. Disney's mission statement is: *To provide the finest entertainment to people of all ages everywhere.*

   Now, wouldn't you agree that that's what Disney does?

   So, consider what you are committed to in the area of real estate. What is your mission statement? What one or two sentences sum up your business strategy in real estate? Now, your office might have a mission statement. But whether it does or doesn't, you should create your personal mission statement. This will give your business some focus and you could also use it in your promotional materials to let buyers and sellers know what you are committed to.

_____

_____

■ **WHAT ARE MY VALUES?** Values are what make up the characteristics of your business. They represent the rules of the game that you will always play by, no matter what, and your actions will reflect these values.

For example, Disney's values include *fun, integrity, service, patriotism, and conservation*. To support this last value, Disney has its own horticulture farm. All of the trees and plants on Disney's property are grown in a special part of the park, so they don't have to be shipped in. This way, they're not cutting down trees, they're creating their own. Another way they conserve is that they have an aqueduct system. If there's a part of the park where the water table is low, the water from another part of the park gets channeled to the part that's low so that it balances out. All of this really shows their commitment to conservation.

So, what are *your* values in the area of real estate?

_____

_____

■ **WHAT ARE MY CREDENTIALS AND ACCOMPLISHMENTS?** Take a look at your production and major accomplishments. What have you done in real estate, in life? Write it down now—all your degrees, certificates, training, experience, and volunteer work. Are you a parent, grandparent, etc.? Perhaps you've won awards in competition or you hold certifications in other industries. List them all.

_____

_____

■ **WHO IS MY TARGET AUDIENCE?** Again, choose your focus: geography, price range, ethnic groups, investors, special type of home, style of home, etc.

_____

_____

■ **WHO ARE MY AFFILIATE CO-SPONSORS?** These are other companies and individuals in our industry that you do business with. They are usually the businesses that directly support you in your effort to list and sell real estate. You should have at least one mortgage company, one title company, one legal person, one termite company, etc. (We delve into this, in a slightly different context, in Chapter 11, "Building a Referral Business.") You recommend business to them and they recommend business to you. And, whenever you want to do some kind of promotion—whether it be a seller seminar, an ad highlighting all of your listings or open houses, or a direct mail piece—they invest some money to help offset your costs. In return, you provide exposure for their name and logo.

Immediate Steps to Start Your Self-Promotion Campaign

Here's how to get started now on your self-promotion campaign.

Slogans

Slogans are easily remembered and help you stand out from the crowd. You use a slogan as a way to help people remember you and the fact that you are in real estate. A slogan can tie into your identity—for instance, it could rhyme with your name—or it can talk about the types of homes you specialize in, the kind of service you deliver, etc. Here are some examples from my *Power Agents:*

- Dan the Real Estate Man
- Bob Shield—The Realtor Who Protects Your Interests
- Gaylin King the Condo King
- Claudia Caesar, "The Classic Realtor"
- John Diamond—The Quality Is in the Name
- Ben Munoz—Call Big Ben for the Right Time in Real Estate
- Lisa Gold: Everything I Touch Turns to Sold
- The Equestrian Specialist

Keep in mind that slogans don't *have* to tie into your name. It can be catchy if it rhymes and it's worth considering. But something catchy about your target market could be just as memorable.

Logos

A logo is a visual key that prompts people to remember you by associating your name and image with an icon. It should incorporate your name and slogan. The golden arches of McDonald's, the hands of Allstate, and the swoosh of Nike are logos familiar to most of us. A logo will add that important element of distinction. Have it designed professionally, because it will stay with you for a long time. A piece of clip art will just look cheap. Here are a few samples:

Figure 9-3. Sample logos

Here are some more expensive designs that combine the logo and the agent:

Figure 9-4. Examples of logos with photographs

Figure 9-5. More examples of logos with photographs

Eight Specific Tips on Self-Promotion

Now, let's take a look at a variety of promotional ideas.

1. **Put your photo on everything.** Earlier, I told you to get your photo taken. What if you don't feel you're very attractive? Get over it. People like the personal touch, and your photo is as personal as it gets. Most important, having a face to attach with a name increases your recognition. And people are less likely to throw away a photo business card than one without a picture.

2. **Always use a call to action.** Your advertising has got to have a call to action. "Call now." "Send for a free…." "Call today for your free CMA." "Call now for a free video on how to sell your home." You get the idea.

3. **Always invest 10%-20% of your income back in self-promotion.** You've got to keep doing that to have the money continue to come in.

4. **Use your area code on all of your printed materials.** It's a little thing, but it makes a big difference—especially if people take a flier or cut your ad out of the paper in a region away from their home.

5. **Don't use 10 phone numbers in your ads and printed materials.** Phone, fax, and toll-free should be sufficient. I strongly recommend getting a toll-free number, if you don't already have one. Toll-free numbers are inexpensive and create perceived value.

6. **Use follow-up mailings.** Plan these in advance. For instance, if you did a mailing of a magnet, you could follow up with something else and

say, "Last month I sent you a magnet. I hope you received it." The point is to make reference to the previous mailing.

7. **Use a lot of white space.** In all your printed materials and your ads, don't get too wordy. Allow sufficient empty space around words and images. Whether the background color is white, blue, or red, you need to avoid clutter.

8. **Work with affiliates.** Remember, these are the businesses that will help to underwrite your costs, send you business (just like you do for them), and support you. Lenders, attorneys, title companies—work with all of those people, as we discussed earlier.

16 Powerful Marketing Tools

- BUSINESS CARDS. Make sure you put your photo on your business card. And, as recommended just above for ads, if you have 10 phone numbers on your business card, take most of them off. You should have only the office number, the fax number, a toll-free number, and maybe a pager number. Just don't put your home number on your card. If you like to give the impression that you're available, here's a better approach.

    Let's say that you're handing out your card to an interested buyer. You would say, "So, you like this house and you want to think about it overnight? My major concern about you sitting on this thing is that somebody could be buying it as we speak. You know what I'll do? In case you should decide tonight, I'm going to give you my home number. Please don't give this out, because I don't give it to everybody. But you should feel free to call me tonight." That works a lot better than printing it on the card. And it makes the buyer feel special.

- **"JUST LISTED/JUST SOLD" POSTCARDS.** We discussed letters announcing this information in our farming chapter. There are advantages to postcards, however. They're cheap, easy to handle, and good for mass mailings. You might use postcards as a change of pace from your other mailings.

- NEWSLETTER. I think the best type of newsletter is something specific to that area. Give quick tips and information relevant to that particular market—whether it's about certain home styles, waterfront property, condos, etc.—whatever you selected as your target market. Above all, make sure your newsletter is worth reading. (There's more on newsletters in Chapter 11, "Building a Referral Business.")

- **FLIERS.** I think fliers are awesome. They are very inexpensive to put together. They can be used for "just listed / just sold," neighborhood updates, special announcements, mini-brochures, résumés, open house invitations. Use a lot of pictures and graphics and stay away from dull, wordy formats.

- **PERSONAL STATIONERY.** This is necessary if you're going to focus on self-promotion. Your photo should be on everything—letterhead, envelopes, thank-you cards—along with your logo and slogan. I think it makes you look a little more professional. Consider purchasing a color printer and producing stationery in-house. With today's prices, this is very affordable.

- **SEMINARS.** Organize and promote how-to seminars for buyers and sellers. Your affiliate co-sponsors—lenders, title companies, lawyers, etc.—help you to promote it and share in the cost. It also may be a good idea to have two or three other agents in your office work with you in getting people to attend. Don't do a seller seminar on your own: it's just too much to manage. By doing it together, you promote each other's farms and share in the leads that come out of it.

- **PRESS RELEASES.** This can lead to great publicity, if you are successful. Some newspapers are looking for newsworthy stuff to print. Consider releases for any courses you've completed, events you've hosted, charitable causes you support, neighborhood events, etc. Some of the events we noted at the end of Chapter 8 are perfect candidates for press releases.

- **VIDEO AND CD BROCHURES.** Video and CD brochures are great. They're high-tech and they're also—what?—expensive. But I'll tell you, once you make that initial investment, you'll make it back over and over again. Once more, we're trying to boost our perceived value.

- **INSTITUTIONAL ADVERTISING.** Magazines such as *Harmon Homes* or *The Real Estate Book* are great vehicles.

- **BUS BENCHES AND BILLBOARDS.** These can be expensive and usually charge by the month. However, some agents across the country have used these as a means of self-promotion with great success. It depends on your market.

- **TELEVISION AND RADIO.** You could use the electronic media, but only if it targets the audience you want to reach. I know some agents who advertise on local cable channels and others who have their own talk shows. When you're on TV, you automatically become a celebrity. You may want to look at it, just for the hay of it.

  One word about this. You may be thinking, "I made only X dollars last year. I'm not ready for prime time." So you won't even look into the possibility of TV, for example, because you're too insecure about it.

  But just think. What does it take to call your local cable company, find out what it would cost to have a half hour of airtime, and then, based on that price, get a sponsor? Besides, in many markets the cable company is required by law to give free airtime. Now, you have your name behind a show and you do interviews … and you charge your guests to get on the show. So, instead of just getting listings, you have a television program and you're now perceived as an expert.

- **NEWSPAPER COLUMNS.** This is a great way to show people in your community that you're an expert. The challenge is to sell an editor on the need for such a column. Or you can simply pay for it like an ad but it would look like a regular column. This is called an *advertorial*. Instead of putting together an ad showing your homes, you write an article on, say, auctions. When people see your face next to the article each month or week, they perceive you as an expert and think that the newspaper has you as one of their contributing writers.

- **"FOR SALE" SIGNS.** You're obviously aware of how important "For Sale" signs are in marketing a home, but if you're going to promote yourself, you need to have a rider with your name and photo on it. I think that's an important thing to do—and they're not very expensive.

- **MOVIE THEATERS.** Can you imagine people sitting in your local movie theater watching previews and then commercials come on for Coke, Tom Cruise, … and *you*! It's great. If you decide to do a video brochure, you can take that and make a 30-second commercial from it. So, now it's cost-effective because you get two things done at once. This also may be less expensive than you think. Make some calls and do the research.

  I caution you here just to be careful with big-ticket items. Make sure that you've put enough money aside. You shouldn't write the check if having your promotion fail means you couldn't pay some of your bills. But if you have money put aside, it's an investment—it either works or it doesn't.

- **PERSONAL LICENSE PLATES.** Vanity plates are a good way to get noticed. What about "REALEST8" or "ISELLHOMES"? Plates will make you stand out from the crowd and easily identify your profession to hundreds of people each day.

- **GIVEAWAYS.** Giveaways are advertising premiums. You can do a mailing of seeds and plants imprinted with the slogan, "Come grow with me," or a highlighter with "Let me highlight how to get your house sold." Isn't that a cool mailing piece? A double-eraser pencil with "Make no mistakes in selling your house—hire Darryl Davis." A coffee mug that says, "Let's see if we can brew up some buyers for your house." Other giveaway ideas include pens, yardsticks, calendars, to-do pads, customized chocolates, magnets, etc.

Keep in mind, though, what I told you earlier in this chapter: you *must* have a marketing plan *before* you implement any idea. You don't want to send out a bunch of different promotional items that don't coordinate and wind up confusing people. Make sure your mailings and giveaways reflect a consistent branding message.

■　■　■

I hope you found this buffet of ideas useful. You now have the foundation for a powerful self-promotion campaign. I want to conclude this chapter by reiterating two things.

First, make sure you have money put aside before you begin your promotional efforts. Don't dip into the monies you need to run your personal life and the day-to-day business of real estate. Every time you get a commission check, earmark a certain portion for self-promotion and deposit it in a separate bank account. That way, when you do self-promotion, you tap into that money. And if it doesn't pay off, it doesn't feel like a loss because you still have the money to run your business and personal life.

The second point I want to stress is that you should plan a full 12-month self-promotion campaign. Look at what kind of promotion you're going to do during the next year and map it out. Be systematic. Make a plan and stick with it. Your persistence will pay off.

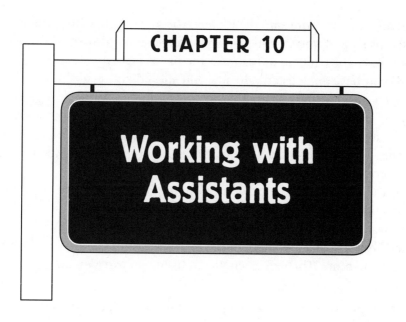

CHAPTER 10

Working with Assistants

Power Fact

Having an assistant requires that you think "outside of the box." You have to dream big. You have to recognize that by having someone else handle the more mundane tasks of your job, you will be freed up to focus on what you do best—sales. In the long run, that can only make you money.

Overview

This topic could be a book by itself. So my focus here will simply be on the beginning stages of finding, hiring, and getting an assistant up and running. The purpose for hiring an assistant is to have someone else do the low-priority activities or hourly wage work to allow you the freedom to do income-generating activities. The key is to make sure that for every hour your assistant is working you are generating more money than you are paying him or her. The differential between what you pay your assistant and what you are earning is the profit your assistant provides.

You can divide the concept of working with assistants into two basic categories. The first would be finding an assistant, training him or her, developing the job description, etc.—in other words, the foundation of working with an assistant. The second category would be the Next Level of working with an assistant. For example, if you've been working with an assistant for a year or so and you've gotten into a groove, what do you do to enhance this? I have chosen here to focus on the first category.

If you have an assistant already, you should still read this chapter with an open mind to the possibilities for increasing the value and profitability of your assistant. And for those agents who can't envision themselves ever getting an assistant, I want you to be open to the possibility that, regardless of what level of income you enjoy, an assistant might be a way to increase your productivity and help you become a top producer.

Let's begin with the job description, to give you the general concept of what an assistant can do. Every time I share something that an assistant can do, I want you to think, "Wow, that's something I don't have to do anymore!" And consider whether or not it would benefit you if you didn't have to do it anymore. The main benefits of hiring an assistant are:

- To increase productivity.
- To free you up so you have more personal time, more family time.
- To keep you on track and focused.
- To improve your attitude and self-esteem.
- To increase income.

One final point: What's the main thing stopping you from hiring an assistant? *Money.* I want you to consider that you don't have to wait to get a lot of money to pay for an assistant. Later in this chapter, I'm going to give you some suggestions for hiring an assistant in a way that it really won't cost you that much. In some cases, you can do it and it won't cost you anything.

What an Assistant Can Do

An assistant can do a number of things that will help you succeed in your business. Here are just a few:

1. **Prepare fliers, fact sheets, and other materials.**

2. **Take photos and handle keys.** You list a property and the assistant can go out and do all the "scut work" associated with this.

3. **Manage the signs.**

4. **Prepare buyer financial sheets.**

5. **Help coordinate brokers' open houses for you.** Your assistant can help you with the food, the opinion sheets, etc. (There's a whole description of this in Chapter 5.) I wouldn't have this person *staff* the

open house; rather, the assistant can be a "facilitator" or "liaison" to make the event flow more smoothly. This would allow you to do what you do best, which is work with the "A" clients. It's important that you use the brokers' open houses as an opportunity to press the flesh and do some public relations and be available for the serious buyers while your assistant handles the "routine" questions, etc.

6. **Manage public open houses.** The assistant can do all the behind-the-scenes preparation, greet people at the door, increase your perceived value, and help you manage the open house.

7. **Write your ads and call them in.** This is especially true if you use my idea of the ad book, covered in Chapter 1. Once you have a great book of ads, your assistant will be able to choose the right one for your new listings, so all you do is approve or reject the ad, saving you time that you can use to generate additional income.

8. **Mail "just listed/just sold" material.** You know deep down you're probably not servicing your farm too well. One of our *Power Program* students used techniques we taught him to start a new mailing campaign and generated 55 leads in one month. However, he was a couple of weeks late following up with these 55 leads, which cost him dearly. An assistant would have freed him up so he could contact these people. Many of us hesitate to hire an assistant because we don't have the money, yet we may be losing a lot of money by not hiring one.

9. **Communicate with your sellers, sharing news, updates etc.** Your assistant is your voice. If somebody shows your listing, the assistant can call and share the results and stay in communication.

10. **Mail, fax, or e-mail the agent's survey.** In Chapter 5, we discussed the agent's survey postcard and the feedback fax. You probably aren't utilizing these techniques to increase your income. Why? Because every time an agent shows one of your listings, you don't have the time to send a letter and one of the cards. Well, your assistant could do that.

11. **Schedule all of your appointments—buyer appointments, seller appointments, etc.**

12. **Input the listings into MLS.**

13. **Do a printout of new and expired listings.** Your office secretary may be doing that now. In my office, it wasn't always done. An assistant could print out all the listings and all the expireds each morning and

put it on your desk. This way, you can see what's happening in the market and follow up on the expireds. You want to call expireds immediately or someone else will be in there.

14. **Cut out the FSBOs for you. Each morning, a pile of these is on your desk.**

15. **Prepare CMAs for all your listing presentations.**

16. **Service your client base.** Your assistant can do the quarterly or every-other-month mailings, he or she can do calls to keep in contact, etc.

17. **Manage mailings to your farm.**

18. **Coach the sellers on preparing the property.** You go over, do the listing presentation, and leave with the listing agreement. The assistant comes by in a couple of days, drops off the sign, picks up the key, does a tour of the property, and gives the sellers some coaching from a civilian's point of view on things they can do to enhance the look of the home.

19. **Monitor your inventory of supplies** and allow you the comfort of knowing you'll never run out of something you need.

20. **Maintain buyer and seller packages** so you'll never be running around at the last minute, late for an appointment, trying to put a packet together. Imagine that! Just pick up your packet and go.

21. **If licensed, the assistant can do many of the tasks that you do yourself** but don't directly contribute to increasing your income, such as meeting appraisers, going to the home inspections, and going to a closing, if you have multiple closings at the same time. (Please check your state laws and the rules of your real estate organizations to learn how a licensed assistant can help you, so you can decide which type of assistant would be best for you.)

22. **Watch out for your own expireds.** If any of your listings are about to expire, the assistant can red flag them for you.

23. **Be in charge of "keeping you organized."** The assistant can remind you about appointments and commitments, remind you to prospect, and keep you focused on attaining your Next Level.

24. **Answer the phone, too.** That has a few great benefits: to screen calls so you don't have to waste time answering basic questions (dates, times, general information); to provide a warm and friendly voice when your prospects, clients, and customers call; to dramatically increase your per-

ceived value. Be honest now. Aren't you impressed when you call an agent's direct line and get her or his assistant on the phone? Wouldn't it be great if other people were that impressed by your assistant?

How to Pay an Assistant

In my opinion, the best way to pay an assistant is with a low base and an override. Here's how an override might work. If you look at your production for the last six months, you may see that you average so many listings and so many sales per month. Let's say you average one sale and two listings per month; the override is for anything over that. If you average two listings, on the third listing he or she gets $100, on the fourth he or she gets another $100, and so on. For any sale that you get over your normal one per month, the assistant could get a percentage of your selling-side commission. So, if the sale was $200,000 and the total sales-side commission was 3% and you're on a 50/50 split, your take would be $3,000. Your assistant could be paid 5% or 10% of your $3,000. A question that comes up: "Can you pay an assistant a percentage if he or she is not licensed?" To the best of my knowledge, yes, you can. But check with your broker or, better yet, get it from the horse's mouth, your Department of Licensing.

Now you can structure your assistant's pay the way I suggested or come up with your own system, as long as you achieve two very important objectives. First is that your assistant's override comes from the income you never would have received without him or her. (That's why they call it "override.") Second is that what the assistant does to earn the override is directly related to the increase in income. What this means is that you don't want to give your assistant a bonus based on the work you did to consummate a transaction, but rather on the work he or she did to help the transaction happen.

Now, why does that format work well? It gives the assistant some incentive to help you. She or he takes some "mental ownership" in your business and is not just showing up everyday. If your assistant had a vested interest in you, because the more money you make the more money he makes, would he perform better? And if you gave your assistant her own business cards that said, "Jane Moss, Assistant to Ed Hunter," don't you think that she would give these out at parties, in the supermarket, to friends, and so on? You've got somebody out there prospecting for you, because she has an incentive to get rid of the cards, to help you prospect, to help you succeed.

Better still, consider giving your assistant a "powerful title" such as

Marketing Coordinator or *Customer Care Representative* or *Personal Administrator.*
The person would still be an assistant, but his or her perceived value would
increase.

By the way, not all people will go for incentive-based pay. Some assistants just want a steady paycheck. The type of assistant who is willing to take
a low base and an override is someone who will be aggressive, an entrepre-
neurial thinker, and that's a good person to have on your team. Somebody
who just wants a steady paycheck may not be bad either; it would depend
on what you need and how you do business. Some agents need a secretary,
someone to keep things in order and do the administrative work for them.
Others want a bit more.

Another thing you can do is partner up with somebody in your office
and share the assistant. You take 20 hours; your partner takes 20 hours. Or,
the assistant can do 20 hours a week total, 10 for you and 10 for your partner. Or, you can hire someone to just do certain projects for you (e.g., come
in once a week and file all your paperwork). Everyone reading this book can
afford an assistant doing it this way.

Here's one other arrangement you might consider instead of hiring an
assistant: partner up with another agent in your office. For instance, you may
have an agent who's not doing as well as he or she would like or just does-
n't want to do some of what we must do in real estate, like prospecting or
attending listing appointments. In fact, it looks like the agent may be leaving on the horizon, although she or he wants to be in real estate. You could
make an arrangement to share the commission—not 50/50, but maybe
80/20 or even 70/30 in your favor. The agreement is this: you go sell, your
partner services. You do listing presentations, buyer's showings, negotiations, etc. Your partner does the other stuff. Open your mind to the possibilities of what you need and create a position that supports and energizes
you. Maybe your partner does the servicing of the seller, the managing of the
contracts at settlements. You're the front-line person and your partner is the
back-line person. And you make it clear that you are the president of this
relationship. Any company only has one president, not two, and the president always overrides the vice president. That needs to be clear. So this other
agent, in effect, serves as your assistant.

Here's another thought: if you hire an assistant, you should have him or
her sign a pay and bonus agreement, to cover pay, hours, vacations, etc. But
the most important thing to have in there is something called a *non-compete*

agreement (see Figures 10-1 and 10-2). (Brokers and managers should do this too; it will reduce turnover.) A non-compete agreement states that if you or the assistant decide not to work together anymore, your assistant agrees not to work for a competitor as an assistant or even as an agent within in a certain period of time—one year, two years, three years. It has to be a reasonable time frame.

Nondisclosure and Non-competition. (a) At all times while this Agreement is in force and after its expiration or termination [employee name] agrees to refrain from disclosing [company name] customer lists, trade secrets, or other confidential material. [Employee's name] agrees to take reasonable security measures to prevent accidental disclosure and industrial espionage.

(b) While this Agreement is in force, the employee agrees to use [his/her] best efforts to [describe job] and to abide by the nondisclosure and non-competition terms of this Agreement; the employer agrees to compensate the employee as follows [decribe compensation]. After expiration or termination of this Agreement [employee name] agrees not to compete with [company name] for a period of [number] months and [number] mile radius of [company name and location]. This prohibition will not apply if this Agreement is terminated because [company] violated the terms of this Agreement.

Competition means owning or working for a business of the following type [specify type of business employee may not engage in].

(c) [Employee name] agrees to pay liquidated damages in the amount of $[dollar amount] for any violation of the convenant not to compete contained in paragraph (b) of this Agreement,

IN WITNESS WHEREOF, [company name] and [employee name] have signed this Agreement.

_____   _____
[employee's name]   [company name]

_____
Date

Figure 10-1. Sample non-compete agreement no. 1

Nondisclosure and Non-competition. (a) After expiration or termination of this agreement, [employee name] agrees to respect the confidentiality of [company name] patents, trademarks, and trade secrets, and not to disclose them to anyone.

(b) [Employee name] agrees not to make use of research done in the course of work done for [company name] while employed by a competitor of [company name].

(c) [Employee name] agrees not to set up in business as a direct competitor of [company name and location] for a period of [number and measure of time (e.g., "four months" or "10 years")] following the expiration or termination of this Agreement.

(d) [Employee name] agrees to pay liquidated damages of $[dollar amount] if any violation of this Agreement is proved or admitted.

IN WITNESS WHEREOF, [company name] and [employee name] have signed this agreement:

_____   _____
[employee's name]   [company name]

_____
Date

Figure 10-2. Sample non-compete agreement no. 2

It's not necessary that you do this. I know plenty of agents who have assistants who don't do this agreement, but I believe it's a real asset for you, for a couple of reasons. For instance, let's say this assistant who has been working with you for a while decides to leave you or you ask him or her to leave. Now, the person goes to work as an assistant for another agent in your same marketplace. Don't you think that somebody who knows about your business, your leads, and your processes and is working with this other agent in another office could be detrimental to you? Obviously, yes. Or, worst-case scenario—and I've seen this happen—the assistant is working with you and sees all the money you're making and begins to think, "This is a great business." So, the assistant gets licensed. Then, she or he decides to go to another office down the street, as an agent. Knowing what he or she knows, that new agent could dramatically diminish your income by using the skills and techniques learned and honed with you. A non-compete agreement will eliminate that possibility.

There's one last thing to bring up in this section. I've suggested that before you hire an assistant, you save some money. Save for three months of her or his salary so it won't be stressful for you when you hire. Also, put aside some funds, because when you hire an assistant, your production may go *down* the first 30 days. Why? Well, what do you think you're going to be spending all your time doing in the first month? *Training your assistant.* So in order to get the person up and running, it's going to take away from some of your production. Be prepared for this monetarily. Of course, if you hire an assistant who has worked for another agent, your training time will be shortened and you might even learn something from him or her.

Where to Find Assistants

Here are some prime candidates to become your assistant:

- **A PART-TIME AGENT.** If you have a part-time agent in your office who's not cutting it, you could work with him or her.

- **EXPIRED OR NEW AGENTS.** "Expired" doesn't mean "dead." They're expired because they used to be licensed but they dropped out of the business for whatever reason. You could also work with new agents who you can mentor. To recruit other active agents, you could use a flier like this one:

Attention Realtors:

Earn a salary plus commission.

Are you willing to work hard and follow instructions?

Would you like to work directly with a strong agent and learn the business from a different perspective?

If so, I will offer the following package:
1. Salary of $1,000 per month, plus
2. Commssion split of 50% on your own deals, plus
3. A new car allowance after 6 months, plus
4. Bonuses tied to team production.

If this caught your attention, let's talk.

Your name
Office
Contact number

■ **PAST CLIENTS.** Here's a letter you can send to all of the people in your client base, to recruit assistants.

It's been some time since we've spoken, and I hope all is well with you. The reason I'm writing is because business is going very well for me, thanks to people like you. As a matter of fact, business is going so well that I can't handle all the details and administrative work without it cutting into the time I can spend with people, helping them with their real estate needs.

I'm at a point where I need to hire a personal assistant. Do you know of someone who might be interested? The hours are flexible, about 20-30 hours a week. Most of the work would be paperwork and follow-up in my office. This person should have dependable transportation and some computer skills and come across as warm and friendly. If you know anyone who would like to get into the exciting business of real estate, please ask him or her to call me. Thank you very much, and I look forward to talking with you soon.

Sincerely,

[Realtor's name]

Besides helping you to find an assistant, a letter like this shows that things are going well for you. And even if you don't generate any assistant leads, it will help you stay in touch with your client base and increase your perceived value as an agent.

■ **FAMILY OR FRIENDS.** This is my least favorite, as mixing business and personal lives often gets messy. However there are many great family/work relationships.

■ **A LOAN PROCESSOR.** These people are worth looking at because they're overworked and underpaid.

■ **A SECRETARY FROM ANOTHER OFFICE.** Just be careful with this one. This is how it might work. When you go to pick up a key or call another office, you might just say to the secretary, "I'm looking for an assistant. If you know of anyone, have them give me a call." Now, if this secretary is unhappy with his or her current office and calls you, I don't think there is anything wrong with that. But what I don't want you to do is go to a competitor's office and say to the secretary, "Are you happy here? Because if you're not, I'm looking for an assistant." That's too aggressive and, I feel, inappropriate.

■ **ADVERTISE IN THE NEWSPAPER.** Here are some sample ads:

SECRETARY PART-TIME
20 hours/week. Basic computer
skills necessary. Wading River location. 631 929-5555. Leave message.

ADMINISTRATIVE ASSISTANT
Local real estate office is looking for
organized secretary to work full
time. Excellent phone and writing
skills required. Send resume to:
Power Realty, 1010 Post Road
Peoria, IL 61602
Fax to: 555 323-1234

SECRETARY, PART-TIME
Flex hours. Excellent phone skills &
knowledge of computer. Microsoft
Word a plus. Start at $10/hour plus
health benefits. E-mail resume to
yourname@youroffice.com.

Here's a good time management tip: when you advertise, consider giving a fax number and an e-mail address, rather than your office phone number, and ask applicants to send a résumé instead of calling. This way, you're
managing the responses and you decide who to call back and when.

- **SOME OTHER PLACES TO LOOK FOR AN ASSISTANT ARE:** court reporting
  school, secretarial schools, colleges, and temp services (usually too
  expensive, however).

The Interview Process

When you talk with applicants on the phone, listen to how they sound.
When you ask them a question, do they elaborate or do they give one-sen-
tence answers? Here are questions for the *telephone interview.*

- Are you currently employed? Where?
- In what capacity?
- Why are you leaving?
- What's your educational background?
- Do you have dependable transportation available to you? (That's an
  important question because she'll need a car to work with you.)

- What type of work appeals to you?
- What is your strongest trait? (I love this question because he usually can't tell you. You can hear him thinking on the phone. This question gives me insight into the person, going beyond the scripted answers he's rehearsed over and over again.)
- What are your skills?
- How many hours are you looking for?
- What salary do you feel you're worth? What is your minimum salary requirement? (Shey'll say, "Tell me, what does it pay?" Ask her to bring in her résumé and a business letter that she's typed, then you'll talk.)

Let me give you some tips on the *live interview*. The first suggestion is to meet in your company office. You may have an office in your home. I would not recommend that you meet applicants there. Why do I say that? First, your office is the center of your business and is probably much more impressive than your home office. In addition, you might make her feel uncomfortable, particularly male agents interviewing women as potential assistants. Instead, have her come to the office. Ask the front secretary to thank her for coming, offer her some coffee, and hand her the application. It creates a professional atmosphere and one where you are in control.

Here are a few specific tips to help you in this process:

- **READ THE APPLICATION WITH A HIGHLIGHTER.** When you go through the application, highlight some of the things you want to ask him. You want it to stand out, rather than making notes on it.
- **LOOK FOR THE NEGATIVES** when reading their application. You can find a reason to hire any applicant. You will want to because you're probably a good person, so you're going to look for the good in other people. What I find works best, however, is when I look for reasons I should *not* hire him. Now, if I can't find a great reason for not hiring an applicant, what should I do? Hire him or her.
- **CHECK HER TYPING AND PROOFREADING SKILLS.** See how fast she types and have her proofread a letter where you've purposely made some mistakes. If a prospective assistant finds a mistake you didn't know you made, try not to look too excited, because you haven't discussed pay yet.
- **DO NOT HIRE ON THE FIRST INTERVIEW.** During the interviews, you're not just checking out the applicants, they're checking you out as well. When you hire right away, you weaken your position. You look too

desperate. If you say, "Let me get back to you," they leave thinking, "Gee, I hope I get the job." It kind of turns the table and puts you in control.

Red flags to watch out for:

- **SHE'S LATE.** I'm not saying you should not hire anybody who shows up late. But if an applicant didn't have the courtesy to phone you and tell you that she would be a few minutes behind, that's a red flag.

- **THEIR APPEARANCE.** Let me give you a rule of thumb. When you see applicants in their interviewing outfits, that's the best you're ever going to see them dressed. Why do I say that? Aren't they trying to look their best on an interview? So if they do all that and they still look terrible, well, it's not going to get any better after that.

- **SHE GIVES YOU TOO MANY SUGGESTIONS** on how to do your business. Now, there's a fine line here. If she seems creative and helpful, that's good. But when she's a little bossy about it, like "Just hire me, darling, I'll tell you how to do your business. You'll be in good hands," you should run the other way.

- **HE INTERVIEWS YOU.** It's natural for and applicant to do some kind of interview of you, right? He wants to check out benefits and find out "what's in it for me?" However, out of respect for you as his potential employer, he should allow you to do your thing. You might explain the job description, your goals, how you see a typical day, then ask him, "How does that sound?" When you're all finished, he might ask you questions: "How much does it pay?" and so on. But if an applicant doesn't even allow you to share your vision before trying to find out what's in it for him, that's a red flag. The applicant is too self-centered.

- **SHE HAS A NEGATIVE ATTITUDE.** Watch out for applicants who come in with a long list of complaints about the weather or the traffic on the commute to your office. I'd be especially wary of applicants who gripe about their former employers and give you a laundry list of ways in which they were wronged. What do you think they'll be saying about you before too long?

- **LONG GAPS BETWEEN JOBS.** This is a red flag unless the long gap was for a good reason, such as caring for an elderly relative, pregnancy, sabbatical, etc. Another version of this is when he's had five jobs in the past four months.

The Live Interview Conversation

Earlier, I gave you a few brief tips on live interviews. Let me go through the specifics on how you might conduct the live interview.

I'm glad you came in. I've set aside sufficient uninterrupted time to conduct the interview so we won't be disturbed. Let me give you an overview of what I would like to cover. First, I want to review your background and experience so that I can decide whether the job is suited to your talents and interests. After we have covered your background, I want to then give you information about our organization and the specifics of the job. Then I can answer any questions that you might have. Sound good?

Work Experience

A good place for us to start would be your work experience. I'm interested in the jobs you've held, what your duties and responsibilities were, your likes and dislikes, and what you felt you might have gained from those jobs. Let's start with a brief review of your first work experiences, those you might have had part-time during school or during the summer, and then we'll concentrate on your more recent jobs in more detail.

- What do you remember about your very first job?
- Tell me about a day you got to work on time, only because of extra effort.
- Tell me about a time when your organizational skills made a project successful.
- How did you organize your work in your last position? How did you handle the unexpected?
- Why did you leave your last job?
- Do you have a computer at home?
- Do you have any sales experience?
- What computer skills do you have? What is your typing speed? Can you take dictation? Have you worked with desktop publishing?
- If I called your last employer, what would he or she tell me?

Education

Why don't we start with high school briefly and then cover more recent schooling and any specialized on-the-job training you may have had. I'm interested in the subjects you preferred and your grades.

- What extracurricular activities did you participate in?
- What was high school like for you?

Activities and Interests

Turning to the present, I'd like to give you the opportunity to mention some of your interests and activities outside of work.

- What hobbies do you have and what do you do for fun and relaxation?
- Are you involved in any community activities and/or professional associations?

Self-Assessment

Now let's try to summarize our conversation.

- Thinking about all we've covered today, what would you say are some of your strengths—qualities, both personal and professional, that make you a good prospect for any employer?
- I'd like to hear about areas you'd like to develop further. All of us have qualities we'd like to change or improve. What are some of yours?

Transition to Information-Giving Phase

You've given me a good review of your background and experience and I've enjoyed talking with you. Before we turn to my review of our organization and the job, is there anything else about your background you would like to cover? Do you have any specific questions or concerns before I give you information about the job and the opportunities here?

At this point, you would share specifics about your company (how long in business, market share, etc.) and the actual job responsibilities. After you've done that, the live interview is over. Tell them you need time to check their references. Let them know when they will hear back from you, one way or another.

Checking References

When you call to check on their references, ask for human resources, assuming there's somebody who does the hiring and letting go. Don't ask for the contact person on their résumé or application.

The reason you do this is because you need to check the title of the person they recommend you call. For instance, they might give you a name for their immediate supervisor, but when you call human resources you find out that the person named is the janitor. In other words, applicants may put the name of a friend who will say nice things on their behalf. So, you're checking the integrity of their application by making these calls.

Here are some good questions to ask when you call and check references.

- What were the dates of employment?
- What was his/her position?
- Who was his/her immediate supervisor?
- What was the reason for leaving?
- What were his/her responsibilities?
- The job he/she is applying for requires _____. Do you think he/she would be a good candidate for this?
- Is he/she eligible to be rehired?

Day One for Your Assistant

Let's briefly walk through your assistant's first day on the job.

1. Have him or her sign the pay and bonus agreements.
2. Take him or her on a tour of the office and introduce your new assistant to everybody.
3. Show where she or he will be working.
4. Have your assistant prepare a phone list. This list would consist of your attorney, title companies, termite inspectors, etc. If you don't already have a phone list like this, have him or her put together a master phone list. Help out by providing the right resources. You might have up-to-date cell and pager numbers, as opposed to your old rolodex.
5. Explain the office equipment, all the mechanical stuff—the copier, the fax machine, the computer, etc.
6. Have your assistant read company literature. This way, he or she mentally buys into the company and its values and understands about the company's history. Now, if somebody calls, your new assistant already has "ownership" in the company.
7. Have him or her send a letter out to the other applicants. What's great about this is you don't have to call these people back … and she or he feels great doing this task.
8. Explain the basic concepts of real estate. *On the first day?* Yes! Now, I said the "basics." I did not say teach him or her 45 hours of real estate. Explain commissions, buyers, sellers, percentages, etc.—Real Estate 101.

Training Your Assistant

- **Computer classes.** Send your assistant for any training needed to be up to speed with the technology skills your office requires. Naturally, you should look to hire someone who already has these skills. But if an impressive candidate just needs to be taught how to use a specific contact management program, take care of it.
- **MLS classes.** Send your assistant to the MLS Board for classes.
- **Company new agent training,** if available. Of course, you should pay for it if there is a charge.
- **Cassette tapes** that might help. These could be motivational or about specific real estate or job functions.
- **Manual,** if you have one. If not, consider creating one. When I had assistants, I used to train them to use a word processing program. Invariably, the next day after I showed them how to do something, they'd come back to me and ask me how to do it again. So I had this brainstorm. Wouldn't it be great if there was a manual with tabs— one for "Computer" and another for "Buyer Appointment" and another for "Listing Appointments" and so on? So, whenever you teach your new assistant something in these general categories of real estate, make sure he or she writes it down in the appropriate tab. (Check to make sure.) This way, your assistant creates a training manual that she or he can check whenever necessary, without bothering you. Another thing that's great about this is that if you hire another assistant, whether a second or to replace this one, you've got a training manual.

One last note. You should *not* hire an assistant and have him or her do telemarketing too. The job description should not be to run the business and then prospect for so many hours a day. Why shouldn't you ask your assistant to do that? Because he or she is not going to prospect, not with other paperwork to do. Face it: *you* don't prospect because you don't have time because you have paperwork to do. So you should hire an assistant who just manages the business. Then, if you want to have someone prospect for you, hire a telemarketer. The only prospecting I would have an assistant do is send out the mailings to your client base and your farm. That's very non-threatening and clerical.

■   ■   ■

Now you have the foundation for working with an assistant. There are two items I want to leave you with if you decide that you're going to work with an assistant. First, in some ways, you're taking on the responsibility of making sure your assistant gets paid. Many people quickly come to recognize when they hire their first employee that there is a human being ... and often a family ... who now will be relying on the income that they promised. Second, in Chapter 1, we talked about various projects and about opening a separate bank account and setting money aside for those projects. I want to remind you of that because I think it's so very important, before you get an assistant, before you place an ad and start interviewing candidates, that you've put aside three or maybe four months of salary. This way, when you hire an assistant, you don't spend the first two weeks upset or obsessing about how you're going to be able to afford your new business investment.

And that's the way you need to look at this. An assistant is an investment in your future. For that investment to start paying dividends, you need to commit to it and move forward, even when it seems difficult at first. This chapter gave you the blueprints for your project. It's up to you to have a bigger vision of your career and all that you can achieve with an assistant supporting you.

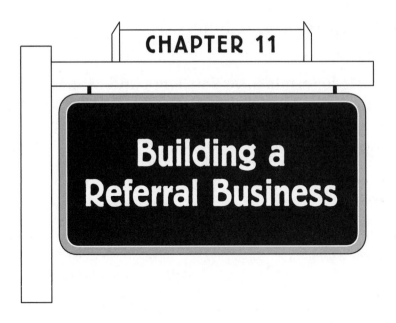

CHAPTER 11

Building a Referral Business

Power Fact

It's been said that a cold lead is afraid of being taken advantage of, while a referral is afraid of being taken for granted. Referrals present a viable and lucrative revenue stream to real estate professionals. The key is to cultivate and communicate with your client base and harvest the referrals you are now missing.

Overview

Building a referral base is about developing a long-term relationship with people by giving them something of value over and over again, creating a reciprocal obligation so they'll want to share referrals and even their personal business. As you read this chapter, I'd like for you to keep one key question foremost in your mind. Ask yourself, "How can I generate more referrals from people who know and like me?" Be committed to this concept and to building your business so it's based more on referrals rather than on FSBOs and expireds. Start considering questions such as "What can I do to stay in touch with my past clients? What can I do to impress them? What can I do to have them be willing to allow me to serve their friends, relatives, colleagues, etc.?"

Three Truths About Referrals

Let's look at what I call the three truths about referrals.

Truth #1: Referrals Save You Time and Money

As you know, we can make money in real estate in several ways. There are FSBOs, expireds, door knocking, open houses, etc. Most of these methods require *active* prospecting, meaning you must generate the lead, appointment, etc. out of your own effort. The referral prospect is *passive* in that you are cultivating your referral base to give you the leads, which then become prospects.

The great thing about referrals is that you can make more money in less time ... and with significantly less aggravation. I'll give you an example of a sale I made a long time ago.

Susan and Tony Boccia—I just liked them. They were really nice people. They were a young couple; I was young at the time. They had one child and two dogs. They bought a ranch from me in Baldwin Harbor on Long Island, New York. It was a corner lot, a really nice piece of property. So over the years I stayed in touch with them. Periodically I'd call them or, if I was in the area, I'd drop by. I had written down notes about the age of their children, about their dogs, and so on. So I would ask them "How are things going with the kids and the dogs?"

About a year later, they called to tell me that they wanted their sister to buy a house near them. They put me in contact with their sister and I sold her a house. Then, a year later, they grew out of their first house and wanted to buy a bigger home. So they listed their house with me; I sold it and then sold them another one.

In other words, from Susan and Tony Boccia, I generated in my pocket $10,000 in commissions over a two-year period. That's an average of $5,000 a year just off of this one couple! You see, referrals already trust you much more than a complete stranger would. So you don't have to spend a lot of time initiating relationships with them. In contrast, when you talk with a FSBO, for example, you have to break down this barrier that he or she has about you—*real estate agents are all the same, they're used car salespeople, you can't trust them, etc.* But the opposite is true with a referral. Most of the time, they're calling you because you have this third-party endorsement. Somebody else is out there saying how wonderful and great you are. So, a referral already has a positive impression of you. This, in and of itself, will save you a tremendous amount of time and money.

The longer you're in this business, the more you should be focused on building your referral base, because you can get to the point where this can generate enough business so you don't have to go out in the cold and talk to strangers.

Here's a terrific example. One of my *Power Agents*, Annette Mena from Long Island, graduated from *The Power Program* in 1993. In that year she made about $68,000. Of the $68,000 in her pocket, 85% came from people she'd done business with before. Oh, and there's one other thing: she worked only six out of 12 months. She could do that because 85% of her earnings came from her client base, which consisted of 352 people she'd worked with before.

Truth #2: Referrals Help with Your Retirement Fund

When you're building a referral business, I want you to think about your retirement. Here's what I mean. In the insurance industry, they have a great setup. Every time a salesperson sells you an insurance policy, that salesperson keeps getting a little residual as long as you're making your premium payments. It's not a lot, but it keeps coming. In the first year, the agents make the bulk of their commission, then after that they just get a little residual. But you keep multiplying those residuals by hundreds of clients. There are some insurance people making a ton of money every year and they're not even actively working insurance anymore. I want you to consider this concept of residuals in your real estate career.

When you decide to get out of real estate, what are you going to do with your past clients? You can take your client base, your referral business, and *sell* it to another agent. But, you can't sell it to another agent if you don't have good systems in place where you can quantify the money you're making from referrals. You need to be able to show another agent, "Here's my system, here's my client base, and here's how much money I've been making from these people." You're selling a system, not just a list of names. So the sooner you get this system in place for yourself, the better that will position you for when you want to get out of real estate.

A perfect illustration of this is Jay Bayliss. Jay lived in Fairfax, VA, and he used to list and sell. When he got out of real estate, he sold his client base to another agent for $10,000. He did this because he could show that agent how much money he generated just from his referrals. Could *you* put a dollar value on *your* book of business?

Here's a formula that I find works really well.

Take your last three years (because three years is substantial enough to show somebody that any given year was not a fluke) of income you generated from your client base and come up with an average. You could sell it for 80% of that average. This percent is not an exact number, but it sounds good to me because it would take less than one year of business from just that client base to pay for itself.

So, let's say that your average comes out to $50,000 a year; 80% of that is $40,000. You would then sell your book of business for $40,000. Now, there's a good chance that the agent you're selling it to is not going to have $40,000 in his bank account to buy your business, so here's the best way to get paid. I would *not* do referral fees—in other words, arranging that every time he does some business with one of your past clients, he sends you a referral fee—because that's a nightmare to track. Instead, you create a note. You tell him $40,000 at X percentage spread out over X years. With a balloon, without a balloon, pay interest only for a period—whatever you like. If you sold your book of business for $40,000 at an 8% interest rate for a period of four years, you would receive almost $1,000 a month. And what's really great is that this is completely passive income. You are now benefiting from the groundwork you laid throughout your real estate career.

Truth #3: Referrals Are Built Through the Client Value Chain

In building a solid and strong relationship with your past clients, it's important that you try to move them up the Client Value Chain, starting with Awareness Bonding and ending at Advocacy Bonding.

1. **Awareness Bonding.** To have people know your name, face, and what you do for a living.

2. **Identity Bonding.** A deeper connection with prospects and customers. This is accomplished through publicity and community service programs, such as fund-raisers.

3. **Relationship Bonding.** You begin to recognize a customer's relationship bond with you by acknowledging his or her devotion. This might be accomplished through special gifts and/or a loyalty program.

4. **Community Bonding.** The bond between the client/customer and you shifts to a bond among clients. An example is residents in a certain subdivision who love where they live and talk about this with others.

5. **Advocacy Bonding.** The customer feels such deep loyalty to you that she

or he will actively promote you and help build your business. You should strive to have your past clients reach the level of Advocacy Bonding.

Nine Tips for Building Your Referral Base

One category of potential referrals would be anyone who has bought or sold real estate through you in the past. Another might be people who haven't done business with you but who know you very well and like you as a person. This might be family or friends. Another could be members of an organization that you belong to outside of real estate, where you're very visible with close associates.

In Chapter 8, "Farming for Dollars," we discussed staying in contact with your farm, which is made up of people who *don't* necessarily know you, like you, or trust you personally. While these people may know of you because you've been mailing them once a month, they don't know you as a human being. These are not potential referrals. For right now, I want you to think, "Who are the people that I know, who like me, who trust me, and who might be willing to directly refer others to use my services?" These would make up your referral base.

Here are some tips to help you move forward.

Tip #1: Interview other top agents. These must be agents who are successfully doing the very thing that we're talking about here—building an effective referral business. Ask them questions. Tell them you want to take them out for dinner or lunch so you can get some coaching from them. Ask them how they're staying in touch with their past clients, how many times a year they're doing this, what types of mailing pieces they're using, what software they're using. Gather as much information as you can and start developing your own plan of attack.

One other thing. When asking for advice, it's vital that you offer to serve them in return. So, ask if there's anything that you can do to help. Perhaps paying for dinner is enough. But if you want to establish an ongoing mentor relationship, consider whether you could do something to help these agents be more successful as well.

Tip #2: Categorize the clients. First, separate out your current buyers and sellers. You see, they're not past clients yet. If some current clients already trust you and you have a good connection with them, put them in. The key is that you are able to pull up this special "hit list" of people in your database with ease.

Regardless of which database or client tracking software you use, you should categorize your referral base. You might divide it into "Special Client A" and "Special Client B," for example. "Special Client A" might consist of people who are most willing to send referrals to you. This is likely the top 20% that's going to generate 80% of your referral business. "Special Client B" might be people who would refer business to you if they knew how or were motivated to do so. You'll have to work this group a little bit differently. You can create other categories if you find it useful.

Tip #3: Treat the referrals right. When you get a referral, you have to treat her or him a little bit differently from the FSBO or the people who came to an open house. Why? Because John, the referral, is going to tell his friend, Mary, who referred him to you, exactly what you did or didn't do for him. Do you see how that's going to impact Mary? If you don't take care of her friend, John, why should she refer anybody else to you? So, be sure you are courteous, that you keep your word every step of the way, and that you deliver impeccable service.

Here's one other tip. When you sit down with this referral, you should manage his or her expectations by telling her or him how you work. This is vital, because it's not uncommon for referrals to have unrealistically high expectations of you. Mary told John how awesome you are, so he might expect you to show him every single house on multiple listing in his price range ... and then some! Or the new listing, who was a referral, might expect you to cut her lawn every week so the house looks good. You get the idea. Be open. Be kind. Tell them how you are ... and aren't ... going to serve them. And do what you say you'll do.

Tip #4: Adopt orphans. If you remember, we touched on this in our chapter on prospecting. An orphan is somebody who has bought or sold real estate through your office and the agent who was involved in that transaction no longer works for your company. So you go to your broker or your manager and ask for all the closed files over the past several years of people who worked with that agent. I'll bet you in that set of files there are many people who are thinking about selling their homes.

Here's an outline of the dialogue you can use to call them:

Step 1: Identify: *May I speak with [Name of person]?*

Step 2: Introduce: *Hi, this is Darryl and I'm calling from Power Realty. How are you?*

Step 3: Reason: *The reason for this call is to apologize. It seems as though you bought [or sold] a house X years ago through our company and the agent who was involved in the sale is no longer working for us. The reason for the apology is it seems as though we lost touch with you. So I've been appointed from our company to be your new representative. If you should ever have any real estate questions, you can feel free to call me personally.*

Step 4: Questions:
- *By the way, how are you enjoying the house?*
- *Have you made any major improvements to the house?*
- *What do you like best about the neighborhood?*
- *Have you ever thought of moving?*
- *If you were to move, where would you move to?*
- *If you could have a larger home or in a different neighborhood, for the same monthly payment, would that be of interest to you?*

Step 5: Invite Action: *One of the services we are now offering is an updated market analysis of a past client's home. It's possible you could move to a larger home and have your monthly payments stay the same. I'd be happy to come by tonight and see what the current value of your home is; you could be amazed at how much it is worth.*

Tip #5: Get in touch with the expired real estate agent. Expired agents have retired from real estate or quit the business for whatever reason. However, they still have their license active. Some Boards of Realtors track when an agent is active or inactive; check with your Board. You can also ask your broker or manager for a list of agents who used to work in your office. When you call them, the dialogue may sound something like this:

Darryl: "Hi, Mary. This is Darryl from Power Realty. How are you doing? The reason why I'm calling is because I know you used to be in real estate X number of years ago, and I wanted to ask if you still have your real estate license?"

Mary: "Well, yeah, it's still active."

Darryl: "OK, great. Let me ask you, would you be interested in some really nice passive income?"

And he'd have to be a bowling ball to say "no" to that. So, assuming he says "yes," you explain that you want to gain access to people he has sold houses to or any listings that he sold. In a nutshell, you want to adopt his client base. Once you do this, you can have that agent send out a letter to his client base introducing you as somebody to call when they are thinking about selling or buying real estate. Here's how it might sound.

You can then do a follow-up call to those people or send your own follow-up letter.

Dear [Name of person],

It's been my sincere pleasure to serve you as your real estate agent in the past. However, at this point in my life, I've decided to move forward onto other interests.

As one of my valued clients, I want to make sure that you are taken care of. I want to be certain that if you ever have any real estate questions you will be represented by someone of excellent character and superior professionalism. One such individual is [your name]. He/she provides a whole list of complimentary services to his/her clients and his/her commitment is to serve you unconditionally.

If you know of someone thinking of buying or selling a home who would appreciate the kind of service I have offered you, [your name] would love to help them. In closing, thank you for the opportunity of serving you in the past.

Sincerely,

Your name

Now, while you're in touch with these agents, you might as well go the extra mile. Tell them that you're building a referral business and ask that they refer anybody that they hear of at the supermarket or the Kiwanis Club, etc., in return for a referral fee. You can do a flat 20% referral fee or a sliding scale. For instance, 10% if they just give you a name and telephone number but no real information or 20% if you get a name and number plus a whole background on these people. You could also do a sliding scale of 10% on the first two leads a month that someone is sending you, then jump it up to 20%, as an incentive.

Dear Michelle,

How are things back in "civilian life"? Do you miss the frantic calls, people who don't show up for appointments, and everyone who says, "I'll get back to you" and doesn't? I didn't think so.

I am writing today because I was thinking of how much time and effort you gave to your real estate business and what a waste it would be for all of that work to be lost now that you are out of the industry. I have an idea that I would like to share with you, in person, about how you can continue to generate referral income from real estate even though you are no longer active.

What I propose, in a nutshell, is that you contact your client base, let them

---

know that you are no longer active in real estate and that I will be taking over your business. In this way your clients and customers will be served with the same dedication and respect they received from you and whenever I close one of the transactions generated from your client base I will send you a referral fee of XX% of my commission.

Michelle, you worked hard for over XX years in real estate and you served your clients and customers well. Wouldn't it be great if they could continue to get the excellent treatment and service you provided? Wouldn't it be a waste to let all that hard work go down the drain?

I'll call you in a few days so we can chat about generating continuing passive income for you. If you're open for lunch one day next week, I'd be delighted if you'd be my guest and we can "talk shop" over a pleasant meal to see how this can benefit both of us.

I look forward to your reply,

Sincerely,

Your name

Tip #6: The endorsement letter technique. I got a letter from Tony Robbins telling me about a great financial planner that he has used and how he highly recommends that I contact this person. Now, I didn't contact the person, because I knew it was a mass mailing and I don't know Tony personally, but I was really impressed with the concept just the same. Anyone who looks up to Tony might call this person because Tony's words add credibility.

To piggyback on this approach, select a target group of professionals, similar to what we discussed in Chapter 9, on self-promotion—e.g., attorneys, CPAs, or insurance agents—and approach them about building a mutual referral system. The basic concept here is that they will send out a letter (on their letterhead) to their client base endorsing your services. The letter would sound something like this:

Dear Mr. Jones,

I know that real estate is one of the most important investments you might own. And, to find a really good agent that you can trust and who is very good at it can be a challenge. I'm happy to say that I've got somebody whom I know very well. His name is Darryl Davis and I highly recommend that you contact him if you ever need anything real estate related.

Darryl specializes in [neighborhood, styles of homes, etc.] and will always look out for your best interests. I feel comfortable knowing that you will be in good hands.

Sincerely,

Your name

Now, in return, you take your whole mailing list and customize a letter recommending that person in his or her industry. Of course, you can't keep hitting your client base every month with a new recommendation, because that might become annoying. I suggest choosing two or three professionals whom you feel comfortable recommending and spreading out your mailings over a year, sending one every few months.

With this approach, each party will benefit tremendously from the "third-party validation" and from reaching people who you couldn't have reached otherwise.

Tip #7: The "Dear Neighbor" letter. You know how you always want a testimonial letter from your clients? Why not make it a *requirement*? When you send a list to your sellers or buyers telling them what to bring to closing, make sure the checklist includes a testimonial letter about your services. It's just one of the documents that they have to execute. When you get that letter, you'll probably want to tweak it and ask them if they would mind if you made the letter begin with "Dear Neighbor." You then take these letters and print them up for future mailings.

Tip #8: The change of address technique. Get a list of friends and family from your current buyers or sellers before the transaction is complete. Tell them that you will provide a free service to them by mailing out a change of address card to their list of people. The whole point, of course, is to build your database. Make sure you get permission to add these names to your database. While you are performing the free service for your present clients, I would add the names and addresses that you receive to your farm database rather than the referral database. (See Chapter 8, "Farming for Dollars," for more details on farming.) The referral database is for people you've done business with before who already know you and trust you … or for those they directly recommend. Individuals receiving a change of address card are not a list of referrals; they are cold leads and belong in your farm rather than your referral database. Got it?

Tip #9: The needs analysis form. When you work with buyers, they typically fill out a sheet indicating the price range they are interested in, their income, their current address, whether they own or rent, etc. But you should also use this opportunity to capture more personal information, such as how many children they have, the names and ages and birthdays of their children, their own birthdays and their anniversary, the kinds of pets they may have and their names, their personal hobbies, etc. Also ask them for their e-mail address, cell phone number, and their preferred contact method. Try to capture as much information as you can get without being obnoxious.

Why do this? When you are mailing to your referral base, you may want to send birthday cards to the kids or anniversary cards to the husband and the wife. Most agents don't know how to get this information. With this form, you can get it up front. Then, once they buy the house and it's six months or a year later, you can send them notes or cards. They probably won't remember filling out this form many months back. They'll just think, "Boy, I can't believe he remembered Alexa's birthday! That's really thoughtful."

To get this information from sellers, create a needs analysis form with the information I mentioned above and have your sellers fill this out when you get their listing.

16 Servicing Tips and Techniques for Your Referral Base

Here are a variety of ways for you to stay in touch with your referral base. I'm providing you with far more ideas than you could possibly implement. You can simply select one or two of these that appeal to you and then implement them.

Two overall guidelines:

1. **Contact them between four and six times a year.** Whereas a farm doesn't know you personally, your referral base does. So, unlike with a farm, you don't need to mail to your referral base on a monthly schedule. If you mail four times a year, you're in good shape. I suggest the following: an anniversary card (for the date that they closed), a Happy Holidays card, and two other mailings. They don't have to be anything fancy, just two mailings that convey the same basic message—"Just wanted to say, 'Hi.' Hope all is well. If you know of anybody thinking about selling or buying, please give me a call."—with a photo on them. It's very simple, right?

2. **Create a marketing plan.** What are you going to send these folks beyond birthday cards? A series of postcards or direct mail letters? A professionally designed newsletter? An informative article reprint? Whatever you send, and whether your list has 50 people or 500, you need a plan.

I'm very visual and would suggest hanging up a calendar for the year

that details what marketing efforts go out and when. Place it somewhere so that it's always visible and stays fresh in your mind. We gave you a sample "marketing calendar" in our chapter on self-promotion.
Specific tips:

- **SEND PERSONAL CARDS.** This builds on the "needs analysis form" covered in the previous section. By sending birthday or anniversary cards, you show how attentive you are, that you are caring and that you are good with details. If you are able to handwrite these, even better.

- **SEND OUT A "REINTRODUCTION LETTER."** Do you have people in your referral base that you sold houses to months or years ago and you haven't communicated with since? If so, you need to send a letter that conveys the sentiment, "I'm sorry that we lost touch." Here's a sample:

Dear Mr. and Mrs. Jefferson,

I'm writing you today to apologize for being out of touch for so long. I often think about you but get so busy helping the families I'm working with that it seems that I never get around to just saying, "Hello." Again, I'm sorry and I want you to know that I value you as people and as clients.

At one time, you were more than just a customer, you were also a friend ... and I'd like to rekindle that friendship. If I can be of any assistance to you now, please feel free to call me. I will definitely be in touch with you soon.

Sincerely,

Your name

After mailing this letter, I would do a follow-up call. If you have a lot of people in your past client base, you may need to stagger this process, mailing only as much at one time as you believe you could call on the phone within a 30-day period.

3. **Send coupons to preferred clients.** These coupons could be from a painter, an accountant, a landscaper, an insurance agency, a dry cleaner, a hair salon, etc. These are the same people who I referred to when we discussed endorsement letters earlier in this chapter. Here's a sample letter that a *Power Agent* shared with me. The letter was accompanied by a coupon and tied into a birthday. (See sample letter on next page.) (Keep in mind, though, that you don't have to tie this into a special occasion; it could just be a monthly or quarterly coupon mailed to special clients.)

4. **Subscribe to a "fruit of the month" or other specialty club for your key clients.** Special clients deserve to eat well, don't they? You can

Dear Paula,

Congratulations on your upcoming birthday. To help you celebrate, I'd like to offer you a very tasteful gift—a custom-made birthday cake! Pick up your *free* cake by presenting this certificate to Marcy at Park Avenue Bakery located at [Address]. Marcy will take great care of you, and I guarantee that you'll love what she bakes. However, if cake isn't for you, you can also use this certificate for up to $20 of Park Avenue's delicious breads and pastries.

Sincerely,

Your name

send fruit baskets or turkey or steak. There are many gourmet companies set up to do this, offering various goodies at various prices. I spend a lot of money on clients of my speaking business ... but they send me a lot of referrals, so it more than pays for itself. And what's really great is you just sign these people up for one of the X-of-the-month clubs and then you have nothing more to do. Each month, the basket of treats is sent out automatically.

5. **Personal stationery.** You can use this as a closing gift. The personal stationery could be little notepaper imprinted with the client's name and new address. These items are so inexpensive. You could also do "to-do" pads with the client's name on top and your name and phone number very small on the bottom for reordering. They'll wind up calling you and asking how they can get more "to-do" pads. It's a great way to have them stay in touch with you.

6. **When you're on vacation, send your folks a postcard.** If you have a thousand people in your referral base, are you going to send a thousand cards when you're on vacation? Of course not. Otherwise, your whole vacation will be devoted to writing postcards. A system that I find works quite well is to call the visitors bureau or chamber of commerce where you are going and tell them that you need a thousand postcards from their city. So if it was New York, you might order a thousand postcards of the Statue of Liberty and have them send it to you before you even go on vacation. You can plan this a month or two ahead of time. Then you or your assistant would write a handwritten note, take these postcards with you to New York, and mail them from there. Your people will be amazed that you thought of them when you were on vacation. Here are a few ideas of what you could write:

> Hey, John and Mary, I was just thinking about you. I'm in New York, having a great time. I hope things are going well with you. When I get back in two weeks, please give me a call if you need anything.

> We are having a great time here and enjoying this much-needed vacation. Whenever I am lucky enough to get away for a few days, I am always reminded how fortunate I have been. That's why I was thinking of you and wanted to drop you a note to say "Hi" and "thanks for being part of my life." This vacation would not be possible without wonderful clients and customers like you.

> I just wanted to drop you a note to say thanks for all your help and support and that I am thinking of you here in Naples. We are having a great time and doing our best to enjoy every moment. The kids think that means doing something every second, while my husband and I were hoping to relax a bit more, but watching the kids have fun is pure delight. I'll call you when I get back home.

> How are things back at home? I hope this card finds you well and that the weather is fine there. We are having a ball on vacation here in Joplin, MO, visiting family and friends. I wanted to drop you a line to let you know I was thinking of you and appreciate your support. Getting away always reminds me of how lucky I am, and when I count my blessings I am delighted that you are on that list.

7. **Mail an updated CMA request letter.** This technique is geared toward people who have bought a house through you before. As you'll see, it works best when the market is good. Write something along these lines:

> Dear [Name of person]
>
> The real estate market has been very impressive lately, with home values rising rapidly. The value of your home may have gone up more than you realize. If you'd like to find out your current equity in your home, please give me a call. I'd be more than happy to go through my records and see how much your house may be worth in today's market.
>
> Sincerely,
>
> [Your name]

I recommend sending this letter at least twice a year because people may not realize how much their house is worth and discovering extra equity might motivate them to buy a new home before they had originally intended.

In addition, you could send out this letter, which my Power Agents have told me is very effective:

Dear Name of person,

If you have owned your home for more than five years, here is a tip that might save you thousands of dollars. Homes purchased with a loan greater than 80% require private mortgage insurance (PMI). The premium is typically 1% to 2% of the mortgage at closing and approximately ¼% to ½% per month for the renewals.

When your equity has increased to 20%, in most cases, you are no longer required to have the PMI but you will have to petition to have it removed. One way for your equity to increase is to reduce the principal to 80% of the original purchase price. However, this usually takes 12 or more years, unless you are making additional principal contributions.

The most common way for your equity to increase is for the value to increase. The difference between the unpaid balance and what it is worth is your equity. The mortgage company may require a new appraisal to prove the current worth, but before you spend the money, ask if they'll accept the assessed value.

Just give me a call at xxx-xxx-xxxx and I'll supply you with the assessed value and sales of comparable homes in your area. If there is anything else I can do for you, please let me know.

Your real estate professional,

Your name

When you get requests for this information, be sure to record the mortgage and values in the person's file in your contact manager. This may be valuable information in the future.

8. **Host a special movie preview.** I know agents who have rented out a local theater for a new movie release and hosted their own special showing for special guests—such as the top 20% of their client base and their children. You can really have a lot of fun with this concept by making it an event like the Academy Awards and telling people to get dressed up, etc. Most movie theatres around the country will do this, especially for children's parties. Note: If you do this, I strongly suggest that you get this sponsored by the special business-networking group you formed (with the accountant, lawyer, landscaper, etc.).

9. **Give a gift for every referral you receive.** This could be chocolate, popcorn, or a clock. I've had agents ask me whether this is against the law. In fact, it's perfectly legal to give somebody gifts to thank them for a lead they've given you.
   Note: Make sure that you have a way to flag files in your contact man-

agement system so that you can follow up with those who referred someone to you, letting them know how it's going. In other words, after you send a gift to the Cole family, thanking them for referring the Johnsons, you will also be reminded to send them periodic updates in a month or two to let them know whether the Johnsons found a home, etc. They deserve a status report.

10. **Produce and mail a newsletter.** This might be on the upper end as far as money is concerned, depending on how you do it. There are several companies that can produce this for you for as little as 20¢ apiece. They have preprinted newsletters: they just drop in your photo and your office information and it's all complete. Some companies like this will even do the mailing for you. Some agents, however, prefer to produce original newsletters—either because they're good writers or because they want to customize the content of each issue. I highly recommend that you do not do this because it's poor time management. Have it written, designed, printed, folded, and mailed by someone else (see Figure 11-1).

   The key with a newsletter, though, is to be consistent. If you're going to launch one, you must send it out regularly. If you send one, then wait another four months, then seven months after that, it will look sporadic and you'll give the impression that you are disorganized. Quarterly is probably the best way to go. But whatever you choose, please stick to a schedule.

11. **Make a donation.** A *Power Agent* gave this idea to me. After the closing, she makes a donation in the name of everybody who was involved in the transaction—the buyers, the attorneys, the title company, the mortgage company, the underwriter, etc. You send a letter to your buyers or sellers thanking them for their business and to your professional colleagues thanking them for their hard work. Say something along the lines of "In appreciation of who you are, I've made a donation to Habitat for Humanity [or whichever charity]."

   This approach makes quite a positive impression and demonstrates that you're committed to causes beyond yourself.

12. **Send recipe cards.** If you've been in real estate for a while, you know about recipe cards. There are a few companies out there that do something like this and there are several varieties of cards ... not all dealing with recipes. For example, there are also humorous postcards, some that give seasonal advice for home improvement, and others that provide maintenance checklists for automobiles. You just provide these

Figure 11-1. Example of a newsletter

companies with your mailing list and they'll do everything for you. Two companies I highly recommend because of the quality of their work and integrity are Sendsations in Orem, UT, 800 800-8197 and You, Inc., Provo, UT, 888 233-5554. (see Figure 11-2).

13. **Advertising premiums.** As we mentioned in the self-promotion chapter, consider rulers, pens, T-shirts, hats, mugs, etc. My favorite concept, though, is a customized magnet with key phone numbers—like the train schedule hotline, the library, poison control, etc. Of course, it also has your number ... and the numbers of the professional referral group

SALISBURY STEAK

Serves 8. Nutrition per serving: Cal. 287, Protein 25g, Carb. 9g, Fat 16.5g, Chol. 131mg

PATTIES		SAUCE	
2 lbs ground beef (lean)	1/2 tsp onion powder	1 can tomato sauce (8 oz.)	1 can mushrooms (4 oz.)
2 eggs	1/2 tsp garlic powder	1 can beef broth	2 tsp Worcestershire sauce
1/2 C bread crumbs		(15 oz. fat free or bouillon)	1/4 tsp salt & pepper

Combine pattie ingredients & form into 8 equal 1/2" thick patties. Sauté in pan browning both sides. Remove & drain off fat. Add sauce ingredients to pan & bring to boil. Reduce heat & return patties. Cover & simmer 10 min.

Printed on recyclable paper with earth friendly inks.
©Copyright 2002, Sendsations®

Key Lime Pie

CRUST	FILLING	
1 pkg graham crackers (apx 16)	2 eggs	2 cans sweetened cond. milk
1/4 C sugar	2 egg yolks	2/3 C key lime juice
1/3 C butter (melted)	(discard whites)	

Preheat oven to 350°. Blend crust ingredients in food processor. Press into 9" pie plate & bake 15 min. For filling, blend milk & eggs well, then add juice. Pour into pre-baked shell & return to oven addtl. 15 min. Chill well. Serve with whipped cream.

Printed on recyclable paper with earth friendly inks.
©Copyright 2002, Realtouch®

Figure 11-2. Examples of recipe cards

Figure 11-3. Examples of advertising premiums

we've discussed throughout this chapter (insurance agent, dentist, doctor, hairdresser, etc.). What are people going to do with this magnet if they already have a dentist or others who are listed? Will they throw it out? No, they'll probably keep it on their refrigerator because there is at least one number on there that interests them. You can find companies through your Yellow Pages, under "advertising premiums."

14. **Whenever you list, whenever you sell, announce it to everybody.** Mail to your referral base, your farm, everybody you might possibly serve. You do this because you want to show people that you're doing business, while keeping your name in front of them. This type of announcement can be done as a letter or a postcard. The advantage to letters is they allow you more space for your message. The advantage of postcards is that they're cheaper to mail and easier to manage.

15. **Send buyers a copy of their closing statement.** As you know, the HUD closing statement has all the closing expenses a buyer pays for, which is also a huge tax write-off for them. Now, most buyers misplace that form (if they even get a copy) and can't find it during tax season. I suggest that January 2 you mail a copy of the HUD form for each buyer you worked with during the previous year—both your buyers and people who bought your listings. Include a brief note that this might help them save money on their taxes. (Of course, they should check with their accountant to be sure.). You will look like a hero!

16. **Host a party for your past clients.** Every year, you do a party for your past clients. I know several top producers who do this faithfully for their client base. Now, for those of you who aren't at that level of production yet, if you've got 15 people who showed up for that party, that's fine. Maybe next year you'll have 30. Maybe the year after that 50, and then 100. You follow me? I know one agent who has 250 people show up. It's always around Christmas and he has ice sculptures and a band. But he doesn't pay for a thing: he has a mortgage company and a title company pay for it. And you can start doing that for as little as 15 people.

■   ■   ■

By now, you should understand the importance of referrals. The most efficient way for you to grow your business and advance to the Next Level in your career is for satisfied clients to recommend you to everyone they know. It's far easier and cost-effective to work referrals than to start out cold. The key is to serve your customers and to consistently communicate with those in your database. I hope that I've provided useful suggestions to help you do just that.

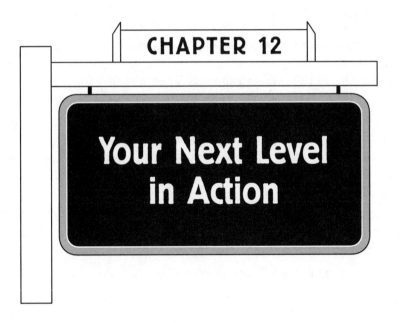

CHAPTER 12

Your Next Level in Action

Lights, Camera, ...

You know what comes next, right? *Action!* (Sorry, with my theatrical background—I just couldn't resist.)

You've just finished 11 chapters loaded with practical, real-world-tested tips and techniques to help you succeed in real estate. If you're like most people, you read this book and found quite a lot of stuff that you can use. Maybe you even began to implement a few of the ideas I discussed. If so, congratulations ... you've taken a step in the right direction.

To help you even more, though, I'd like to briefly review *Three Power Principles of Real Estate* that we first touched on in our introductory chapter. These principles form the foundation for success in our industry. After this review, I'll give you an action plan to help you reach the *Next Level* in your career—whether you're a new or advanced agent.

The Three Power Principles Revisited

Principle #1: The Coaching Philosophy. Said simply, *coaching* is when you are more committed to someone else achieving his or her goals than you are to fulfilling your own agenda. This is very easy to understand in the sports world, as coaches at the professional level are judged mainly by their won-loss records. If you're a tennis coach, for instance, you will be successful when the player you are coaching is successful on the court. If you get paid good money to coach that player, but she never wins and seldom enjoys herself, you've done a poor job regardless of your personal income and fame.

The same holds true in our business. Truly effective coaches are part strategist, part psychologist, and part motivator. As a *Power Agent* in real estate, you are indeed all of these things. You are not "in the game" to simply earn a commission. Rather, your role is to enable buyers and sellers to achieve their personal goals (buying their first home, selling a piece of property, moving to be closer to their family, etc.) in the most efficient way possible through a real estate transaction. You can succeed only if they come out a winner.

Principle #2: The Next Level Design. Throughout this book, I've given you a slew of valuable concepts about a variety of real estate topics. Everything I provided was based on helping you reach your Next Level. Remember the Oliver Wendell Holmes quote? "Once the mind of man is stretched, it can never go back to its original form."

Here's what's so interesting about this. You've already moved up a level just from reading this book! You can never go back. If you approached these pages with the conviction that the solutions you want and need were all within these pages, you received the greatest possible value. You had an intention and a definitive mission: this book was going to make a difference in your life. If, on the other hand, you read this book passively without any upfront goal, you also benefited ... but likely not to the same degree.

The same principle applies with your Next Level. While you can sometimes gain new heights by accident, a far more effective method for anyone who wishes to become a top producer in real estate is to set objectives and systematically work to achieve them. Later in this chapter, I will provide you with exercises to help you do just that.

Principle #3: Maintaining Focus. Of course, it's not enough to simply know where you want to go. The key is to FOCUS on your goals and to be consistently in ACTION to achieve them.

In *The Power Program*, my students meet once a month for 12 consecutive months, providing them with a wonderful forum to maintain focus on their Next Level. By systematically looking at their goals every 30 days, they are constantly reminded of their commitments and develop a sense of urgency.

So, since this is a book and not *The Power Program*, how can you reach your Next Level and become a *Power Agent?*

Moving Forward

There are three steps that I would recommend to help you gain the most value from this book.

Step #1: The Reference Method. In the future, I hope that you'll use *How to Be a Power Agent in Real Estate* as a reference manual for your career. Whenever there's an area where you feel weak or you need assistance—handling objections, for instance—go to that chapter and review it. Implement some of the specific steps I discuss and improve your performance until you've mastered that area.

Step #2: The Focus Method. Now that you've read this book, go back and review one chapter each month. (In this way, you will be mimicking the sequence and timing of *The Power Program*.) After you complete, for example, "Servicing Listings to Sell," maintain focus on that one single area of real estate until you master it. Read with a "to-do" pad next to you. As you find items that solve your current challenges, you'll think, "Here's something I can implement." Jot down those thoughts. Then, when you complete each task, use a highlighter to signify your accomplishment. (Remember, in our time management chapter we discussed the motivational benefits of highlighters versus checkmarks!)

Step #3: The Exercise Method. To get you started and into action *immediately*, in the pages that follow I've provided detailed action plans. For *agents who are new to the business*, I offer a *60-Day Action Plan for New Agents*. Over the course of eight weeks, this plan will get you up on your feet and proactively pursuing your goals. I cover everything from learning how to use your voice mail system to role-playing a listing presentation. If you follow these simple checklists, I promise that you will start moving forward toward your Next Level.

For *experienced agents and top producers*, the challenge is often to recognize what has been working for you thus far and to strengthen the areas where you might be lacking. My *30-Day Action Plan for Experienced Agents* will help you assess your present status, identify your strengths and weaknesses, and create a plan and take action to work on any vulnerabilities.

■   ■   ■

Well, there you have it. I sincerely *thank you* for dedicating the time and effort to read through these pages. But don't stop here. As your coach, I encourage you to remain committed to reaching your Next Level. Do whatever it takes to live a productive life, to have a successful and fun career, and to become a *Power Agent* in real estate!

Now, go ahead, get started....

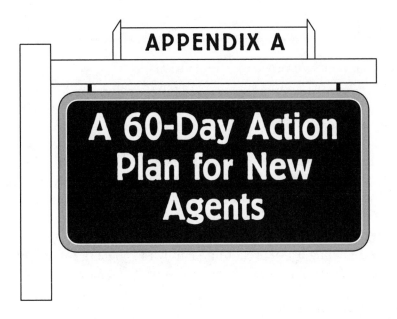

APPENDIX A

A 60-Day Action Plan for New Agents

Beginning on the next page, you'll find a set of actions you can take to become a power agent in real estate. Be disciplined as you undertake these activities, but also have fun. Understand that you are taking actions that will help move you to the elite among real estate agents and brokers.

Week 1

DATE:

- Pick your desk and program your voice mail.
- Notify Board of Realtors and Department of State of affiliation.
- Get a digital color photo to your manager and two film photos with your name written on back.
- Items to give to your manager:
  - Bio: years in business, previous work experiences production
  - Personal info: Social Security number, birthday, family members' birthdays and names
  - Affiliations with groups, clubs, societies, etc.
- Order business cards and stationery.
- Create a mailing list of friends and family (a sphere of influence).
- Visit five houses a day (first company listings) and take notes as you preview.
- Purchase local area street maps.
- Schedule to attend classes for MLS.
- Buy an organizer to keep track of schedule. *Note*: You may use a "hard copy" or paper organizer, a PDA (personal digital assistant), or a laptop with organizer software. The key is to make sure you have a method to remain focused on your Next Level.
- Connect your notebook computer to the company's network.
- Learn the operation of your office:
  - Phone system
  - Up-board and incoming call process
  - Security system
- Make sure your name and phone numbers are on the office phone list.
- Call five agents you know and let them know of your affiliation.
- Get a beeper, a wireless PDA with paging, or a cell phone
- Attend brokers, open houses, buyer appointments, and listing appointments with a fellow agent.
- Review tasks completed with your broker or manager.

SUMMARIZE WHAT YOU FEEL YOU'VE LEARNED OR ACCOMPLISHED THIS WEEK AND SHARE IT WITH YOUR BROKER OR MANAGER:

Week 2

DATE:

- Preview a total of 20 houses.
  - Log your feelings or perceptions of each home's pluses and minuses.
  - Write down your "gut" feeling of what you believe the selling price of each home will be and why you feel that way.
  - Be sure to check your price with the actual selling price when the home sells. This is a great way to learn how to "comp" homes for your listings.
- Mail an announcement to members of your sphere of influence, whether they live in your local area or not. Remember, you can send a referral to agents almost anywhere.
- Meet with a lender to understand the mortgage process and the call capture program.
- Role-play how to answer incoming buyer calls. Do this role-play on three days and use three different scenarios each day. Make it as real as possible.
- Learn how to search for information on the MLS computer. Make sure to search by various criteria. Learn what the most common searches are and discover how to do those first. Then learn how to do other searches that may come in handy when working with buyers or finding "comps" to do a CMA.
- Understand the crisscross directory and how to use this tool to find an address or a homeowner's name when all you have is the phone number.
- Learn how to access your company's Web site and familiarize yourself with the various pages and features of the site.
- Write a press release and distribute it to papers in and around your market area.
- Make sure an ad is placed about a new agent (*you*) joining your office team.
- Attend brokers' open houses, buyer appointments, and listing appointments with a fellow agent.
- Review tasks completed with your broker or manager.

SUMMARIZE WHAT YOU FEEL YOU'VE LEARNED OR ACCOMPLISHED THIS WEEK AND SHARE IT WITH YOUR BROKER OR MANAGER:

Week 3
DATE:

- Set up houses to show for a fellow agent.
  - Role-play how to hold a buyer interview.
  - Learn how to present your state's disclosure forms (if applicable).
- Focus on creating buyer loyalty and need awareness.
- Ask your secretary to place you on the up-board.
- Preview a total of 20 houses.
- Perfect doing searches on computer.
  - You should be doing advanced searches by now.
  - Learn ways to use the computer to "forward" your business by asking other producing agents in your office how they use the computer and what software programs they find most beneficial.
- Pick a farm area and create a mailing list with phone numbers.
  - Ask your fellow agents for guidance in choosing your farm.
  - Drive through the area before finalizing your choice. Decide if that farm area is a place where you'd be happy working with the folks who live there. You'll always do best working in an area you'd be comfortable living in.
- Attend brokers' open houses, buyer appointments, and listing appointments with a fellow agent.
  - Start to make notes about what you like and dislike about how the other agents are holding brokers' open houses.
- Review tasks completed with your broker or manager.

SUMMARIZE WHAT YOU FEEL YOU'VE LEARNED OR ACCOMPLISHED THIS WEEK AND SHARE IT WITH YOUR BROKER OR MANAGER:

Week 4
DATE:

- Call five members of your sphere of influence a day.
  - Make sure to make the call personable and friendly.
  - Keep notes about the conversation that you can refer to when you call them again in the future.
  - Be sure to ask them for a referral or if they need real estate help.
- Preview a total of 10 homes and call to find out the status on 20 houses already previewed.
- Learn how to fill out contracts and what the process is in presenting offers.
  - Ask other producing agents how they present the offer in your market.
  - Make sure to familiarize yourself with all of the paperwork.
- Pick at least two community activities to get involved in.
  - Choose activities that you personally enjoy.
  - You might choose a charity, club, association, or group.
  - The purpose of getting involved is to give of yourself while you are increasing your sphere of influence and creating relationships that will refer business to you in the future.
- Prepare a market analysis on a total of 10 houses you've previewed.
  - Learn how to price the home appropriately.
  - Learn how to present the market analysis in the most positive way.
- Create a listing conversation book.
  - Make sure it's neat, concise, and professional-looking.
  - Include photos about yourself, your company, and your office.
  - Include graphs, charts, and facts to support why people should choose you when they decide to sell their homes.
- Show five houses to a buyer.
  - Make sure you know how to get to each house and not get lost.
  - Understand how to develop rapport.
  - Remember to ask questions and enroll the buyers in chatting, sharing, and letting you know what they want and need in the purchase of a home.
- Attend brokers' open houses, buyer appointments, and listing appointments with a fellow agent.
- Review tasks completed with your broker or manager.

SUMMARIZE WHAT YOU FEEL YOU'VE LEARNED OR ACCOMPLISHED THIS WEEK AND SHARE IT WITH YOUR BROKER OR MANAGER:

Week 5

DATE:

- Call five spheres a day.
- Preview a total of 10 homes and call to find out the status on 20 houses already previewed.
- Hold a public open house for a fellow agent's listing.
  - Treat the open house as if it's your listing.
  - Focus on the three goals of holding an open house: a) to sell the home, b) to find buyers, and c) to find people who are sellers.
  - Ask each person attending the open house if he or she has a home to sell first.
- Go to a closing.
  - Observe the closing process.
  - Make sure to understand the part the agent plays.
- Knock on 40 doors around a new listing.
  - Let them know who you are and your company/office.
  - Tell them that you'd be happy to answer any of their real estate questions.
  - Leave something with them—a flier, a brochure, etc.
- Role-play a listing presentation.
  - Do this in a place you won't be interrupted.
  - Videotape the conversation, if possible.
  - Review the videotape and see how you did.
- Learn how to pull expireds from the MLS system.
  - Make sure to find out the initial listing price, which is often higher than the price of the home when the listing expired.
  - Notice which companies/agents have the most expired listings.
- Start calling FSBOs and expireds.
- Attend brokers' open houses, buyer appointments, and listing appointments with a fellow agent.
- Review tasks completed with your broker or manager.

SUMMARIZE WHAT YOU FEEL YOU'VE LEARNED OR ACCOMPLISHED THIS WEEK AND SHARE IT WITH YOUR BROKER OR MANAGER:

Week 6

DATE:

- Call five spheres a day.
- Preview a total of 10 homes and call to find out the status on 10 houses already previewed.
- Prepare a listing flyer for one listing. Try to use an established format or template rather than creating a flier from scratch.
- Read policy and procedure manual.
  - *Note*: The purpose of reading your policy and procedure manual is to give you a sense of your company's mission, the job descriptions of the various people who support you, and how you fit into the picture. Most agents have never read the policy and procedure manual—and that's another reason you should. It will help you understand what is expected of you as an agent and let you know how your support team is there to help you before, during, and after each transaction.
- Role-play the listing conversation with a fellow agent.
  - Learn the various tools, benefits, and advantages of your company.
  - Learn how to present the benefits and advantages of your company in a conversational and compelling way. Remember that you are the ambassador of your company to the families who wish to sell their home.
  - Remember that the listing appointment is where you get to shine. Treat the role-play as an actual appointment and ask your fellow agent if he or she would have chosen you to list his or her house and why.
- Attend brokers' open houses, buyer appointments, and listing appointments with a fellow agent.
- Review tasks completed with your broker or manager.

SUMMARIZE WHAT YOU FEEL YOU'VE LEARNED OR ACCOMPLISHED THIS WEEK AND SHARE IT WITH YOUR BROKER OR MANAGER:

Week 7

DATE:

- Prospect for three listing appointments.
  - Schedule time to make your prospecting calls in "blocks," meaning that you will schedule two hours of prospecting at a time to start. This will allow you to prospect without the feeling that you're "stuck" calling all day.
  - Be sure to write down your approach to prospecting and have that approach in front of you when you call. Don't be afraid to use what you've written if you're concerned that you won't know what to say.
  - Be helpful, courteous, and happy on the phone. Studies say that if you are actually smiling you'll increase your chances of success. Some professionals have found that looking into a mirror while calling makes them feel more comfortable. Others keep a sign with an affirmation or a thought for the day where they can see it and it reminds them to stay focused.
  - Your goal is to schedule an appointment, rather than trying to take a listing over the phone. Take your time talking and try to ask as many questions as you feel comfortable with and maybe one or two more.
  - Get the person you've called enrolled into talking with you, sharing information about herself or himself, the area, the neighbors, or anyone he or she even thinks might be selling or buying a home in the near future.
  - Ask for an appointment or referral. You must actually ask them to help you because some of them might be unsure of what you want.
- Attend brokers' open houses, buyer appointments, and listing appointments with a fellow agent.
- Review tasks completed with your broker or manager.

SUMMARIZE WHAT YOU FEEL YOU'VE LEARNED OR ACCOMPLISHED THIS WEEK AND SHARE IT WITH YOUR BROKER OR MANAGER:

Week 8

DATE:

- Read and review this Action Plan and repeat anything you don't feel comfortable with.
- Take a day off.
  - *Note*: Taking time off is something you must start to do. We did not recommend this previously, because you're new to the business and it's OK to stay focused for a few weeks until you get rolling. At this point, you should be thinking along the lines of prospecting for business, following up on the business and prospects you already have, and taking care of your personal and family life. Having a balance of all three is crucial if you want to become a top-producing agent and enjoy a lucrative career.
- Attend brokers' open houses, buyer appointments, and listing appointments with a fellow agent.
- Review tasks completed with your broker or manager.

SUMMARIZE WHAT YOU FEEL YOU'VE LEARNED OR ACCOMPLISHED THIS WEEK AND SHARE IT WITH YOUR BROKER OR MANAGER:

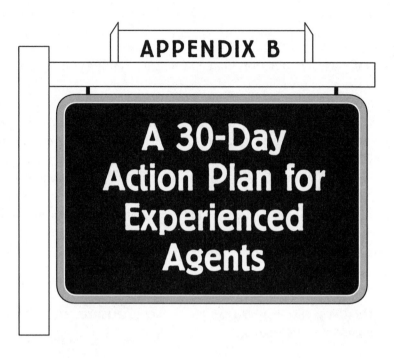

APPENDIX B

A 30-Day Action Plan for Experienced Agents

The key to taking action for experienced agents is to analyze what you are currently doing, create an immediate Next Level, and design a plan to attain that Next Level. Here is a way to develop your own Action Plan that allows you to focus on what you need to accomplish to bring your business to the Next Level.

Step 1: Self-Assessment. The key to self-assessment is to objectively view your current strengths and weaknesses. One of the best ways to do this is to use the Ben Franklin technique, as shown below. List your strengths in one column and your weaknesses in the other.

My Strengths	My Weaknesses

My Strengths	My Weaknesses

Step 2: Target a Weakness. Since your goal is to improve your current business practices and reach your Next Level, you can now choose an item listed in your Weaknesses column and turn that weakness into a strength.

For example, let's say that one of your weaknesses that you would like to target is "I need to utilize automation in my planning and in sending letters, faxes, and/or e-mails to my clients, customers, and support people."

Step 3: Set Your Next Level Goal. Each goal that you set has some individual elements that should always include:

A. What you want to accomplish.
B. When you will attain your goal (also known as the "due date").
C. The reward or benefit that you will receive when you attain your goal.

Our example might look like this:

A. To learn and use my computer and its programs for business planning and keeping in touch with everyone.
B. I will have this done by _____ (date by which you will have achieved this goal).

C. Better time management, improved follow-up, consistent updating of clients, customers, and other agents who are involved in my deals, as well as my support staff/administration department/management team.

Step 4: Create a Plan to Achieve Your Goal. This is where you list every step you need to take, in the appropriate order, and how you plan to take that step.

Example:

A. List the tasks needed to achieve my goal:
  1. Learn to use my computer for planning and scheduling.
     a) Weekly planning
     b) To-do lists
     c) Client and customer follow-up
     d) Prospecting
     e) Farming

  2. Find out how other top agents use the computer to be more effective.
     a) Who are the successful agents who are automated in my office/company?
     b) What are they doing and what software/computers are they using?

  3. Learn how to automatically send update letters, faxes, or e-mails for:
     a) Updates to homeowners who listed with me
     b) Updates to buyers currently in contract
     c) Tickler letters/faxes/e-mails to prospects
     d) Mail-merging letters to my farm, sphere, past clients, prospects, etc.

B. List the resources you think you will need. Please understand that as you go through the processes of planning and taking action you will uncover many unexpected items (both positive and negative) that must be considered or accommodated in achieving your goal and reaching your Next Level.

C. Fill out your Action Plan Task List in the order of what you need to do and when you want to get it done. An example of the Task List is below.

   The following task list is an easy way to get a hard job done. The key is in the old adage: "How do you eat an elephant? One bite at a time." Your objective in using this concept is to learn (mostly from trial and error) how to organize your ideas into a specific list of what you must accomplish in order to achieve your goals. Your success as a real estate agent and in life is directly proportional to your ability to create your own plan of action and to be in action toward achieving your goals.

DUE DATE	ACTION PLAN TASK LIST	DONE DATE

Step 5: Take Action Consistent with Your Goal. This is where you tackle each item in your Action Plan one step at a time. The best way to do this is to remember to always adjust your Action Plan to include each step you must take to achieve your goal. In addition, you should always re-analyze what you are trying to achieve and how you are going about achieving it. My best advice here is "Don't try to reinvent the wheel"—meaning you should always be looking at how other top producers in your field and even in other businesses do what you are trying to do. For instance, if you're trying to automate in real estate, you should probably use an established real estate automation program like "Top Producer," so you can take advantage of what's already out there and being used by thousands of others in your industry who are currently doing what you are trying to do.

Index

A
ABC technique, 46
"A" buyers
  filing, 13
  versus other types, 21–22, 110
  what to show, 123–124
Accomplishments, focusing on, 7–8, 169
Action, inviting. *See* Inviting action
Activities and interests of assistants, 191
Ad books, 10
Addresses, withholding from phone conversations, 112
Advertising. *See also* Self-promotion
  for assistants, 186–187
  by FSBOs, filing, 13–15
  idea books, 10
  institutional, 174
  investor ads, 39
  in movie theaters, 175–176
  other agents' listings, 164
  in specialized publications, 102
  TV and radio, 175
Advertising premiums, 176, 211–214
Advertorials, 175
Advocacy bonding, 198–199
Affiliate co-sponsors, 169–170
Agent evaluation cards, 105–106
Agent Qualifier, 57–58

Agents
  advantages over FSBOs, 25–27
  assessing competitors, 57–58
  as assistants, 182, 185
  client openness to working with, 30–31
  negotiation tasks, 26
  open houses for, 52–53, 96, 97–100
  presenting offers in person, 131–132
  promoting (*see* Self-promotion)
  promotion techniques to other agents,
    102–104, 105–106
  successful, 106, 109
  validating, 51–52, 115–116, 118,
    119–120
  wrong reasons for hiring, 54
Agents' surveys, 98–100, 179
Airplane technique (objection handling), 78
Amsterdam Printing, 161
Analogies, 62
Announcements, 214
Appearance (of assistant candidates), 189
Appointments
  guidelines for booking by phone, 30–35
  listing, 46–57
  preparing for, 35–36
  scheduling with buyers, 115–116
  tentative for shiny pennies, 122, 123,
    125

About the Author

Darryl Davis is a speaker, trainer, and business coach for many of the largest real estate brokerages and franchises in the United States and Canada. He started his real estate career at age 19 and became a top producer in his first year. As an active agent he generated an average of six transactions a month. In 1993 he created The POWER Program, the only training course for real estate agents that meets once a month for 12 consecutive months. He has helped thousands of real estate agents double their incomes. For more information, go to **www.darryldavisseminars.com** or call 800-395-3905.